How to Start Your Own Business on a Shoestring and Make Up to $500,000 a Year

Revised 3rd Edition

Tyler G. Hicks

Prima Publishing
P.O. Box 1260
Rocklin, CA 95677
Telephone: (916) 632-4400

Cover design by Paul Page Design, Inc.

Library of Congress Cataloging-in-Publication Data

Hicks, Tyler Gregory
    How to start your own business on a shoestring
and make up to $500,000 a year / Tyler G. Hicks—Rev.
3rd ed.

        p.   cm.
    Includes index.
    ISBN 1-55958-564-1

    1. New business enterprises.   2. Home-based
businesses. 3. Self-employed. 4. Success in business.

HD62.5.H527   1994
658'.041—dc20   94-19877
                                     CIP

Printed in the United States of America

96 97 98 99 AA 10 9 8 7 6 5 4 3

You Can Make a Million, Starting with Only a Little Cash

And that cash need not even be yours—if you use the easy, proven, practical, money-studded techniques given you in this book. Yes, by following the step-by-step tips in each chapter, you can start your own business on a shoestring and quickly make from $100,000 to $500,000 or more per year! In a few years you, too, can be a millionaire.

What a Shoestring Start Can Mean to You

Why invest thousands and thousands of dollars in a factory, machinery, computers, delivery trucks, and other equipment when you can avoid most of these expenses when starting your own business? During the last twenty years I've started and made big money in a large number of businesses. Yet my starting capital for each business was only a few dollars—a shoestring. And thousands of people I've advised have done the same. Some of these people were laid-off corporate managers who thought their earning years had ended. Instead, they're in the BIG money today. Starting your own business on a shoestring can mean

* Bigger profits—sooner
* Faster wealth for you
* Fewer business problems
* Greater personal independence
* Better tax deals
* Wider expansion of your markets
* Freedom from layoff worries

There's Big Money All around You

You needn't step outside your home to make really big money— $2,000, or more, per week. For instance, in this book I show you how

* A widow started a greeting-card business in her basement. Within three years her income was more than $1-million per year (Chapter 1).

* A mail-order rare-book dealer who regularly earns $125,000 per year never leaves his study at home (Chapter 2).

* Two city firemen opened a picture-framing business with $50 in cash. Today, four years later, their annual business volume is $500,000 (Chapter 1).

* A newly married couple started, and still operate, a $500-million business in their home (Chapter 2).

* A housewife began a bakery in her own kitchen—today her products sell in half the nation, and gross $50-million a year (Chapter 11).

* Two of the largest computer companies in business today started in garages in northern California; current sales of each company are multi-billions of dollars annually.

Use Big-Money Techniques

In my own businesses I aim at, and hit, the big money. I don't fool around with a business that brings in just a few dollars each week. And I want you to do the same. In fact my aim in this book is to help you make *at least* $2,000 a week. That's why this book gives you, for the first time in print, my BIG-MONEY wealth-building techniques—starting with only shoestring capital.

These sure-fire success-laden techniques help you

* Pick a high-profit, low-investment business
* Make big money every day
* Earn a million in a few years
* Use ALL your many money skills
* Diversify to maximize your income
* Make cash flow build income pyramids

Profit from Fabulous Wealth Know-How

Stop making false starts on your path to enormous riches—begin, here and now, to profit from the fabulous wealth know-how and secrets presented in this book. Put an end to your endless struggle for a pittance income. Convert each hour of the day to a golden rush of profitable dollars that put you on easy street sooner than you ever thought possible.

Knowledge is power. The crucial wealth knowledge you need to build a fortune starting with only a shoestring investment is in the pages of this book. No matter what kind of business interests you, the key, confidential secrets to making big money fast are yours. All you need do is read this book from cover to cover.

Succeed in Your Very Own Business

During my years as a highly successful consultant to thousands of beginning wealth builders, I've watched with delight as one after another of my trainees has built an enormous fortune in

* Mail order and direct mail
* Booming service businesses
* Low-cost manufacturing
* Unique personal services
* Computers and software for a variety of applications

There's big money to be made in your shoestring-capital business. What's more, this money is only a few steps away from where you sit at this very moment. But to start and continue this gold rush you must use the proven techniques you are about to learn. I *know* my system works because after using it to put a wad of profit dollars into my own bank, I watched others do the same under my careful guidance. Now that same guidance which others paid so much for is yours at a cost of only pennies per page—thanks to the publishers of this valuable book.

Know the All-Important Wealth Secrets

Getting rich in your own shoestring-start business is not a matter of luck—it takes know-how developed by an expert. *Your* expert advises you on every page of this book and shows you how to

* Convince yourself of your right to wealth
* Find the ideal business for yourself
* Pick an achievable income goal
* Build enormous riches quickly
* Actionize your big-income plans
* Schedule your business profits
* Use the secret of the century
* Keep business problems at a minimum

Don't go wrong switching from one unsuccessful business to another. Right at this very moment you hold in your hands the clearest road map to riches that is available today. Use it as directed and you're certain to hit the big money quickly and surely.

Learn Invaluable Profit Techniques

There is a great and amazing new way to figure your business profits. This new technique is used by the largest and most profitable firms in the world. Yet it is so simple that you can use it within minutes in your own business. This book shows you, with interesting and practical case histories, exactly how to use this invaluable profit technique. See Chapter 3 for this and many other money-laden profit ideas.

In the same chapter you'll find unique wealth building tips on

* How to profit from greater business volume
* Turning your personal time into big profits
* Using your personal computer to make charts and diagrams to build your profits

Profitable ideas surround you. All you need is a guide to show you where they are. This book *is* your guide. A few evenings spent reading it will put you on the path to great riches.

You Don't Need Big Cash

Learn how an airline pilot took over real estate worth more than $300,000 without putting a penny down! And he didn't spend a dime while negotiating the deal. As you'll see in Chapter 4, he invested a commodity we all have—*time*.

Follow the business adventures of a cab driver in Chapter 5. See how he built his business from one cab to a lucrative limousine service grossing $120,000 a year.

Or if cultural activities interest you, learn how a young secretary started an art rental business. As Chapter 5 shows, she has a booming art rental service with more customers than paintings. Yet her cash investment was minimal—she even rents some paintings from museums. In turn she rents these out to companies and individuals for a big profit.

Or run your business in a room in your home, as a successful portrait photographer does. Chapter 6 tells you his success secrets.

Get free advertising for your shoestring business. Learn, in Chapter 6, exactly how to get thousands of dollars worth of *free* advertising for just pennies and a few hours of your time.

Need products, parts, or materials in your business? Nearly everyone does. But you can go broke if you overpay for your needs. Chapter 6 shows you where to find low-cost sources of the items you need. Using these sources you invest less and earn higher profits.

Are you just plumb broke without a dime to your name? Yet you hunger to start your own business? Then use one or more of the half dozen *no-cost* money sources listed in Chapter 6.

Share in Profitable Business Experiences

Each chapter in this book contains numerous real-life shoestring-capital business experiences. Each of these case histories is written in such a manner that you live through the experience while you're reading about it. This develops your business judgment, improves your perspective, and puts you solidly on the road to great wealth.

Thus, Chapter 7 shows you how to earn enormous profits from products. All kinds of products are considered. If you want to make, sell, or market a product, Chapter 7 is your personal key to an enormous kingdom of product wealth.

Build Your Fortune in Mail Order

Products don't interest you? You're in love with mail order or direct mail? Great! Come with me, in Chapter 8, and spend a day in the life of one of the world's most successful mail-order men. Learn how he cuts costs, how he earns fabulous profits in mail order. Then go out and do the same, using the step-by-step special techniques I give you in this chapter. This one chapter alone could be worth more than a million dollars to you. Why? Because it shows you *what* to do, *when* to do it, and *how* to do it to earn incredible mail-order and direct-mail profits. I call my system *The Seven Magic Steps to Mail-Order Success.*

Get Rich in the World's Most Needed Business

"A service business is what really interests me," you say. "I've been mechanically inclined all my life—I love to work with my hands." Fine! Chapter 9 is made to order for you.

In Chapter 9 you'll learn why today *good* service is wanted and longed for by millions of people everywhere. People will pay almost any price to have their service work done correctly the first time, and on the day they need it. So use the techniques in Chapter 9 and watch your shoestring service business grow into a big company that puts $100,000 to $500,000 or more a year into your pocket.

And even if your skills come more from the brain than your hands, you can still make a quick fortune in the service business. Chapter 9 shows you exactly how to do it, no matter what kinds of brain skills you may have. And if you're a personal computer (PC) enthusiast, you can combine your love of PCs with a business idea to earn an enormous fortune, using your brain skills. You'll find plenty of practical ideas in Chapter 9.

Turn Your Know-How into Money

Once you start your own shoestring business you must make it earn you a steady profit which increases each year. Chapters 10 through 13 show you, with numerous real-life case histories how to

* Build your daily income to the maximum
* Use leisure and travel time to earn bigger profits
* Keep your taxes low
* Double your hourly income
* Pyramid riches by expanding your business
* Use borrowed money to build riches
* Set up a franchise system
* Solve many more business problems
* Set up a franchise system
* Solve many more business problems using your PC

Make this book your guide to great riches. It is full of practical techniques that work for you. I know this is true because these techniques have, and are, making millions of dollars for thousands and thousands of people.

In this book I give you my wide know-how, my foolproof special techniques, my step-by-step systems, and show you the extraordinary wealth potentials open to you. Then I take you, step-by-step, along the way from a low income to riches. Turn now to Chapter 1 to begin this wealth-laden adventure with me.

Contents

5. Pick Your Wealth-Building Home Business (*Continued*)

skilled workers. Check out business facts. Aim at middle-income markets. Low incomes are steadily increasing. Shun high labor hours. Avoid small-demand businesses. Six powerful money-making tips. Take action now. Aim for the big-money profits. Stimulate your thinking. Actionize your wealth planning. Profit from the right associates. Choose your home wealth business.

6. Start Your Business for Maximum Profits 86

Know how you can operate your home business. Consider a sole proprietorship or partnership. It's easy to form your business. You may want to form a corporation. Pick a place to work. Your work place can be beautiful. Line up some money sources. Try this valuable tip. Here's your key secret to home wealth. Put your key secret to work. Sell before you spend. How to get free publicity. Big sales for a pittance. How to write your news releases. A technique for any business. Spend time instead of money. Time is money. Develop low-cost sources. Four steps to lower costs. Five keys to low-cost sources. How one fortune builder keeps costs low. Emphasize your profit builders. Why home profits can fall. Profitable bill collecting. You can start with no money. Six no-cost fund sources. Other sources of business funds. Should you borrow some starting capital? Think positively and win. Experience is a good teacher. Facts can help you. Use the magic riches checklist. Six outstanding fortune builders.

7. Earn Enormous Income from Good Products 104

Classify product needs. Pick your type of product. How widely used products pay off. Unusual products find their market. Which is your best product? Where to find profitable products. Evaluate available products. Plan your marketing. Four whose products hit it big. How to finance your new products. Seven powerful financing techniques. Make your fortune selling products.

8. Become Incredibly Rich with These Mail Order Secrets 123

Why mail order is booming. Mail order is the ideal home business. A day in the life of a mail-order man. A fortune in your mail box. What the mails bring you. Keep simple records of orders. How to start your mail-order business. Seven magic steps to mail-order success. How to start with a smaller investment. Volume doesn't always mean profit. How to make mailing lists pay off. Know your indirect costs. Which mail-order product for you? Find, or develop, a unique product. Sometimes you must research new products. Test your product in the market place. Market a unique service by mail order. A service should help people. Mail-order service in the living room. Your quick guide to mail-order millions. Is mail-order training worth the money? What will mail-order training teach me? Where can I get mail-order training? Is mail-order drop shipping profitable? Work through mail-order dealers. What mail-order dealers do. Successful dealer product promotion. You have a BIG mail-order future.

9. Get Rich Fast in Home Service 143

People hunger for good service. What type of service business for you? Three important types of service businesses. You have a good friend near

9. Get Rich Fast in Home Service (*Continued*)

you. How to pick your home service business. Make your choice now. How to try again. Three examples of success. Start small; grow big—fast. Know your risks. Use the little-bit technique. The little-bit technique really works. Know where you want to go. What is planning? Put your plans into action. Valuable planning guide for your business. Other profitable aids. Home service wealth can be yours.

Follow a regular schedule. Work at a steady pace. Ten rules for a big income. Find an easy income measure. Keep a daily record of your work. Why income records are important. Keep other business records. How records can pay off. Take a regular day off. Time off can increase your income. Travel and entertain for business. Use your legitimate deductions. Be willing to do anything honest. Never refuse honest income. Pyramid your working time. Developing a home-business skill. How to double your hourly income. Be wary of partnerships. Read widely in your business field. Keep tight control of all costs. Solving cost-control problems. Build your home fortune with will power. "I willed my way to home wealth." Ideas make a business grow. Build your daily income to the maximum.

Why pyramiding builds wealth. Tie your wealth growth to cash flow. Cash flow builds income pyramids. Use OPM to pyramid your riches. Buy another profitable business. Expand your production equipment. Hire more help to increase your profits. Don't overlook employment laws. Use better materials in your business. Advertise your business more. Run contents to increase your income. Use give-aways to increase business. Give bonuses to improve sales. Enter new markets. Pick the best new market for your business. From farm kitchen to nationwide market. Set up a franchise system. There's money in franchises. How to do low-cost research. How to project research results.

Know the tax laws. Build a tax library. Keep up with the tax news. Where to find tax-free dollars. Seven steps to greater home income. Search for legitimate business deductions. Use depreciation whenever possible. Using depreciation in a home business. Two ways to figure depreciation. Advantages of each method. Explore research and development costs. Make your hobby a profitable business. Avoid tax problems. How to stay out of trouble. Take full advantage of home deductions. Consider property rental value. Watch your entertainment expenses. Don't overlook special expenses. Profit from capital gains. How to figure your capital-gain time. Keep more of your earnings by using capital gains. Make your future more profitable. Get expert tax advice when you grow.

How to use this checklist. Method of business operation. How much capital do you need? How much experience do you need?

Know the Joys of Getting Rich at Home

There are many ways you can get rich. But none are as attractive as getting rich in your own home business. Why? This chapter shows you the joys and advantages you obtain when you get rich in your own home business.

Forget the 9-to-5 Grind

Work at home and you work your own hours. Forget forever time clocks, secretaries who check the exact minute you arrive, and nasty looks from a slave-driving boss when you're one minute late.

Pick the hours you want to work at home—you're the boss. Fish or golf in the morning; sleep late, or have two extra cups of coffee in the morning. Start work when *you* want; stop when you're tired.

Take a nap after lunch, or at 4 P.M. Play all day; work after dark. Sleep until 4 P.M.; work until 3 A.M. Work fourteen hours a day for two days; take two days off. Or do as I once did—work twelve hours a day for three weeks; then take an entire week off.

You can get rich at home on your own schedule. Forget the 9-to-5 grind forever! Read on to learn how you can get richer—faster—at home than on any job you might ever hold.

Say Goodbye to Surly Bosses

Some bosses are dreams—others are slave drivers. If your boss is average, he's unpredictable, demanding, surly at times, and a tight-wad when it comes to raises. Why put up with such a situation when you can be your own boss?

Life is short. If your working day is full of frustrating demands, conflicting orders, back-stabbing, and constant competition, you can't be completely happy. Is it worth being miserable for years just to get a modest weekly paycheck? Work at home and know the joyous freedom of being your own boss. After all, who's nicer to you than yourself?

Rid Yourself of Job Fear

Do you dread being fired, laid off, down-sized, excessed, furloughed, demoted, terminated, reposted, "promoted" horizontally, kicked upstairs, or phased out? Are your skills obsolescent? Is a younger man or woman about to be given your responsibilities?

Are you sickly, physically incapacitated, or a little slower than other people when it comes to learning new skills? Does your family situation require that you take time off? Are you a single parent?

These are just a few of the conditions that can put a cold fear in any worker's heart. You can lie awake, night after night, sweating out job fears ranging from fear of your boss to worry over a chance remark you made to the office clerk who's a known gossip.

Men and women weren't born to live in fear. You need never fear anyone or anything again—if you are your own boss in your own home business. Resolve, here and now, to rid yourself of useless, body-wrecking job fear, by becoming independent forever.

Jump Off the Promotion Treadmill

Do you hanker after a promotion that never comes? Are others promoted while you stand still? Does your boss have favorites in every department except yours? Have you spent ten, twenty, or thirty years on the same job doing the same boring work?

The promotion treadmill can make enemies of good friends, can keep you chasing a star that recedes forever, can give you the biggest ulcers known to man or woman.

Promote yourself to the ownership and presidency of your own company, in your own home. Why hang onto a job for years, waiting for a promotion that gives only a pittance of a raise, if any at all? Work for yourself and know the joys of fabulous income earned at the hours, and in the place, you choose. Save your health; conserve your strength; be infinitely happier; start and succeed in your own home business! And STOP WORRYING ABOUT LAYOFFS FOREVER!

Use All Your Skills

Are you trapped in a job where only one-tenth, one-quarter, or one-half your skills are used? Are your talents growing rustier every day because a jealous, surly, insecure boss refuses to give you greater responsibilities? Do you feel yourself falling behind younger people because your skills are bottled up by ancient work rules, procedures, or red tape?

Begin your own home business and use ALL your skills—and then some. Know the glorious joy of functioning one-hundred per cent of the time as a fully integrated personality using all your skills. You'll also experience the infinite delight of stretching your mind to new horizons, new knowledge.

H. A. Callahan, a long-time friend of mine, is the author of ten books in the boating field. Early in his career he worked for advertising agencies. This was followed by a stint as a Naval officer. Cal's career really blossomed when he founded, in his garage, his own business to sell marine products to the boating field. Starting with a high-grade varnish, Cal soon expanded to other quality products. Today he has a full-time staff but Cal uses all his talents writing what some think is the best advertising in the boating field, testing his excellent products, calling on boat yards, seeking new products, and being a friend to boatmen everywhere.

Don't allow your skills to die. You have but one life on this earth. Live it to the fullest, using ALL your skills to build your wealth, happiness, and independence while helping others. You'll never regret making a full commitment to outstanding success.

Scuttle the Age Barrier Forever

Does your boss call you *old* at forty? Thirty-five? Is he or she ready to throw you to the wolves—unemployment, discouragement, loss of ego—after you've given the best years of your life to the company? Are you faced with a constant barrage of sarcastic remarks designed to undermine your ego and make your life a mass of insecurity?

Stop singing the overage blues. Start, or buy, a business of your own that can be run at home. With such a business you can be proud of your age, instead of ashamed of it. You can proudly advertise your years of experience and highly developed skills. Instead of losing money because of your age, you'll earn bigger profits. Escape the age barrier forever in your own business—the freedom you obtain will be more joyous than any you've ever known.

Move Ahead Faster, More Surely

In a few corporations you can start at the bottom today and rise to the top—if you're lucky and if you're willing to wait thirty to thirty-five years. By the time you reach the top you may be so weak and so worn out from the competition with other people that you can't enjoy the results of your labors. Worse yet, you may work for years, giving all your energies and time to the company. Then your department may be reorganized, down-sized, or merged with another, and you may be demoted, discharged, or laid off "until business picks up a little."

You can move ahead ten times faster, and with much greater satisfaction, in your own business. Why spend thirty years waiting for the big promotion when you can earn as much, or more, in your own business within three years, or less? Hundreds of top executives say to me every year "If I worked as hard for myself as I do for this company I'd be a millionaire many times over. Yet, what do they pay me here? Peanuts!"

The older you get, the more important it becomes that you move ahead *fast*. A business of your own has the ideal advantage of combining fast success with a disregard for age. Try it and see!

And if you want to retire early, after building a fortune in your own business, you can sell it, or lease it out, and get away from it all on some sandy beach or clear-air mountain top. What's more, you can set up your own pension plan while you're running your business. Payments into the plan for *your* future pension are legally tax-deductible to your corporation while *not* being taxable to you! Compare this to using after-tax money to set up a pension plan for yourself. No, you can't get a better deal than having your own home business today.

Earn BIG Money Every Day

Most companies and organizations try to hold down the wages they pay because labor is a big part of the cost of doing business. This means that your chances for earning really BIG money—say $100,000 per year, or more—are very small. You can work for thirty years in many companies and still earn less than $40,000 per year simply because the company has a tight salary policy.

Form your own low-overhead, home-based business and earn BIG money every day of the year. Why do you earn more in your own business? Because all the profit is yours—you don't have to deduct the cost of big executive offices, high executive salaries, enormous expense accounts, and bonuses before you figure your profit. You can, if *you* want, have the joy of a big expense account, a chauffeured car, etc. But these are *your* joys, not the joys of someone you've never met who is just a shadowy figure sending nasty memos to the staff.

Remember the following facts whenever you think about the small salary you receive on a job. Your employer must take in at least $2 for every $1 he or she pays you. In some companies your employer must take in at least $3 for every $1 he or she pays you. When you work for yourself, much of the $1 or $2 now going to your employer becomes yours because *you* are the employer. And if you keep your overhead (rent, light, heat, etc.) low, you can earn BIG money—$500 to $2,000 per day—every day you work for yourself. So don't settle for half a loaf when there's an entire bakery available to you!

Work in Comfort

Do you enjoy working in a sport shirt, slacks or jogging shorts, and sneakers? Or do you prefer neat khaki work clothes? Perhaps you have other favorite clothes in which you feel comfortable. No matter what your favorite clothing is, you can wear it when you work at home.

Other conditions which can make you more comfortable while you work are lack of noise, a cool working space, freedom from interruption, proper light, a pleasant view, and handy equipment and supplies. You can have all these and more conveniences when you work in your own home. Will they be expensive? No; you can furnish your office or shop at low cost when you start your business. Then, as profits increase, you can replace worn out or inefficient equipment.

One of my good friends, Tom B., worked for several large companies without much success. Finally, after twenty years of poor luck, he told me his troubles. He couldn't hold a job because he disliked taking orders but liked to work on his home computer to solve problems. As we talked it became clear that Tom, while ambitious and capable, was actually an independent thinker. He was really cut out to be in his own business, instead of taking orders from vice presidents in large companies.

"Tom," I said, "did you ever consider going into your own business?"

"I've dreamed of it many times," he said.

"Then what's stopping you?" I asked.

He pondered this for several minutes before he said "I guess you might say I'm afraid."

"That's foolish, Tom. You're afraid you won't make good with a large company because you're an independent thinker. And you're also afraid to go into business for yourself. Give fear the boot by deciding what you want to do. Then do it."

Tom did. He went into the chicken feed business because he lived in a poultry farm area. Today he works his own hours three days a week and works on his PC the other four days. As he remarked recently, "I find it very comfortable working at home, away from nasty memos, insolent vice presidents, and bossy secretaries. I should have done this years ago."

Gain Liberal Tax Advantages

When you work at home you are entitled to a number of liberal tax deductions. You can, for example, deduct the cost of the following items used in your business:

Electricity	Autos
Telephone	Trucks
Office Supplies	Rent
Water	Repairs
Insurance	Gasoline
Computers	Computer Supplies

There are many other legitimate deductions you can take. For example, you can deduct a portion of your home expenses if you actually earn money in a basement room, attic, garage, den, or another room or part of your home. You can depreciate your house, if you own it, taking the portion of the depreciation assignable to the business as a tax deduction. The business portion of the depreciation can be figured on an area basis. Thus, if your house has a floor area of 2,000 square feet and you use a 200-square-foot room for your business, the Internal Revenue Service will probably allow you to deduct $200/2,000 = 0.1$, or 10 per cent of the depreciation assignable to your home.

Note that you "own" a home as soon as you take title to it. You need not have paid off a home to "own" it. Thus, you can have a depreciation credit while you're still paying for the home.

If you rent a home or apartment, you can deduct that portion of the rent chargeable to the business. Suppose you pay $750 per month rent and 10 per cent of the space rented is used for business. Then you can deduct $(0.1) \ (\$750) = \$75$ per month for business rent on your tax return.

Legitimate deductions enable you to reduce your taxes while living better and earning more from your business. For accurate guidance on what you can deduct, consult Chapter 12 and a Certified Public Accountant. CPAs will earn their nominal fee many times by the savings they help you make.

Save Travel Time and Costs

Many people spend two hours a day traveling to and from their job. This time is wasted, so far as earning income is concerned. Also, the longer it takes you to get to and from work, the more it costs you.

So you really suffer a double loss—nonproductive time and non-deductible travel costs.

Did you ever stop to think how much you could earn in two hours if you worked at home instead of traveling? Add to this your travel-cost savings and you'll probably have a good day's pay, if you travel two or more hours per day.

People are motivated to start their own home business for many different reasons. When I point out these travel facts to some people, they say "I don't care how little I might earn in a home business. All I want to do is get away from the miserable crowds on the train I ride."

Others say "A day's pay in two hours? All I'll have to do is work four hours a day and I can double my income—without traveling! That's great!"

Don't worry about your motives—just so long as you want to earn money at home. Given this basic desire, you'll welcome the fact that you don't have to travel to and from work. And once you've picked and started your own home business you can forget about catching the 6:13 train or bus every morning, or zooming onto a jammed free-way with other harrassed drivers, and concentrate on earning big money at home. You'll never regret the fact that you don't have to catch a train, bus, or freeway car pool ride every morning of the week.

Be Closer to Your Loved Ones

Few of us today can spend as much time with our loved ones—children, wife, husband, relatives—as we would like. Why? Because we're too busy earning a living. Your job can take nine to sixteen hours a day, depending on how much time you spend traveling to and from work, and how many hours you work.

Work at home and you'll be closer to your loved ones all day, every day. A friend of mine had a sickly wife who was constantly under a doctor's care. This friend was suddenly furloughed from his job because of a big cutback in government contracts. With his wife ill, my friend decided to work at home for awhile to see if he could help her. He opened a mail-order business using his own catalog, which he put together to feature products from several carefully selected unique suppliers.

His business boomed. Today he's a wealthy man and his wife is healthy. She helps him in his business; the activity keeps her mind on things other than her minor pains. Privately my friend attributes his wife's cure more to her interest in his business than to medicine. But he hasn't told her this because, as he says, "She's too happy this way."

Work at home and you'll have more time to share with your growing children. They'll appreciate you more and understand you better. After all, a child is young only once. If you are too busy with a job away from home, your child may grow to manhood before you realize that the time the two of you might have spent together is gone. Don't let this happen to you.

Improve Your Standard of Living

When you work at home there are certain facilities you need, such as an office, a shop, a car, perhaps even an airplane. The cost of all these is a legitimate tax deduction if you use them in the production of taxable income. You may also need pencils, pens, paper, a type-writer, a desk, a personal computer, a printer, a modem, and a CD-ROM. Again, the cost of these is deductible on your tax return.

Jerry K., an author who works at home, had a $55,000 addition put on his home to house his study, books, and research materials. This addition has markedly improved the value of his home while giving him greater comfort during his working hours. Jerry's standard of living is increasing daily because the pleasant surroundings enable him to work more efficiently and turn out better articles and books. Thus, his home business is improving every aspect of Jerry's life.

Tony M. loves sailing. He could never afford his own sailboat until he decided to open a sailing school in the backyard of his shoreside home. Today Tony owns twenty sailboats—from a seven-foot dinghy to a forty-foot ketch. He does as much sailing as he wants and earns big money at it from the tuition his students pay. Meanwhile, his standard of living has improved considerably.

Many of us dream of great wealth. You need not earn millions and millions of dollars to enjoy the rewards of wealth. My observations of many people show that once your income exceeds $100,000 per year you can begin to live as though you have great wealth. At this income level you can have your own home, a big car, a fairly big (30-foot) boat, charge accounts at the best stores, etc. As your income increases, you can gradually change to more expensive things, if you wish. Thus, you can shift from an $18,000 auto to a $75,000 auto, if you like big cars.

Too many people hunger for large sums of money, failing to recognize that they can begin to live richly on smaller sums. Start to earn a fortune at home and you'll improve your standard of living to a level you never thought possible.

Rocket Ahead in Your Own Business

You can move up in life faster in a business of your own than in any job where you work for someone else. And when the business you run operates in your own home you move ahead even faster because your expenses are so low. Thus, you hardly have any real overhead (rent, light, heat, etc.).

Mrs. Liza M. started a high-grade greeting-card business in her basement. She features "the world's most unusual cards." With no previous business experience to guide her, Liza M. built a million-dollar-per-year business in her home basement in three years. Had she been working in an office for someone else, Mrs. M. might have earned about $50,000 in the same period.

What I want to do for you in this book is to make you so successful in your own home business that you'll have to consider getting your own factory. If you reach this level of success I'll consider my job well done. Whether you move into your own factory, or stay at home, is your decision. But either way you'll be earning such an excellent income that the decision should be an easy one to make.

Two friends of mine, Tom and Ed, were San Francisco City firemen. When Tom and Ed reached the age in life where hauling a heavy hose up six flights of stairs was no longer any fun, they began doing spare-time work to earn extra income. They worked as carpenters, paper hangers, and mechanics.

One day a friend suggested that they open a picture-framing business in the Bay area because it was a growing community free of strong competition. With $50 in capital, Tom and Ed bought a used saw and some lengths of molding. They began business in Tom's garage. Soon they needed more space so they moved one of Tom's children to another bedroom and used the child's room for the business. Still this space wasn't enough. So Tom and Ed moved their equipment to an old, but artsy looking, barn. They outgrew the barn, and moved to a factory. Recently they moved again—to a bigger and newer factory. The business they started in a garage with $50 in capital today has annual sales of half a million dollars. Tom and Ed resigned their Fire Department jobs long ago.

You'd think that a man in prison would not have a chance to operate successfully a "home" business. Yet an inmate of a midwestern prison operates a clipping service during his idle hours. He clips items from newspapers and sends them to clients who pay him a monthly fee. This man is preparing for a productive future while earning money in his temporary home. Compared with the nominal prison wages he receives, his clipping-service income is truly permitting him to rocket ahead.

Take Off for the Future Today

Resolve, here and now, that you *will* build a big income at home. Why? Because a home business is probably the safest way you can start earning big money. You can

- Begin in your spare time
- Continue your present income
- Start with minimum capital
- Work with almost no overhead
- Expand at a convenient rate
- Verify the business potential

There are very few home businesses that fail. Most of them earn back the owner's investment in a short time. From then on, you're on a wonderful profit path to riches. You can build your business to a large activity, employing many people. Or you can keep it small enough to pay you just the income you want without an expensive payroll.

We're ready now to explore the many ways in which *you* can make a fortune in your own home business. I'm sure that amongst the thousands of ways of building a home fortune which you'll learn in this book there is one way ideally suited to *you*. Once you discover the way you like most, you can blast off to riches. So let's get started, here and now, to build your home income to $100,000 to $500,000 or more per year. With this high income you'll soon be able to do all the things in life you've always dreamed of doing.

Hopefully, you may become as successful as Richard S. who owns 51 shopping centers in the northeast. He runs these various properties from an office in his home. He is an active sportsman who enjoys skiing, tennis, and sailing. For a number of years Richard S. has sailed his beautiful 66-foot yawl in the Newport, R. I. to Bermuda race. He is also active in a number of philanthropies.

Or you may prosper like two friends, Sharon and Ginny, in Virginia, who started their own business selling cheerleader uniforms and accessories to high schools, middle schools, and little league teams. The two women also serve as a clearinghouse of useful information on cheerleading competitions held at colleges and universities. Know someone who'd like to get a college scholarship as a cheerleader? Ask Sharon and Ginny—they're experts on this interesting, healthy, and rewarding activity for young women and men.

Their business started with the sewing of cheerleader uniforms. From there it was a logical step to a store having a full line of uniforms and accessories—socks, T-shirts, etc. Today their business is booming—they've expanded to mail order to supply customers who don't have access to a local cheerleading supply store.

Another woman, Jane, started, from home, a newsletter for church secretaries. She chose this market because there were no such newsletters available. Today her newsletter goes to church secretaries nationwide.

I started my monthly small business opportunity newsletter, *International Wealth Success,** from home for the same reason. Today we have thousands of subscribers worldwide and operate from a large modern office. To help subscribers we offer financing in the form of business loans and grants.

The joys of working at home are great. You now know many of them. If a home business appeals to you, the remainder of this book shows you exactly, in step-by-step fashion, how to start and succeed in your own home business. I want you to earn at least $100,000 to $500,000 per year in your home business. If you're ready to earn that kind of money, let's stop waiting and get going! Then you can write me a letter like this one:

> *Just a note to let you know that, based on my few telephone calls to you, being a steady subscriber to your* International Wealth Success, *and following your advice, my net worth is $3.5 million.*

*Available for $24 per year (12 issues) or $48 for two years (24 issues). Send check or money order to IWS, Inc., POB 186, Merrick NY 11566-0186. You do *not* have to be a subscriber to apply for, or obtain, a loan or grant.

2

You Can Earn
Big Money in a
Home Business

Many people scoff at the idea of earning spare-time money at home. "Why work at home?" they ask. "You can only earn pennies."

"It depends on what you call pennies," I always reply. "If you call a minimum of $10,000 to $100,000 per year pennies, then I suppose that there's no point in working at home."

"Oh, I had no idea you could earn that much," the scoffers usually say quickly. "But how many hours do you have to put in to earn money like that?"

"Oh, about 10 to 20 hours per week," I reply as casually as I can. "Figure 500 to 1000 hours per year."

This is when a scoffer's eyes usually bulge. "Tell me how I can get in on a deal like that," he or she almost begs.

"You understand that I'm only talking about spare-time work when I mention an income of $10,000 to $100,000 per year," I usually add. "If you work full time you can earn $100,000 to $500,000 per year, or more!"

Most scoffers begin to drool when they hear this. Others start to shake, anticipating that enormous income.

Believe You Can and You Will

Thousands of people, while reading my other self-help fortune and wealth books, write me each year telling me how much the books have helped them. Often they write "I never believed your system would work until I saw the money rolling in. Then I couldn't believe my eyes!"

This disbelief is one reason why it takes some people so long to hit the big money. Disbelief keeps other people from *ever* earning big money.

Resolve today that you *will* believe, that you *will* accept the guidance this book offers you. I am so anxious to see you get rich in your own home business that I've planned this book so it covers every important aspect of the topic.

The stories in this book are all true. These stories show how people just like you started a business at home and carefully guided it to a strong, prosperous organization. You can do the same—if you believe in your own abilities. *Believe you can and you will!* Then you can write a letter like this to me:*

> *I have been a subscriber of your newsletter for about 1 year and have learned a great deal from it and from your books. I started a successful business and all is going well. I am a dealer for a log home company and have sold six homes in the last five months. I am planning to expand my business.*

Know How You Can Earn Money at Home

Knowledge is power—when you *know* how you can earn money at home it is easier for you to believe that you can. If you make a study of how people successfully earn big money at home you'll find they do it in one of four general ways:

* Services
* Manufacturing
* Mail order
* Personal skills

*Letters quoted in this book are available for free inspection in my office. Just give me a few days' notice and we'll ready the letters for you.

Think about people you know who earn money at home. You'll find, I believe, that almost all fall into one of these four general categories. Thus, knowledge of these categories can be helpful to you when you are searching for a successful business to build a fortune in *your* home. Let's take a quick look at each category.

Services Are Booming

Today people spend almost as much money on services—cleaning, laundering, repairs, etc.—as they do on food, clothing, shelter, and entertainment. Why does so much of our income go for services? There are several reasons.

People today are busier than ever. They have little time to spend washing, cleaning, or repairing the various things they own. Products—autos, washing machines, personal computers, TV sets, etc.— are more complex. The average man has neither the skill nor the desire to repair the complex products he owns. While he may dislike calling a TV repairman to fix his new color set, the average man really has little choice, unless he happens to be a TV specialist, which few of us are.

Everyone in the world today is slowly becoming wealthier. In highly developed nations, such as the United States, greater wealth encourages people to use, and pay for, more services. Thus, a woman who formerly washed clothes at home will send the clothing to the laundry as soon as she thinks she has enough money to afford it.

As a man you may have washed your car every weekend, partly to pass the time, partly because you like the exercise, and partly because you didn't want to spend the money to have the car washed. But now that you have a few more dollars in your pocket you take your car to the auto wash. Within minutes you have a sparkling new gleam on your car which makes you feel more prosperous.

And so it goes. As time passes, we use more and more of our income for services. Soon we will spend more on services than we do on the necessities of life (food, shelter, medicine, etc.).

You can cash in on the boom in services by working in, or out of, your own home. Why? Because service businesses are ideally suited to being worked on in, or from, your home.

Later in this book you'll find hundreds of home services listed. You can start any of these services—like floor waxing, income-tax consultation, furniture repair, word processing, auto towing, etc.—using your present knowledge, or new knowledge you acquire by self-training or by attending a course. If you open a franchised service business, your franchiser will give the course.

Manufacturing Returns High Profits

Travel through some sections of the United States and you'll see huge factories built to manufacture a variety of products—autos, trucks, airplanes, stoves, refrigerators, etc. These factories have enormous payrolls. The salary expense for just one month is more than many people earn in a lifetime.

"How," you ask, "can I compete with factories like these? Where would I ever find the money to pay for the machinery?"

The answer is simple. When you manufacture products at home you concentrate on specialty items that usually are too expensive for large factories to handle. Also, you select products that are simple to manufacture—products that do not require expensive machinery. If high-cost machines are needed to perform a certain operation on a product, you subcontract the work, farming it out to firms owning such machinery. The operation may cost a little more than if you did it on your own machines. But you avoid the large investment in machinery.

Seven key secrets to successful home manufacture of any product are:

* A simple product
* Minimum production steps
* Fast production
* Low-cost materials
* Small labor cost
* Simple or no machinery needed
* Mass production possible

Look for these seven characteristics whenever you are considering a product to manufacture. The product you pick may not have all these desirable features, but if it has most of them you may decide to go ahead.

Here's a typical example of a successful home manufacturer. Clara C. is a happily married woman who never had any children. Once, while working with some orphan children, she devised an attractive doll made of strands of thick yarn. The doll was so popular with the children that she was soon making it by hand at home and selling it to expensive department stores. Sales were slow until she fitted a knitted hat to the doll. While the hat cost almost as much to make as the doll, the push it gave to sales made it worthwhile. Sales of the doll began to boom. Today the doll is more popular than when first introduced.

In analyzing the success of this doll made of yarn, there are several important facts we can learn from it. These are:

(1) The doll is a simple product
(2) It is easily made—only six steps are needed
(3) The doll can be made quickly—one woman can turn out twenty per hour at home
(4) Except for the knitted hat, the doll is made of low-cost materials
(5) Labor costs are low because unskilled women can make the doll at home
(6) No machinery is needed to make the doll

Thus, the doll has almost every desirable characteristic of the ideal product for home manufacture. This is the main reason why it sells so profitably.

Later chapters discuss hundreds of items you can manufacture at home. You'll also learn how to set up your own manufacturing business so you earn maximum profits.

Mail Order Is Better Than Ever

Some of the biggest fortunes earned at home are made in mail order. Why? Because mail order is ideally suited to work at home. A mail order business is

* Simple to operate
* Requires little investment
* Needs only minimum help
* Can be operated anywhere
* Is easily expanded
* Can sell hundreds of products

* Is ideal for family operation
* Can be highly profitable
* Requires no previous experience
* Can be operated by young or old
* Is an ideal spare-time business

You can hit it big in mail order if you apply your unique experience and background. Each of us has certain knowledge which sets us apart from others. If you put your special know-how to work in mail order you may go from no income to big income within a few days.
few days.

Later chapters show you exactly how to earn an enormous income in home-operated mail order. Sid K., a rare-book dealer, wasn't having much luck in his bookstore. Some days he didn't have a customer in the shop. I suggested that *he* go to his customers, using an attractively prepared mail-order catalog. Sid was doubtful at first but eventually agreed to my suggestion. The response was almost instantaneous—Sid received an avalanche of orders. What's more, the flow of customers to the store also increased. Sid's mail-order business grew so rapidly that the post office in his town was changed from a Class 4 to Class 1. Today he's the best customer the post office has.

Many of the techniques used by Sid K. and other successful mail order operators are included in the *Mail Order Riches Success Kit* (K-3 at the back of this book). Using the techniques given in this *Kit* will increase your chances of success in the great field of mail order. You—too—might become a mailbox millionaire, as so many others who study and work hard do!

I'm so determined to make you rich at home that I've included in this book every possible variation of mail order that I know of, based on my own experience and that of hundreds of others in the field. You'll learn how you can use mail order in almost any business you might go into. Thus, you might choose a service-type business to build your fortune at home. As your income increases, you may find many opportunities to use mail order to further expand your profits. I'll show you exactly what steps to take on your path to riches.

Use Your Skills at Home

Almost everyone in the world has certain unique skills. Thus, if you're a man, you might know more about repairing tractors than anyone in your area. Or if you're a woman, you might bake the best pies this side of the Rockies. With either skill a person could earn an excellent income working at home.

When you use your skills in a home business you

* Save office or shop rent
* Eliminate travel time to and from your job
* Have more time available to earn money
* Build local business

Many a big factory started in someone's garage, basement, barn, or attic. I know of at least six important electronics companies that started this way. Two large computer companies started in home garages. A number of large mail-order businesses started the same way.

Other ideal home attic or basement activities using personal skills include real-estate sales and rentals, telephone sales, poultry or animal breeding and raising, tree or flower cultivation, etc. Later chapters list hundreds of ways to put your skills to profitable use.

One of the greatest thrills you'll ever receive in life is that of earning money at home by using your skills. Once you experience this thrill you'll realize why the craftspeople of old were so content to work in their own homes. These men and women never had any fear of passing their skill and knowledge on to their children because they knew the great satisfaction their children would receive from their work.

With a careful approach to business, you can build a lucrative income at home. You will have little difficulty earning $100,000 to $500,000 per year, or more. Later chapters show you exactly how.

Learn the Other Ways

There are thousands of other high-profit ways to earn big money at home. Almost all involve one or more of the four methods mentioned above—services, manufacturing, mail order, or skills.

Thus, a neighbor of mine, Basil K., who has a physical handicap, came to me when his job was terminated after his employer sold the business. Basil was distraught because he didn't think he could find another job. I recommended that he take a free eight-week evening course given by a local stock-broker. At the end of the course he could take a simple test and become a Registered Representative. Then he could sell stocks, bonds, and mutual funds.

Basil did as I recommended. Today he is a highly successful stock salesman working out of his own home using his PC. He combines services with mail-order and personal skills. His business is growing so fast that Basil plans to hire several salesmen of his own. Then he'll earn money from the efforts of others. When you expand this way, your income zooms and you can easily reach the $500,000-per-year level.

As you read on, you'll learn many of the other ways to earn big money at home. My main intention in this chapter is to start you thinking about the ways *you* can earn money at home.

Show Yourself You Can Earn Money at Home

Many people lack self-confidence when they think of earning money at home. "Sure," they say, "Joe Jones can earn big money working in his garage. But I'm not as lucky as he is. Also, he knows a lot more than I do."

Yet when you meet Joe Jones and talk to him you wonder; is he as smart as people say he is? My observation of many home fortune builders is that some have more ambition than anything else. Their strong ambition makes up for everything else they may lack—education, skill, brain power, etc.

Other home fortune builders are near-geniuses. They work at home because there they can do as they please, without being restrained by strict rules. Many great inventions began in a basement, attic, or kitchen. Today many of these inventors, who began at home because they lacked capital, are rolling in money.

Let's check on *your* home fortune building self-confidence. I'm sure you have the necessary confidence—if you didn't, you'd be reading another book. Here's a handy checklist that will help you see how much self-confidence you really have.

My Self-Confidence Checklist

	Yes	No
1. I believe I can earn big money at home.	....	....
2. Past business failures will prevent success at home.	....	....
3. The cost of getting a business started frightens me.	....	....
4. Competition may make me go broke.	....	....
5. I'm afraid my family will complain about the business.	....	....

6. The decision to start a business is difficult.   ....
7. I'm taking a big financial risk in a home business.   ....
8. I may have legal problems in the business.   ....
9. I can't make up my mind on what to do.   ....
10. I often wonder if the effort is worth the return.   ....

Look over your answers. Do they discourage you? Let's see what a typical successful home fortune builder's answers might be.

1. *Yes;* by all means I *can* earn big money at home.
2. *No;* past failures are behind me and I've forgotten them.
3. *Yes;* investing money—even $5—frightens people. So what!
4. *Yes;* but competition keeps you alert, can make you rich.
5. *Yes;* let the family complain—until the profits roll in!
6. *Yes;* starting a business is a difficult decision for anyone.
7. *Yes;* but everyone who starts a business takes financial risks.
8. *Yes;* most businesses do have legal problems.
9. *Yes;* indecision is a common problem.
10. *Yes;* so does every other businessperson wonder, at times, if the return is worth the effort.

Compare your answers with those of the typical successful home fortune builder. Note that he or she:

* Is ready to forget past failures
* Is frightened by the investment he or she must make
* Is frightened by competition
* Is in a family that complains
* Is in a dither over decisions
* Is taking a big financial risk
* Is sometimes doubtful about a home business

Now here's an interesting and an important fact.

The typical beginning home fortune builder resembles, in many ways, the typical successful home fortune builder. Thus, the typical beginner is undecided—attracted to big money but fearful of the penalty he or she must pay. If they forget their fears and push ahead, they'll earn rewards far greater than those in their most hopeful dreams. When you meet them a few years after the start of their march toward their fortune, you'll find they

* Have forgotten past failures
* Are no longer frightened by an investment

* Like competition because it helps business
* Ignore the idle complaints of their family
* Make decisions quickly, confidently
* Enjoy taking big financial risks
* Are convinced that a home business earns big money

Have confidence in yourself and your abilities. You can—and will—build a fortune at home if you follow the easy steps you'll learn in this book. Then you too may write me a letter, like so many of my other readers have, saying "Your system works; it *really* works!"

Certainly it works—*if you do*. And the system will continue to work as long as you want it to. Just try it and see for yourself!

Look at the Record

Some of the largest companies in the world today started in someone's home. Some of them, like a $500-million mutual fund which was started by a young married couple in a Brooklyn Heights apartment, still operate from a home. Others, like one huge auto company, started in a man's backyard. Today the auto company owns enormous factories, its own ships, and other expensive equipment.

I know you are interested in a home business. My experience shows me that if I can bring you to the point where you're earning $500,000 per year, you won't have any trouble deciding your future workplace—home or factory. Incidentally, many home wealth builders tell me "I used to hate working in a factory. But now that I own a factory I really enjoy working in it!"

As I often say to people "It's amazing what a difference a little money can make in a man's or woman's life."

So look at the record. On nearly every page of this book you'll learn about people just like yourself who hit it big in their own home business. If they can do it, so can you. Now, let's start, here and now.

So look at the record. On nearly every page of this book you'll learn about people just like yourself who hit it big in their own home business. If they can do it, so can you.

For example, one of the bravest home business builders I know of is a woman who, after having four sons, built a real estate business with her husband. Unfortunately, the marriage turned bad and the husband left, taking the business away from his wife and children.

Desolate and emotionally wrecked, this 50-year-old woman pulled herself together and started another real estate company on her kitchen table. She trained three sales agents in her home and sent them out to work. Today she has more than 300 sales agents and staff people in her booming business. In her latest year in business she—through her company and agents—took part in more than 3,200 real estate deals! Her company today is probably the most successful in its region of the country.

Today she is happy, content, and full of life. Her business—started in her kitchen—helped her recover her self-esteem, her place in society, and her financial freedom. You—too—can do much the same in your chosen field if you follow the hints in this book. So let's start—here and now!

3

Analyze Your Home Income Needs

Much of my working time is spent on jet airplanes flying all over the world. An airplane, as you probably know, is an excellent thought-generator—particularly on long flights.

During these long flights I often analyze my life, my work, and my family. I also analyze the lives and work of my friends and business associates. The many hours I've spent bouncing along the world's airways have taught me that analysis of one's life and work is an excellent way to improve your ability to cope with life and its many problems.

Equally important is another truth the analysis-in-the-sky sessions have taught me. This truth is: *Every time my business associates or I have a planned goal in life, we achieve it. Our greatest financial successes come when we plan for them.* This secret truth can be worth millions of dollars to you. Let's see why.

You Must Have an Income Goal

Without an income goal of a certain number of dollars per year or a specific sum by a given date, most people have trouble directing their moneymaking efforts. They wander from one idea to the next, earning little or nothing from each idea.

This lack of a specific income goal has, I believe, caused me the loss of nearly half a million dollars in my lifetime. Why? Because for about fifteen years I had only four goals in life. These were (a) to earn more money, (b) to hold a top executive job, (c) to write successful books and articles, and (d) to run several profitable spare-time home businesses.

For about five years these goals worked well for me. My income and responsibilities increased, as did the number of books carrying my name as author. Then my income levelled off—for about six years it didn't vary by more than $1,000 per year.

It was during one of my "sky-analysis" sessions that I suddenly realized that I was in a rut. True, it was a fur-lined rut that 99.5 per cent of the people in the world would love to be in for the rest of their lives.

But I wasn't making progress. Why? I had goals; I worked hard; I lived a wonderful life; I was happy, but unhappy. Why was I unhappy? I wanted to earn more money. And why didn't I earn more; why had I topped out at a high level? Because *I lacked specific income goals.*

Your Income Goals Must Be Specific

I made a very common error. I mistook a general desire to earn more money for an income goal. A general longing to earn more money is an excellent motivator. But to convert this longing to dollars you must have a *specific income goal.*

What's a specific income goal? It's a goal that

    (a) Specifies the exact dollar income you seek
    (b) States the date by which you'll earn this amount
    (c) Tells how you'll earn the desired income

Thus your goal tells you the *what* (amount), the *when* (date), and the *how* (method) of your home fortune hunt.

Choose Your Home Income Goal Now

Here's a handy form on which you can record your home-business income goal now. Decide how much you'd like to earn. Be realistic—you might want to earn one to two million dollars per year at home, but this is almost impossible, unless you turn your home into a factory or go into the mail-order business. You can, however, easily earn $100,000 to $500,000 per year at home without turning your living room into a warehouse. So, during the course of four or more years, you can earn one to two million dollars in the privacy of your own home. But if you want to earn, let's say, two million *per year*, you'll have to rent, buy, or build a factory or office/warehouse and work away from home.

Enter your income goal in the form below before reading further. Just the act of writing down a realistic income goal puts you one step closer to that flood of wonderful money you can earn in your own home.

My Home-Business Income Goals

By . . . . I want to earn $ . . . . per year.
    (date)
By . . . . I will begin my . . . .
    (date)   (type)
business in my own home.

Recognize Money's Most Important Characteristic

Money has many important characteristics. Probably the most important one to you in your search for home riches is that money will never seek you out. *You must seek out money.*

Sitting and dreaming about what you'd do if you had a million dollars is a good way to prepare yourself for the home riches you seek. But these riches won't come to you until you take action—until you *actionize* your search for riches. Dreams, plans, schemes, and hopes mean little until you go out and do something about them. But once you begin your search for home wealth using the ideas in this book you'll find that big money is easier to earn than you ever thought possible.

Build Riches in a Business

Look around your neighborhood today. Note who has the largest income. In most neighborhoods you'll find that people in business for themselves have the largest incomes. True, a few corporation executives earn as much, and possibly more, than certain people in business for themselves. But, in general, successful men or women in business for themselves earn more than people working for someone else.

In my visits to all kinds of home-operated businesses—electronics, metalworking, boatbuilding, printing, desktop publishing, and many others—I see many highly successful people in business for themselves. They are prosperous, happy people who enjoy earning large incomes. Their home business activities are a constant challenge which keeps these men and women active, alert, interested, and busy. It almost seems that their way of relaxing is to work harder in their own business. As one businessman notes, "My home business is my hobby; my hobby is my home business. I'm the happiest guy in the world—and someday I may be nearly the richest."

Successful home businesspeople usually have the best cars, nicest homes, longest vacations, and other evidences of a larger-than-average income. When you build your riches at home you can obtain similar possessions, if you want them, or you can spend your money in other ways. Perhaps you'd like to own a fast, fully equipped private jet airplane, or a healthy young racehorse, or an expensive antique car. All these can be yours if you have the money to buy them.

For example, Gail M., mother of three children, trades stock using her personal computer at home. This allows her to care for her three youngsters directly, without leaving them in the hands of a baby sitter, as she would have to if she worked in someone's office.

Relying heavily on research done with her PC, fax machine, and telephone, Gail showed a $50,000 profit last year. Gail regards her computer-guided investing as a serious business—in her home. So she expects, and is glad, to pay taxes on her home-based profits! Meanwhile, her small children get the loving care they deserve—in their own familiar home.

Actionize your search for riches now by deciding that you, too, will build riches in a home business of your own. You'll be your own boss, free of worry over layoffs, firings, and the political intrigues of the usual job in a large or small corporation. What's more, if you have a physical handicap of any kind, or if you're over 65 years old, you can "hide" behind a home business having a well-chosen name and a good reputation. Nothing will stop you in your search for wealth at home, if you put your plans into action. Let's see how you can start.

Know the Cost of Doing Business at Home

I've helped several thousand people get started in their own home business. Not one of these people failed. Several went on to earn more money each year from one home business than I earn from all my many activities. As I tell these more successful ex-students when I meet them "I'll be over to negotiate a loan!"

What is the outstanding characteristic of these highly successful home business operators? It is this:

> **The big successes in a home business are achieved by those people who know the cost of doing business at home.**

Is the cost of doing business at home high? Most people don't think it is. Let's see if *you* do.

To start your own home business you'll generally need these items:

Business registration	$ 25
Letterheads and envelopes	100
Pencils, paper clips, stapler	8
Cardboard file	4
Total	$137

Thus, you need only a small sum — $150 or less — to start *your* home business. The registration fee, shown here as $25, could be higher or lower, depending on where you live. It seldom exceeds $25 and can be as low as $1. You can easily start your home business on money you save from your regular salary.

In some businesses you must, of course, invest in some inventory—i.e. in items you will offer for sale. To keep your starting cash as low as possible, I recommend:

(1) Obtain orders *before* you invest in inventory.
(2) Use borrowed money for inventory purchases.

Later in this book you'll learn how to use each of these important techniques in *your* home business. Why spend thousands of dollars to start a home business when, in most cases, less than $200 will do?

Learn the Other Costs of a Home Business

There are other "costs" in starting your own home business. I call these "costs" even though you don't have to invest a penny for them. Why do I call them "costs" when there is no investment? Because these other "costs" involve you, your mind, and your energy. If you're willing to invest a large amount of yourself and your time in your home business, you're sure to succeed.

How do you "invest yourself" in your business? Here are seven lucky ways that I know you can use to put new magic and greater home wealth into your life.

1. Start with enthusiasm. Keep your hopes high at all times.

2. Work hard; you can't earn unless you work steadily to produce a profit.

3. Be alert for new profit opportunities. Introduce new ideas or products whenever you can.

4. Know what your competition is doing. Seek, and find, ways to best your competitors.

5. Keep negative emotions—envy, anger, and discouragement—out of your mind. Replace these negative emotions with positive ones—ambition, drive, and helpfulness to others.

6. Serve your customers or clients well. Attention to details builds big profits.

7. Act in a professional, businesslike manner at all times. People enjoy dealing with a professional and will give you repeat business which is highly profitable.

Once you recognize the start-up and mental costs of doing business in your own home, you're well on your way towards wealth. Thousands of people dream of earning money at home but their dreams never materialize. Why? Because these people never take the trouble to analyze and actionize their search for riches.

You can compliment yourself right now because you're one step closer to great home wealth. Continue reading to learn the next steps to take in your search for home wealth.

Estimate Your Potential Home Profits

In any home business you have two kinds of expenses—(1) *fixed expenses* which are also called overhead expenses, and (2) *variable expenses,* also called volume or out-of-pocket (oop) expenses.

The beauty of any home business is its low fixed costs like rent, depreciation, manager's salaries, etc. Why? Because the lower your fixed costs, the sooner you break even. In any business you reach break even when your sales income equals your fixed plus variable costs. Let's see how this works.

Suppose you have a home business in which you sell one product—a large cut-glass bowl. You sell this glass bowl at $10, after paying $7 in variable costs (cost of bowl, shipping cost to customer, etc.) on each bowl. Your fixed costs (rent, depreciation, etc.) are $300 per year. What is your break-even point?

On each bowl you sell you have a *contribution* of $10 − $7 = $3. When you've sold just enough bowls so that the sum of the contributions from each sale equals your fixed expenses, you will break even. Or, fixed expenses / contribution per sale = break even. For this business, break even = $300/$3 = 100 bowls. Once you reach break even, the contribution per sale = profit per sale = $3 per sale in this business. And your profit percentage, after you reach break even = contribution $/ sales $ = $3/$10 = 0.30, or 30 per cent.

Now what is your potential home profit in this business? We know that you'll earn a profit of $3 on each bowl you sell, after you reach break even. But how many bowls will you sell per year? If you sell 100 bowls your profit will be zero because you will just break even. Let's say, however, that you think you can sell 500 bowls a year. What will your profit be? Find the difference between your expected sale and the break-even quantity and multiply this by the profit per sale, or (500 − 100) ($3) = $1,200. Thus, you'd have a profit of $1,200 per year, or $100 per month, from your home business.

Suppose, however, that you could increase your sales to 2,100 bowls per year without increasing the fixed costs (rent, light, heat, etc.). What would your profit be? Use the same method as above, or (2,100 − 100) ($3) = $6,000 per year, or $500 per month. Now we're getting somewhere.

You've just learned a powerful way to estimate your potential profits in a home business. You can use this method in minutes to come up with an accurate forecast of your potential profits. When you use this method be sure to remember that the contribution of a sale equals the selling price minus your variable or oop costs.

The breakeven method is very powerful if you decide to form an export-import company in your own home. Exporting can help build home riches faster than most people realize. Here's a letter from a reader showing how she's building home export riches:

> Enclosed is a copy of my first commission check from my export business. It was for the sale of a cotton-ball machine to a client in Pakistan. The sale was for $32,000 and my commission was $4,269.60 (13.3%). Not bad for starting with $100 capital and your *Export-Import Riches Kit*. They are getting ready to order two similar machines.
>
> The buyer is now a steady client and I am serving as a buying agent for them in the United States, as well as an import agent for their finished products. Their group is the largest exporter of cotton in Pakistan, and they operate 7 other companies.
>
> I am working on a joint venture with the Pakistanis and a gauze machine company in Georgia. It is for the installation of a complete gauze factory in Pakistan. If it goes through I will make about $82,000 in commission. I am also negotiating the design and sale of another complete factory in Mexico with a commission of $50,000 for me. (A cotton-ball machine makes items used in surgery and other medical procedures.)

Consider the Effects of Business Volume

Many people think that their biggest problem in business is getting a large enough sales volume. This is correct—up to the break-even point. Beyond break even, too large a volume can drive you out of your home into a factory. Of course, this may be the sweetest problem of your life because with such a large volume the dollars will flood into your bank so fast you won't be able to count them.

You know that once you reach break even the contribution from each sale becomes your profit per sale. But as your volume increases you may find that

> Fixed expenses increase
> Variable expenses increase
> Profit per unit decreases
> Problems increase

Knowing your income goals, break-even sales level, and contribution, you can decide how large a volume of business you wish to do. In making this decision, keep in mind that a business volume exceeding your home capacity will drive you into a factory, possibly increasing your fixed and variable expenses, and the problems you'll have with personnel, withholding taxes, etc. But don't let these problems discourage you—particularly if you can really hit the big money — $100,000 to $500,000 or more per year. Several home businesses I know grew from a nominal annual income (less than $1,000) to more than one million dollars per year in less than five years, but the owner had to move from his cellar or garage into a factory or office to reach this large sales level.

To summarize, volume is good for any business. But you may find that too large a volume puts you out of your home business and into a large factory or office of your own. If this book does that for you I'll be delighted, because if you achieve that large a sales level I'm sure you can solve the problem of staying at home vs. moving into a factory or office.

Set Up Your Personal Time Plans

In your own home business time is more important than in almost any other business. Why? Because when you start your home business the most important commodity you'll have to sell is your time. Every business you learn about in this book was chosen because it requires only a small amount of capital. Under these conditions, the time you invest in your business becomes an important segment of the founder's "capital."

You need two time plans for your home business: (1) a positive achievement time plan, and (2) a daily time plan. Let's take a look at each type of time plan to see how you can use it to bring a steady stream of dollars into your home business.

Positive Achievement Time Plan. This plan helps you schedule the dates by which you intend to accomplish specific objectives. You can begin such a plan right now, using the date for finishing the reading of this book as your first time goal.

Recognize, here and now, that few major successes in life are achieved without a time plan. We all need time plans of some kind to urge us on to our intermediate and final goals. Since I want to help you get as rich as possible, as soon as possible, in your own home business, I've prepared a typical set of time goals for you. These time goals are designed to be used as is, but you can change them in any way you want—adding to or deleting from them, depending on your particular situation.

My Positive Achievement Time Plan

Action	Planned Date
1. Finish reading this book	. . . .
2. Select home business to enter	. . . .
3. Obtain needed money	. . . .
4. Register business name	. . . .
5. Start advertising and publicity campaigns	. . . .
6. Evaluate results of Step 5	. . . .
7. Begin sales campaign	. . . .
8. Reach first sales goal of $.	. . . .
9. Begin first planned expansion	. . . .
10. Start investigating possible diversification	. . . .

Your time plan ends with a study of diversification because by the time you reach this stage you won't need my help. Time plans will be so much a part of your regular routine that you'll be more enthused about them than I am.

A personal time plan can mean the difference between failure and success in your home business. So use this simple planning device—all it takes is a pencil, a piece of paper, and some thought. It's the thinking part of time plans that really pay off. For as Richard S., builder of several home fortunes remarked to me recently, "When a man in his own home business begins to make time plans, he's sure to hit the big money, sooner or later. With a time schedule, he can't miss." So start your personal time plans today.

Use Charts, Diagrams, and Spreadsheets

Today you live in a world of pictures. A picture used to be worth a thousand words—today's carefully prepared business charts and diagrams are often worth a million words. (And possibly a million dollars, too, especially if you use your personal computer for charts and diagrams.)

How can you use charts and diagrams and your PC to help you in building a fortune in your own home business? Here are six ways.

* To plan any business task
* To plot your personal time plans
* To show how sales are increasing
* To indicate profit trends
* To study expense changes
* To detect problem areas

The biggest businesses in the world—General Motors, General Electric, Ford, etc.—make wide use of diagrams and charts in their planning, controlling, and evaluation of business activities. So why shouldn't you? "My home business is too small," someone says? Nonsense! When you adapt big-business techniques to a small business, you're using your head. You're jumping far ahead of the next guy, who's outlook is so limited he'll never make more than $100 a week in his own home business. What I want you to make — provided you're willing — is $2,000 to $10,000 per week or more, nothing less.

What kinds of charts and diagrams can you use in your home business? Start with the simplest, such as bar charts, pie charts, etc. Here are two simple charts you can use today. The first, Fig. 1, is a time bar chart for starting your own home business. To use this chart, just insert your dates on a copy of the chart, or on the chart itself. Pin the copy on the wall in front of your desk and watch the results. Mark on the chart the date on which you reach each goal. There are a number of personal computer programs on which you can, easily and quickly, set up such bar charts and enter data for each date on the chart. You'll find that you accomplish more, sooner, and with less work.

Figure 2 is a line-of-balance chart for any task in which you have two or more things to do which require different time intervals. To schedule different tasks, you just move to the left the number of days you think each task will take. Join the task lines where parts or jobs come together. With a line chart like this you can easily see which item or task is the critical one. Which do you think is the critical task in Fig. 2? Why? The answer is in the legend for Fig. 2.

That diagrams can be highly important in any home business was dramatically pointed out to me by the well-known Billy Rose. When Billy became interested in the stock market he installed a ticker tape in his home. From his "board room" he conducted all sorts of intricate stock deals. The walls of this room were lined with charts and diagrams Billy prepared for the business deals he was working on. Billy made a fortune in stocks, *after* he made a fortune on Broadway, *after* he made a fortune in swim shows, *after* he made a

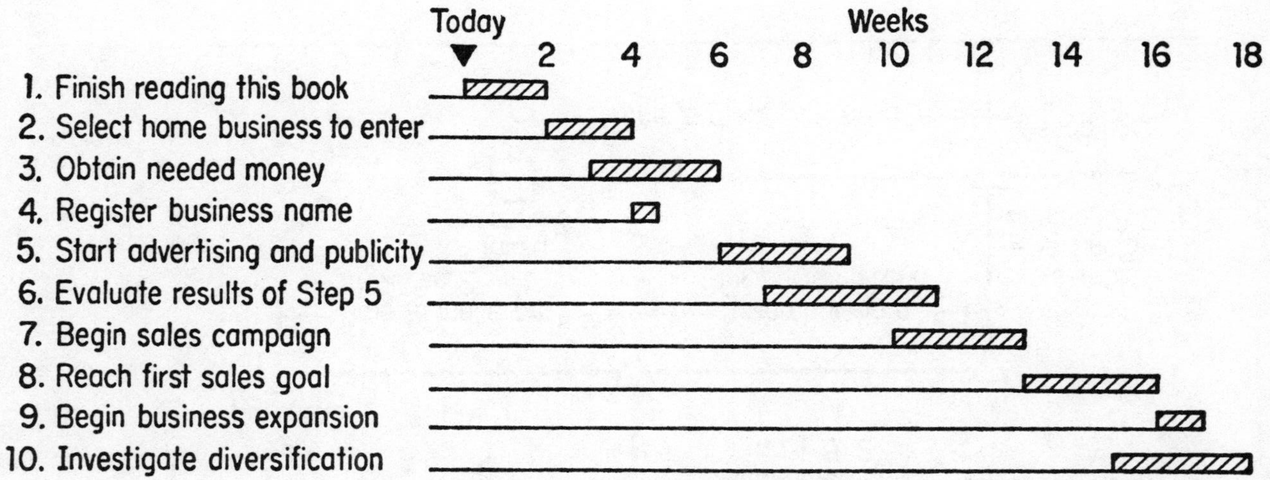

Today

Weeks

2   4   6   8   10   12   14   16   18

1. Finish reading this book
2. Select home business to enter
3. Obtain needed money
4. Register business name
5. Start advertising and publicity
6. Evaluate results of Step 5
7. Begin sales campaign
8. Reach first sales goal
9. Begin business expansion
10. Investigate diversification

Fig. 1: A bar chart is useful for planning your business activities. This bar chart shows the steps you can follow to select, and start, your own home business, and the probable time required for each step.

35

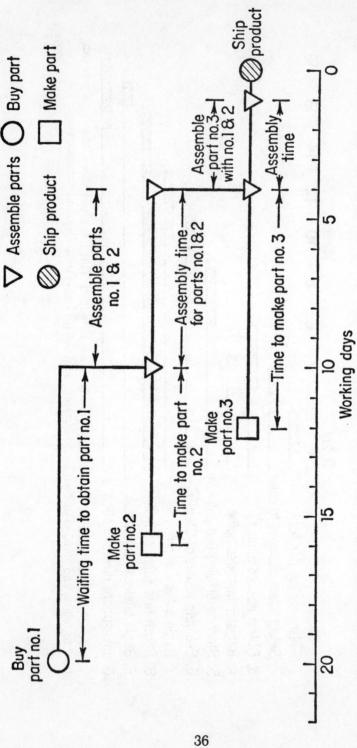

Buy part no.1

Assemble parts ▽ **Buy part** ◯

Ship product ◐ **Make part** ▢

Assemble parts no.1 & 2

Waiting time to obtain part no.1

Make part no.2

Assembly time for parts no.1 & 2

Time to make part no.2

Make part no.3

Assemble part no.3 with no.1 & 2

Assembly time

Time to make part no. 3

Ship product

Working days

0   5   10   15   20

Fig. 2: Line-of-balance diagram shows how long you must allow to obtain or make parts for a product you assemble and sell. Part #1 is critical here because you must depend on an outside source for it. Outside sources are less dependable and less controllable than your own group.

36

fortune writing hit tunes. Yet his first fortune was made like his last, in the privacy of his home where he wrote more than 100 hit songs.

"I don't need a six-inch thick carpet and a two-ton mahogany desk to make money," Billy told me. "All I need is a quiet place to work. I wrote my hit songs at home, and did the same with my column 'Pitching Horseshoes.'"

Actionize Your Income Plans

You're now at the point where, I hope, you are ready to take action on your home income plans. Please believe me when I tell you that one of the happiest days of your life will be the day you first receive a payment for a product or service you've sold from your own home. A whole new world of money, leisure, freedom, and happiness will open to you. Why? Because, possibly for the first time in your life, you will see a path to independence, and you'll have the beginnings in the form of hard cash.

What actions should you take on your income plans? Here are the six best positive actions you can take on your income plans:

(1) Finish reading this book
(2) Begin looking for your ideal home business
(3) Start reading the business section of your newspaper
(4) Review your financial situation
(5) Learn what's in your public library
(6) Convince yourself the money is there

Now let's take a closer look at each of these actions to see how *you* can take them starting today.

(1) **Finish reading this book.** That's *not* an idle recommendation of an author who's overimpressed with his own importance. It's because *you* are the entire focus of this book. *Your* home business and its zooming success are the only concern of the book. You and yours, I assure you, will prosper if you read, and understand, every word in this book.

(2) **Begin looking for your ideal home business.** Don't spend too much time trying to learn what the other person does at home. Concentrate instead on yourself, and what you can do best at home. Remember, also, that just because a certain home business that interests you—say TV and personal computer repair—has yet to run successfully in your town, is no reason for you to get discouraged. Sometimes just

opening a business in your home will give your activity a novel touch
that builds an enormous volume and starts an avalanche of dollars
across your doorstep.

(3) **Start reading the business section of your newspaper.** This
will keep you up to date on the newest developments in many
business subjects. Also, you'll be closer to stocks, bonds, and com-
modities. Since you may want to invest in the stock or commodity
market once you have some extra money from your home business,
the knowledge you gain from daily reading of the business section
of your newspaper will be a big help.

Incidentally, the stock market is an ideal place to invest excess
funds from your home business. A number of successful home
business operators have built enormous fortunes in the stock market
by making careful investments. This is one profitable way to pyramid your home business income with little investment of time.

(4) **Review your financial situation.** You *will* have to spend some
money to start your home business. There's hardly a business in this
world which doesn't require some starting capital. But one of the
purposes of this book is to show you how to get started on the least
money possible. Set up a simple balance sheet like that below when
reviewing your financial situation.

Assets	*Liabilities*
Cash on hand	Short-term debts
Cash in bank	Long-term debts
Stocks (at market value)	Judgments
Bonds (at market value)	
Other assets (real estate, etc.)	

Find the sum of your *liquid* or *quick* assets, i.e. ready cash in the
left-hand column. From this subtract the sum of your liabilities—i.e.
money you owe to others. The result is your net cash assets. Once you
know this number you are in a better position to take action. For as
Paul B., a well-known home real-estate operator says "When I have
some numbers to work with, even inaccurate ones, I'm on the trail of
profits. Without numbers any businessperson is lost."

When it comes to financing your great home business idea you can
sometimes work miracles just by asking, as these two readers told me:
"Thank you for mentioning small business loans for women. I called
my bank and they immediately offered me all the money I need for
my business at a good rate of interest. That call opened the bank vault
for me! Everything you said was true." And: "After reading a few of

your books I applied for a business loan at the bank here and got it. I paid it back early and I'm finishing paying off a second loan. I'm a BWB and I'm enjoying it."

(5) **Learn what's in your public library.** Visit your local public library Spend several hours examining the business books on the shelves. You'll find much of interest to you and many helpful ideas for your home business. Since I want you to get into a home business to earn the biggest profits possible in the shortest time, with the smallest investment, I strongly recommend that you visit your public library. It is an excellent source of free information.

Here's a list of a number of useful books for the home business specialist. Look for them in your public library, if you have the time. Used in conjunction with the book you are presently reading, these basic references form a profit-laden shelf of knowledge that can put you in the millionaire class sooner than you think.

Valuable Home Business Reference Books

U.S. Census Bureau, *Statistical Abstract of the United States,* U.S. Government Printing Office. (Issued annually.)

Coman, E. T., *Sources of Business Information,* University of California Press.

Manley, M. C., *Business Information: How to Find and Use It,* HarperCollins.

Hicks, Tyler G., *How to Build a Second Income Fortune in Your Spare Time,* IWS, Inc., POB 186, Merrick NY 11566-0186.

Hicks, Tyler G., *Smart Money Shortcuts to Becoming Rich,* IWS, Inc., POB 186, Merrick NY 11566-0186.

Hicks, Tyler G., *199 Great Home Businesses You Can Start (and Succeed in) for Under $1,000,* Prima, POB 1260, Rocklin CA 95677.

Lasser, J. K., *Business Management Handbook,* McGraw-Hill, New York NY.

Rapp, Stan and Collins, Thomas, *Beyond Maxi-Marketing,* McGraw-Hill, New York NY.

Rothfeder, Jeffrey, *Privacy for Sale: How Computerization has Made Everyone's Private Life an Open Secret,* Simon & Schuster, New York, NY.

Internal Revenue Service, *Tax Guide for Small Business,* U.S. Government Printing Office.

(6) *Convince yourself the money is there.* The most successful home business operators I know are energetic, enthusiastic, and full of ideas. Those that "have it made" are, if anything, more enthusi-

astic than the newcomer. Convince yourself that there's a pile of money to be made in your den, garage, basement, kitchen, living room, or attic. That pile of money *wants* to wind up in your bank account. And you can make all of that money yours regardless of where you live—in a one-room studio apartment or a thirty-room house. Convince yourself the money is there and you'll make more than you've ever earned before in your life. I firmly believe that if you *convince* yourself there's money to be made at home, that you can overcome every obstacle in your way. Belief in yourself and what you want to do is one of the world's greatest, but least understood, forces.

Lou D., a highly intelligent businessman, believed in the future of the mail-order business when he founded his direct-marketing mail-order sales catalog as a sideline activity. Even the manufacturer of Lou's first mail-order product—a pocket-size rubber stamp—tried to discourage him. But using his knowledge of people, Lou personalized the rubber stamp by putting the buyer's name and address on it and calling it a pocket printer. Despite the manufacturer's discouraging prediction, Lou was able to sell about one million of these useful and handy printers.

Fifteen years after starting his mail-order sales catalog with one product, Lou's company is an outstandingly successful $14-million-per-year business. Its first Christmas catalog contained 77 items and was mailed to 50,000 people. The current catalog, at the time of this writing, contains thousands of items and has a total press run of 50 million copies. Lou's firm exceeded 500 employees as it grew from a spare-time activity to a major force in the catalog direct-marketing field.

Yet Lou lost money on his first product. However, he stuck with his idea and did not get discouraged. You, too, can get rich in mail order if you start with a salable product and keep adding new ones to your line as your sales increase.

Refuse to Get Discouraged

Your refusal to get discouraged is the belief in yourself, your ideas, and your abilities which I have been urging on you in the last few paragraphs. To hit the big money in any business you must like yourself. Yet I see hundreds of struggling home businessmen every year who don't like themselves—as a result they are working under an enormous emotional strain. Once they realize how big a load they are carrying because of their lack of confidence in themselves, their lack of belief in their own ideas, and their dissatisfaction with the progress they are making in life, they change their way of thinking. *Seek the positive; shun the negative* is an approach that will help you more in your own home business than you realize.

When you first start, or take over, a small business you may lead a lonely existence. Your own family may even have trouble understanding what you're trying to do. Some of your potential customers may be completely unsympathetic to your ideas and products. You may even operate at a loss for awhile. For these and many other reasons, you need courage and belief in yourself if you are to prosper. If you have courage and believe in yourself, you *can* get into the $500,000-per-year earnings bracket in your own home business. This book shows you exactly how.

One More Suggestion

This chapter wouldn't be complete from your standpoint if I overlooked one more suggestion. If you have trouble:

* Getting ideas for profitable businesses
* Finding banks that will lend you money
* Developing mail-order ideas
* Earning finder's fees
* Doing business overseas
* Finding money for your business

or any of hundreds of other home business problems, I have a valuable suggestion for you. The monthly newsletter *International Wealth Success*, available from Prima Publishing, P.O. Box 1260HB, Rocklin, CA 95677, is full of profitable money and business leads for you. This newsletter, which you can subscribe to for $24 per year, contains items such as:

* New wealth ideas every month
* Finder's fees of all kinds
* Many sources of business loans
* Part-time moneymaking ideas
* Mail-order opportunities
* Franchise sources
* 100% financing for business ideas

* New, good wealth-building books
* World-wide international business opportunities
* Patents and inventions wanted
* Capital available for investment
* Businesses for sale at low cost
* Home moneymaking opportunities
* And many more wealth-building features

Thousands of home wealth builders regularly read this newsletter and profit from it. You should try it for a year because, when combined with this book, it gives you thousands of opportunities each year to hit the big money in the quiet and privacy of your own home.

As publisher of *International Wealth Success* (IWS) since its start, I've talked on the phone, met with, and written to thousands of people like yourself whom I call Beginning Wealth Builders—BWBs. Any number of these people have become big successes, using ideas from the IWS newsletter. As a subscriber you can call me day or night and bounce business and real estate ideas off me. I answer on the first ring and I'll spend as much time with you as you need. See later chapters and the back of this book for other services offered to BWBs by the IWS newsletter.

And I'll even consider lending you the money you need for your business ideas if you're a 2-year, or longer, subscriber to my newsletter. While it is not a requirement that you subscribe to my newsletter, I have found that readers of it are usually better equipped to handle business ideas and borrowing. Most BWBs I meet have great business ideas. Where they run into problems is financing these ideas. So I try to help by funding good ideas through my company, IWS, Inc., where such lending is permitted by local statutes. As the president and chairman of the board of another lending organization I see—almost every day of the week—how people can benefit from quick, low-cost funding of their business and personal needs. That's why I try to help as many BWBs as I can—with sensible business advice and fast, minimum-cost financing of workable and promising business ideas. A number of our borrowers have done well in business using the loan funds we provided to them.

So subscribe to my newsletter (see the back of this book) for two years, or longer, and ask for our loan application. Again, it is not necessary to subscribe, but I believe you will be happy if you do.

Now let's take a look at several sure-fire ways to pick a home business for yourself that will earn you at least $100,000 to $500,000 per year. The next chapter shows you these ways.

4

One Thousand
Profitable Home Businesses
for You

You should be happy in the work you do at home. Why? Because the man or woman who is happy with his work does a better job. Customers are satisfied and they return to give you more business. But let's understand one basic rule about doing business at home:

Earning money at home is such a wonderful experience that most people are happy with any business that does not overburden them mentally or physically.

Keeping this rule in mind helps you pick a home business sooner. You don't waste months agonizing over which business is *exactly* right for you. Instead, you pick your business and get to work to start the profits rolling in. And profit, after all, is the force which spurs every home wealth builder to greater efforts. Without profit there is no point spending time and energy in a home business.

Know the Profitable Businesses

I've advised thousands of home wealth builders; I've built several highly successful home businesses; and I've rescued a number of floundering home wealth builders. These experiences have taught me many valuable lessons. I want to pass these lessons on to you because they will help you know which business is the *right* business for you. Putting you on the exact path to a home income of at least $100,000 to $500,000 per year is my goal with every word of this book.

Basically there are, as we showed you earlier, four kinds of home businesses. These are:
  (1) Manufacture or sale of products
  (2) Mail order
  (3) Services to individuals and firms
  (4) Sale of personal skills

No matter how far you search for a home business you will find that it is one of these types, or a combination of two or more. What you must decide, with my help, is which type of business is best for you. I'm ready to spend as many hours as necessary talking or writing to you if I can help you find the right home business for yourself.

Knowing the types of home businesses you might start or buy gives you a definite advantage over other people. Why? Because you can narrow your search to the kind of business you *know* will be interesting to yourself. If a business interests you, you're certain to be a success in it. To get you ready for a home income of at least $100,000 to $500,000 per year, let's take a quick look at each of the four types of home businesses you might enter to earn your fortune.

What Each Home Business Offers You

PRODUCT BUSINESS

In a *product* home business you either make or buy products—toys, autos, boats, furnishings, etc.—which you sell to others for a profit. To sell these products you may run a store, an auction gallery, a mail-order business, or any of several other kinds of outlets. The important concepts of a product business which you'll find worth keeping in mind are:

(1) You must obtain or make the products you offer for sale
(2) You need some type of outlet in your home so you can sell the products
(3) You will probably have to advertise your products to sell them

King Camp Gillette invented in his home the safety razor with the removable blade. Starting with less than $10, which he spent for materials to build the first safety razor, he went on to become a multimillionaire. Though he had only one product at the start of his business, he quickly built his business into a world-wide organization. Today the Gillette name is one of the most highly respected in the world and you see it on a wide range of superior products.

MAIL-ORDER BUSINESS

In a *mail-order* business you use space advertising in magazines or newspapers to promote products which you make or buy. You may also use *direct mail*, i.e. ads sent through the mail to promote your products. Some mail-order operators neither make nor buy the products they sell. Instead, they arrange with a product manufacturer to *drop ship* various products to the customers ordering them. With this mode of operation you don't need a warehouse, shipping facilities, or any other high-cost buildings. Truly, mail order is an ideal home business for anyone who wants to get rich quickly in his or her own home.

SERVICE AND SKILLS

In a *service* business which you run in your own home you generally perform some kind of personal service for your customers. Thus, you might repair appliances, teach special courses, advise unhappy people, or perform any of hundreds of other important services. You can say that in a service business you

(1) Often work for people instead of companies
(2) Use your personal skills
(3) May have little capital invested in equipment
(4) Become very close to your customers

Sam B. began an income-tax service business in his basement. For a few dollars each he made out and filed Federal and state income-tax forms for people in his neighborhood. Because he kept up to date on the latest changes in the tax laws, Sam was able to save money for many of his clients. His reputation as a tax saver spread and soon Sam had more clients than he could handle. To cope with the extra work Sam trained some neighborhood people in a little school he set up. To be sure he got people who really wanted to work at home in their spare time, Sam charged a nominal tuition fee for his course. Soon Sam expanded his business to one nearby city, then two. Today he operates tax services in some 80 cities and his home income exceeds $350,000 per year. Even his school, in which he trains his future employees, shows a profit!

Products You Can Sell

In this chapter I want to show you where you can quickly, easily, and cheaply find lists of more than 1,000 home businesses. As you look over the lists I recommend to you, I hope that you'll find one or more businesses that appeal to you more strongly than others. Once you find the right business for yourself you can take the actions suggested in the next chapter. Let's start with the source of the list of products you might sell.

I am about to let you in on one of the most important home business secrets existing today. This is the first time I've ever revealed it to anyone. Knowing this secret could be worth at least one million dollars to you. Why? Because this secret shows you exactly how to target your home business interests so you find a product that interests *you* and that you'll enjoy selling. I call this the *Secret of the Century*.

The Secret of the Century

To earn a *big* income at home you have to get a clear, wide-range view of the opportunities open to you. And I say, here and now, that if you have a telephone in your home, you have that view available to you. Even if you don't have a telephone, if you can get to a public library, you have the same advantages as a person who has a telephone.

What is this great secret? It is the single source of more than 10,000 home business ideas. This source is the *Yellow Pages* of any large city phone book. Which large cities am I talking about? Here are three: New York, Chicago, Los Angeles.

Recently I checked the *Yellow Pages* of the Chicago phone book. In it I found more than 11,000 potential home businesses listed! Just imagine that. To avoid sensational claims, I took less than one-tenth of the listed businesses as potential home businesses. Yet I sincerely believe that at least half the businesses listed in the Chicago *Yellow Pages* are potential home businesses for the average person. And if you take the larger listings of the New York and Los Angeles *Yellow Pages*, you certainly have more than 1,000 potential home businesses available to you. Now what can these lists do for you? They can:

(1) Suggest specific businesses needed in *your* town or city
(2) Indicate which businesses are *not* operating in your town or city
(3) Show you thousands of home businesses in which many people are earning good profits
(4) Act as idea stimulators for home businesses which are needed in your area, based on activities which are *not* listed
(5) Expand your home business horizons so you understand more about what is going on in the world of home businesses
(6) Serve as a lead on the services and products which are available to you in your present or future home business

How to Acquire Home Business Ideas Quickly

Must you study every item on every page of the *Yellow Pages?* No; certainly not! All you need do is study the alphabetical listing of contents of the *Yellow Pages* beginning about page 7, 9, or 11 of the *Yellow Pages* of the city you select. Truly, the contents of the *Yellow Pages* for a large city contains a GOLD MINE of information for you. Believe me when I say this—I know what I'm talking about. I've had more than twenty years of experience in earning big money in the privacy of my own home.

To mine the home wealth that lies hidden in the *Yellow Pages* of your phone book, take these ten steps today.

(1) Tear out the contents pages of the book. This will give you anywhere from twenty to forty conveniently handled pages.

(2) Study each page, beginning with the letter "A."

(3) Read all the main (boldface or dark-ink) entries, and all the subentries (lightface ink).

(4) Keep a pad and pencil handy.

(5) Write down each entry that appeals to you as a potential home business, *exactly as it appears in the contents of the Yellow Pages. Don't make any changes—yet.* You'll see why in a few minutes.

(6) Devote at least four hours to preparing your list of attractive potential home businesses.

(7) If you have the time and the desire, I strongly suggest that you study the *Yellow Pages* for New York, Chicago, and Los Angeles. Why? Because the listings are *not* the same. Home businesses active in one city are not necessarily functioning in another city. By studying the lists for these three major cities you get a view of a wide variety of successful home businesses.

(8) When you finish either one, two, or three sets of large-city *Yellow Pages,* turn to the *Yellow Pages* for your local area and list, from A to Z, the home businesses which appeal to you.

(9) Compare the big-city list with your local list. On a third sheet list the big-city home businesses which do *not* appear on your local list. This third list provides you with a home business gold mine—that is successful home businesses which are not functioning in your town or city. You have money-laden information which could hardly be obtained in any other way.

(10) Narrow your choice of businesses which appeal to you to those ten you like the most. Get ready to analyze these ten businesses.

The Four Basic Rules for Analyzing Home Businesses

"Business is business," is a favorite saying of people who are trying to explain why they made an unpopular decision, took a course of action which inconveniences other people, or did any of a number of other things which displease someone. The implication in this statement is that you may have to do things in your business which you would not do in your personal life. These actions are completely honest, but they may lead to disappointing someone, such as when you can't hire a person, or must lay off people when business is slow.

To analyze potential home businesses you must be completely objective. While you may buy a car because you like the shape of its fenders, you wouldn't buy trucks for a home business for this reason. Why? Because trucks with pretty fenders may be a poor business investment. When buying trucks for a business you try to obtain the make of truck which gives you the most mileage for each dollar you invest in the truck.

The same principle applies when you analyze home businesses that interest you. Thus, while you may be interested in opening a fine-food restaurant in your home, you'd be silly to do so if your only reason for opening such a business is because you personally like good food. After all, you can't earn money on the food *you* eat—the only way you can earn money on the food served in your restaurant is to have customers who are willing to pay you for the food.

To analyze potential home businesses which appeal to you, four items must be carefully considered. These are:

(1) Profit potential of the business
(2) Need for the business
(3) Capital required for the business
(4) Experience required for the business

Let's take a quick look at each of these items.

PROFIT POTENTIAL OF THE BUSINESS

Some home businesses have twice the profit potential of others. Why work in a low profit potential business when you can just as easily work in a high potential profit business? As a general rule a high potential profit business

(a) Requires unusual or special worker skills
(b) Provides a product or service that is not readily available from many sources
(c) Adapts its product or service to the special needs of its customers or clients
(d) Is not driven to lower its prices by extreme competition from others
(e) Serves the needs of wealthy people or profitable companies
(f) Renders its service quickly and efficiently

Claude M. analyzed a list of 32 home businesses which he compiled from the *Yellow Pages* using the technique described above. His study showed him that a home business in which he used his personal skills would probably be most profitable for him. The home business which seemed to promise him the highest potential profit from his personal skills was a jiu jitsu school. However, Claude knew little about jiu jitsu.

But after applying the methods which you will learn in the next chapter, Claude chose the jiu jitsu school as the best way to build his fortune in his own home. He studied several books on jiu jitsu and then took a short course in it. Once he finished the course, Claude opened his school in his basement. The school was an immediate, highly profitable success because it (a) filled a need in his local area, (b) provided a service not readily available in his town, (c) altered its lessons to the special needs of his customers, regardless of age, financial means, or reasons for taking the course—self-defense, physical development, etc.—and (d) gave lessons quickly and efficiently in a short period of time.

Paula S. discovered personal computing and its business potential after she bought her son a PC. Tying into an online service when her son wasn't using the PC, Paula soon found a broker doing online sales at a discount. Recognizing that stock trading on a PC had a huge profit potential (and just as large a risk of losses), Paula decided to start trading via PC.

She also began collecting valuable trading data from her online connections. Today Paula is showing a nice profit from her home PC stock trading. Her profit potential is enormous, compared to the few fun hours she spends on her PC. For Paula, PC stock trading is an ideal home business.

NEED FOR THE BUSINESS

You'd do well to think twice before opening a florist shop in a small town which already has three such shops. Keep in mind at all times this fundamental fact about a home business:

> For any given product or service there is a basic potential market. When this market is served by several competitors they split the potential business amongst themselves. If another competitor enters the market he or she only causes a further split of the potential business. And, most important of all, entrance of a new competitor does not increase the potential market.

So don't assume, as many beginning home wealth builders do, that a large number of people in a business indicates that there's a very large demand for their services or products. All but a few of the businesspeople may be going broke. Actually,

> **The greatest need for a business exists when no one is in the business but people require the product or service the business would furnish.**

Thus, Joe T. opened a locksmith shop in his garage after he found that there wasn't one such shop in a city having a population of 65,000 people. Joe's only competition was two hardware stores in town. While these stores would duplicate a key for their customers, they couldn't render fast service because they were more interested in pushing hardware. Why? Because hardware was more profitable.

Soon after Joe opened his locksmith shop the two hardware stores closed down their key departments and sent their customers to Joe. He gives better, faster, and more efficient service. The hardware stores keep the goodwill of their customers because they recommend a competent locksmith. Joe profits and the stores rid themselves of an unprofitable service which was a constant nuisance.

CAPITAL REQUIRED FOR THE BUSINESS

No home business, in my opinion, should require you to invest more than $200 to get it started. Why do I recommend such a low starting capital when, I'm sure, you've heard of people spending hundreds of thousands of dollars to get a business started? I recommend this low starting capital because I believe you have a better chance to hit it big if you put more of yourself and less of your money into your new home business.

Now the *Yellow Page* approach you learned above is excellent for discovering the type of home business you might enter. But most of the businesses listed in the *Yellow Pages* are *not* home-operated. Instead, they are run in a store, a factory, a warehouse, etc. But that doesn't prevent you from getting the basic *idea* for your home business from the *Yellow Pages*. As a general rule, avoid home businesses requiring

(a) Expensive machinery
(b) Special work areas such as air-conditioned rooms

    (c) Large storage spaces
    (d) High-cost signs, lighting, heating, etc.

Don't fall in love with an intricate production process just because the machinery intrigues you. If you must fall in love with a production process, go for one that is simple, fast, and low-cost. Above all, keep this general rule in mind:

> **The less money you invest in a home business the more energy you will put into the business. And the less money you invest, the greater your chances of success.**

So invest yourself and your energies in your business. You'll be delighted with the enormous payoff you receive.

EXPERIENCE REQUIRED FOR THE BUSINESS

There are some home businesses, like diamond cutting, that require many years of exacting experience. Yet there are other home businesses, like vending-machine operation that require no previous experience—just some common sense.

You'd be foolish to go into a business requiring extensive experience, unless you had, or could acquire, the needed experience. If you have no idea of how much experience a home business requires, talk to one or more people in the business. You'll find that most businesspeople are ready to talk about their business, its problems, and the experience required to succeed in it.

Don't rely on the opinions of just one businessperson—talk to several, if you can. This will give you a cross section of opinion. You'll find there is a consensus as to the experience required. Where the businessperson you consult tells you that you need five years or more of experience, proceed carefully. I don't want you to fail because you lack experience—this is a silly error which you can avoid if you carefully analyze the businesses you are considering.

Other Sources of Home Business Ideas

The title of this chapter promises you one thousand home businesses. Since I want you to believe that this book gives you your money's worth several times over, the following paragraphs are designed to give you many other good ideas for home businesses.

The United States Government Printing Office, Washington, D.C. 20402, is one of your finest sources of low-cost business information. Called GPO for easy reference, this government agency publishes many excellent booklets prepared by the Small Business Administration (SBA). Some of these publications which might interest you are listed below. To obtain a copy of any of these useful publications, contact the GPO to obtain the current price and availability; send a check or money order for the correct amount to Superintendent of Documents, Government Printing Office, Washington, D.C. 20402. Here are some publications you may find useful when they are available:

Public Accounting Services for Small Manufacturers
Cutting Office Costs in Small Plants
Making Your Sales Figures Talk
Executive Development in Small Business
The Small Manufacturer and His Specialized Staff
A Handbook of Small Business Finance
New Product Introduction for Small Business Owners
Profitable Advertising for Small Industrial Goods Producers
Technology and Your New Products
Ratio Analysis for Small Business
Practical Business Use of Government Statistics
Equity Capital and Small Business
Guides for Profit Planning
Management Audit for Small Manufacturers
Insurance and Risk Management for Small Business
Management Audit for Small Retailers

You can also obtain copies of current issues of "Management Aids for Small Business," "Small Marketers Aids," "Management Research Summary," "Technical Aids for Small Manufacturers," and "Small Business Bibliographies." Simply visit the nearest office of the Small Business Administration to obtain your copies.

The monthly newsletter, *International Wealth Success*, available from Prima Publishing, P.O. Box 1260HB, Rocklin, CA 95677, is another valuable source of home business ideas. Besides listing hundreds of home businesses each year, *International Wealth Suc-*

cess, which costs $24 per year for a 12-month subscription, runs free ads for its regular subscribers and contains exclusive listings of:

> Finder's fees available
> Sources of business loans
> Mail-order opportunities
> Franchise facts and figures
> International business opportunities
> Unusual business deals
> Hundreds of highly profitable businesses

One of the subscribers to my *International Wealth Success* news-letter—working from home—wrote me to say:

> *I'm writing this letter, with much elation, after our recent telephone conversation. Thank you very much for helping me obtain an LBO (leveraged buyout). It was only through your books, which I have read over and over again, and the helpful and very informative conversations we had, that I was able to successfully accomplish this takeover.*
>
> *The business I took over is an office leasing and secretarial service company. I purchased this company for the outrageous cost of two dollars ($2.00). For this cost of two dollars I received all of the out-standing stock, $180,000 in fixed assets, $200,000 in gross income, and $14,000 in bank accounts. This all was made possible only through your help and expertise.*

A Gold-Laden List

In the last chapter of this book is a list of more than 1,000 home businesses which I think you ought to consider entering. What I want you to do after you finish reading this and the next paragraph is:

(1) Turn to the list at the end of this book
(2) Glance down the list
(3) Read, and think about, every business listed
(4) Check those home businesses that interest you most
(5) Get more information on each business you checked from your public library, people in the business, or trade associations

The list at the end of this book has been specially set up for *you*. Take a moment to read the instructions with the list. With the idea behind the list in mind, you can easily expand upon the items shown. Using such an approach, the list might suggest two to three times the number of businesses listed.

Never Stop Looking

Cal E., an airline pilot, bought a motel as a start for a home business which he plans to run when he retires from the airline. The motel is doing well but Cal thinks there are other chances for him. Recently a very attractive apartment house containing 48 furnished units was offered for sale. The mortgage payments are about $3,000 per month.

Since the apartment house would make a nice combination with his motel, Cal watched it closely. The owner listed the apartment house for several months but couldn't get anyone who was willing to take on the large monthly mortgage payment. After waiting for three months, Cal made his move. He offered to take over the apartment house, which is valued at $315,000, for no cash down. By this time the owner was so anxious to sell that he jumped at the chance.

So Cal, who never stops looking, became the proud owner of real estate worth more than $300,000 without putting up one cent! By careful balancing of tenants between his motel and apartment house, Cal is keeping both rented at almost full capacity. Although the mortgage is a heavy burden, Cal feels he can soon "get out from under" by refinancing. When he does, he'll be in clover because his net worth will be enormously increased.

Helen K., a highly competent business executive, saw the need for other part-time female executives in companies of various sizes. So she formed her own consulting company and lined up a number of professional women who are also mothers wanting to spend more time with their children.

Seeking women with 10 years or more of business experience, Helen pays them $30 to $50 per hour while they're on assignment. The women she recruits are primarily certified public accountants (CPAs) because this is a skill sorely needed by her client businesses.

Since all her female consultants are computer literate, they can work on the computer in the office, or at home using a modem. This makes it easy for the women to spend more time at home with their children—a desire all of them have.

Helen's business is booming because she can offer dedicated, competent, hard working people at a price about half of that charged by her competitors. Her bright idea is paying off for herself and her consultants! Her consultants get the part-time work they seek while earning an excellent wage without having to leave their children for more than a day or two at a time.

Start Looking in Your Spare Time

Don't put off getting ideas for home businesses one more day. Thinking and looking costs nothing. What's more, every time you check out a new home business possibility, you learn something. And the more you learn about various home businesses, the better prepared you'll be to start to earn $100,000 to $500,000 or more per year in your own home business.

If you'd like to start your home business in your spare time, I'd suggest that you buy a copy of *How to Build a Second-Income Fortune in Your Spare Time*, written by the author of the book you're now reading and available from IWS, Inc., POB 186, Merrick NY 11566-0186, for $10.00.

Also, if you're in a big hurry to build your home fortune, buy a copy of *Smart-Money Shortcuts to Becoming Rich*, written by the same author and available from the same publisher, IWS, for $10.00. Both books will repay you your purchase price many times over. Readers keep writing and calling me, saying "Gee, what you say really works!"

Certainly it works. Why? Because I never make a recommendation in any book until after I've used the method myself. *It must make money for me or I won't recommend it to you.* And if I have to spend money to make money, I have to earn at least five times what I invest. If I don't, I discard the method. Here's a good rule to keep in mind:

> **Aim at earning $5 for each $1 you spend in your home business for materials, advertising, and overhead. Make this goal and you'll earn a hefty profit.**

Try the spare-time and smart-money ways of building your home fortune. I like both because

- Spare-time work teaches valuable methods
- There's less chance of spare-time failures
- You build wealth fast in your spare time

- Shortcuts put you into the big money faster
- With big money rolling in you zoom ahead

There are so many other advantages to the spare-time and short-cut ways to building your home fortune that I could go on listing them all day. What I want you to do is try them. Then you may be one of the thousands who write or call to say "Gee, it really works!"

A Successful Spare-Time Businessman

Joe T. was somewhat doubtful when he first talked to me because his product was, he thought, very special. What was his product? Dog food. Joe mixed it in his garage and the neighborhood dogs just loved it. In fact, when a neighbor's dog was lost he always knew where to find it—outside Joe's garage waiting for some of that delicious dog food.

"Try putting display racks into local stores," I told Joe. "You don't have to quit your job; you can call on the stores on Saturday, in your spare time."

Joe mumbled something about not wanting to make a fool of himself.

"You'll make a fool of yourself if you don't push a good product when you have a chance to," I said. "If you can bring more business into a store, the owner will love you."

Joe sold pet food to the first six stores he called on when he went out the Saturday following our talk. "Gee," he said on the phone, "it really works!"

"Certainly it does," I said. "Why do you think I pushed you into doing something?"

Today Joe has pet food racks in more than 500 stores in his area. His line now includes food for many pets—dogs, cats, birds, fish, hamsters, etc. Some people call his racks a pet store in a supermarket. Meanwhile, of course, Joe's profits are excellent.

Be Ready for Fights

I've earned an enormous amount of money in my various home businesses. And today these businesses, and the income they produce, is better than ever. But before you pick a home business for yourself, as you will in the next chapter, I want to warn you of one big problem you may face in starting and running your own home business. This is the problem of fights. Let me explain.

Be prepared, if you're the typical home business builder, to have your nearest and dearest call you

> Stupid
> Slow-witted
> Thick-headed
> Money-mad
> A poor manager
> Failure-prone
> Etc., etc.

Ready yourself to have your ideas and plans laughed at, ridiculed, and spoofed by these same people. Expect to see your nearest and dearest, who in many cases know nothing about what you're doing, set themselves up as experts in everything you're thinking of doing in your home business. And their "expert" opinions will, in most instances, be completely wrong.

I've seen home business operators who, when they were listed in *Who's Who*, were ridiculed by their nearest and dearest who commented "I wouldn't let them list my name in a book like that!" Yet when a friend of this same nearest and dearest mentioned that she, the friend, would be listed in *Who's Who*, the comment by the nearest and dearest was: "So-and-so is listed in *Who's Who*. That shows how important she is."

The ridicule, laughter, and unpleasantness that your desire for home wealth can cause may be a greater hindrance to your success than any other resistance you meet. Competition from other businesses, price-cutting, and cheaper products may be meaningless, compared with the lack of understanding of your loved ones.

But don't despair, fellow home business operators. I've lived through many years of this and can tell you exactly how to handle this difficult and often perplexing problem. Since my businesses grow stronger every year and the income they generate gets larger and larger, the method I've developed is practical and useful. Here it is.

How to Reduce Family Strife

To reduce family strife to the minimum when considering, founding, or operating a home business

(1) Resolve to engage only in honest activities

(2) Tell your business plans to no one at home

(3) Make your own business decisions

(4) Never, never mention a failure

(5) Keep your business funds in your own name

(6) If you must talk business, talk about your successes

(7) Share some, but not all, of your income with your family

(8) Get what *you* want from your home business—i.e. a new car, more clothing, etc.

You must take a cold, hard look at family criticism of your business activities. If you talk too much about your home business activities you will spend a lot of time defending your ideas and plans. Why waste time this way, particularly when it may also cause your nearest and dearest ones to lose their tempers? Take my advice and follow this rule:

> **Figure out what you want to do in your home business. Tell no one at home, if you can avoid doing so. Take the business action you've decided on.**

Why People Resist Business Ideas

Your nearest and dearest resist your business ideas for several reasons, including

(a) They don't understand your ideas

(b) They're envious of your ambition

(c) They resent your attempts to succeed

(d) They're afraid you'll outgrow them

(e) They're insecure and want you to be the same

The man or woman who has the courage to start his or her own home business is a unique individual. As such, you can expect other people to be envious of you because these people would like to be as courageous as you are. When these people realize that you have more ambition than they do, they react emotionally instead of logically. That's when the criticism, sarcasm, and snide remarks begin.

Shun Small-Minded People

If you're starting your own home business, you're a big man or woman from a personality standpoint. Don't allow small-minded people to get in your way. Do what you want to do, when you want to. Shut your ears to idle envy and ignorant remarks.

Why do I recommend action instead of hours and hours of patient explaining, justifying, and filling-in of those near and dear to you? Because actions produce results. And results can be ten thousand times more convincing than all the arguments you could ever dream up. So don't waste time talking—get to work and start earning!

As soon as you start earning you'll see a strange change in your critics. Instead of truculently disagreeing with everything you say, their arguments will be milder. If you follow the tips in this book your income will soon increase, possibly to the level where you're earning more in a few hours at home than other people are in a week in an office.

At this point your critics may stop talking altogether, and start listening to you! They may even agree with you—once in awhile.

As your income increases, your critics become your warm friends —at least that's the way they'd like to have it. Soon they're asking you to spend money on them, or lend them money for "brilliant" business ideas they have.

Take my advice—I know what I'm talking about. Follow this rule:

> **Keep your money to yourself. Spend some on your loved ones, even if they've been your worst critics. But, as a general guide, spend less than you earn and keep control of your money.**

Don't Let Criticism Get You Down

Never allow criticism to bother you. Keep your goal of a home fortune in view at all times. Follow the tips in this book and you'll soon have a big income flowing into your home. Then when one of your critics asks you for a loan or some other part of your home income you can say, with mock surprise, "But you've been so critical of my home business ideas, you certainly *couldn't* accept any of the money I earned from them. You're so much smarter than I am that accepting money from me would probably be an insult to you!"

Remember: There's a day of reckoning for everyone in life. If you spend your time in a useful activity, such as a home business, your day of reckoning will be a pleasant one. But if a person spends his or her time criticizing others, his or her day of reckoning will often extend to years, and every day in every year will be unpleasant.

Beware of Posers

As you move ahead with your home business plans, various types of people will try to attach themselves to you. The worst kind of person of this type is, in my opinion, the poser.

The poser *pretends* to be more capable than he or she actually is. They will often pretend to be an intellectual—thinking that occasional attendance at the opera and visits to art galleries increases their brain power. Let me tell you a secret—it doesn't!

Don't think that I'm anti-intellectual. I'm not. What I am against is the automatic assumption by some people that just because they read poetry and listen to classical music they therefore know so much that they can tell you how to pick and run your home business. The ability to read poetry and listen to music does not necessarily mix with the ability to run a home business. In fact, my experience shows that the two abilities usually do not occur in the same person, though either ability can be developed if the other exists first.

Be friendly with posers—you may be able to put them to work in your business when you need some *cheap* help! For when you probe the posers' real worth you find you can't afford to pay them much because their skills are so limited. They sense this and are willing to work for the lowest kind of wages so they can pay for more poetry books and classical records. Meanwhile, your home income will increase because of the work they do for you. So:

Be friendly with posers but keep them out of the financial areas of your business.

Get Ready to Select Your Home Business

You now have your list of home businesses that interest you. Also, you've been alerted to some of the general problems you may meet in starting any home business. So you're now ready to pick the most profitable home business for *you*. The next chapter shows you exactly how to pick a home business from the list you prepared while reading this chapter — a business that will make you happy and rich and pay you at least $100,000 to $500,000 per year.

Pick Your Wealth-Building Home Business

You *can* control the money that will be yours in the future. How? By choosing a wealth-building home business that appeals to you, excites your imagination, and provides you with a deep sense of accomplishment. When these personal satisfactions from your business are linked with a good idea, your income zooms to new highs, powered by the fuels that have no equals—belief, energy, and enthusiasm. Throughout this book I want to introduce you to these highly potent ideas so you'll hit the big money as soon as possible.

Know What You Like

Some people stumble through life, wandering from one job to another without a specific goal in mind. These people never bother to do some serious thinking about what they really like to do to earn money, and what they want out of life.

Don't let this happen to you. I want *you* to have the best of everything you desire in life. This book shows you how to get what you want by working in your own home business. The book helps you lead a *planned* business life, instead of a life which is a series of compulsory adjustments to circumstances over which you have little control.

What do you like to do best? Make a list of your favorite activities in several areas. Enter *your* favorites in the spaces below.

Favorite Activity Checklist

Item	Favorite Activity
Work	....
Hobby	....
Education	....
Sports	....
Social	....
Recreation	....
Other	....
Favorite activity area (indoors; outdoors)	....

Study the entries in your checklist. Does the same activity appear under more than one heading—such as Work and Recreation, Hobby and Social, etc.? If so, you may find that you're about to make a new discovery concerning yourself and your favorite activities.

Learn More about Yourself

Why, you might ask, must I learn what I like? "What I like best," you might say, "is a five-letter word—money." Sure, I say, most people do like money. But if you earn money doing what you like to do, you

(1) Earn more money
(2) Earn this money faster
(3) Give better service to customers
(4) Obtain greater satisfaction from your work
(5) Have a professional attitude towards your work

When people find a reliable, productive professional engaged in his or her own home business they will flock to his door. Almost everyone misses the day of the true craftsman. So, in knowing what you like, you are preparing yourself for a profitable home business.

Most of us *like* money. But to earn really *big* money we must also like to do something which will earn an income for us. Knowing what you like is a powerful guide to the home business that will earn you a fortune in a short time.

A great home business that requires little more than a typewriter and telephone is Loan Portfolio Brokering. In this business you locate collections of loans—called a portfolio—and bring the collection to one or more buyers. You are paid a commission by the buyer for locating the loan collection. Thus one reader in the Midwest told me he went into the business of buying written-off credit-card bad debts. Working with three other brokers, the four bought some $31-million of bad debt chargeoffs for 3¢ on the dollar, or $930,000. Within days they sold the same $31-million in bad debts for 4.25¢ on the dollar. Each of the four brokers netted some $78,000 on the deal, after expenses were paid. Not bad for a business that doesn't need a big factory, lots of machinery, a huge staff, etc. And, as this portfolio broker says, there's some $8-billion out there of bad debt paper of various types just waiting to be bought and sold. An ideal home business for many people! (See back of this book for more information on this great business.)

Review What You Do Best

There are certain things that come easy to you—things you do so well that you hardly have to think about them. Perhaps you're a linguist—you speak three or four languages and you can pick up a new language in a few days. Yet you're so accustomed to this skill that you hardly think of it when you analyze what you like and what you do best.

Recently, while guiding a new client towards the selection of a profitable home business, I asked him about his hobbies. "Oh, they're not important," he said. "My main hobby, which is putting ship models in bottles, wouldn't earn me a dime." "What!" I almost roared at him. "Wouldn't earn you a dime! Man, you have to bring yourself up to date. Ships in bottles are big business today."

Craftsmen Earn Big Home Incomes

I explained to him the growing interest in older crafts. Young couples, in decorating new homes, want a dash of the past amongst their modern furnishings. A ship in a bottle is a colorful, compact conversation piece. It is "just right," many homemakers believe for that touch of early American New England in an Italian Provincial living room.

"And since skilled ship bottlers are scarce," I told him, "you have a lifetime job ahead of you helping decorate the homes of America at a highly profitable price. After all, your materials cost pennies, your overhead is negligible, and quality control is simple. Yet you can sell ships in bottles at prices from $10 to $10,000, or more." Today this client has a booming ship-bottling business. Yet he almost overlooked this profitable skill because he mistakenly assumed it was worthless.

Pinpoint Your Many Skills

To help prevent this kind of an incident from robbing *you* of profits, here's an easy-to-use, what-I-do-best checklist. Take a few moments, here and now, to fill in this list. You'll be surprised—and pleased—with the number of skills you uncover.

Best Skills Checklist
(A list of what I do best in my life)

At Work	At Home	At Play	Elsewhere
1.	....	....	....
2.	....	....	....
3.	....	....	....
4.	....	....	....

Study your list when you finish it. Is there any skill you might use directly in a home business? Compare your do-best list with the many home businesses discussed in Chapter 4. Are there any businesses mentioned in Chapter 4 in which *your* talents would earn you money? I'm sure there are. Make a list of them right now in this space.

Potential Home Businesses for Me

1. . . . .   4. . . . .
2. . . . .   5. . . . .
3. . . . .   6. . . . .

Understand What You're Getting Into

Every business requires some of your time, energy, thought, and creative powers. You can't run the usual home business by remote control. You must be on the scene, directing the business. This means that you must understand what you're getting yourself into when you open your own home business.

As a strong believer in the dry-run or virtual-reality technique—i.e. studying a business on paper or your computer monitor screen before ever buying or starting it—I recommend you try this method. I believe you'll find it a valuable profit builder.

Start a dry run by listing what the business or businesses you're interested in will require of you. Here's a handy checklist of the usual requirements of a business. Fill in the spaces that apply to your business.

Business Requirements Checklist

Item	*Requirement*	
1. Time	Hr. per day	week . . . .
2. Capital	$ per week	year . . . .
3. Travel	Days per week	year . . . .
4. Labor	Persons per day	week . . . .
5. Overhead costs	$ per week	year . . . .
6. Professional advice (taxes, etc.)	$ per week	year . . . .
7. Customer complaints	Hr. per month	year . . . .
8. Work area	Indoors	Outdoors . . . .

Let's take a quick look at the most important items in this checklist. You'll find it easier to apply the list to *your* business once you've explored these items.

Study Your Business' Time Needs

How many hours per day will you have to spend (a) working at serving your customers, (b) preparing for and cleaning up after the customers, (c) ordering supplies, checking inventory, tracking down errors of all kinds, (d) doing the bookkeeping, depositing money in the bank, obtaining change, etc.? To earn money in a home business you must put in time. True, your business may require different activities from those listed. But any way you look at it, you have to put in the hours. So:

> Know, in advance, exactly how many hours of your time your home business will require. If you can't devote this much time to your home business, look elsewhere for another business.

Plan to Pay Off Loans

If you start your own home business you'll have to make an investment of some kind. Hopefully, you can supply this from other earnings until your home business starts paying you a profit. If you buy a home business, you'll probably have to pay off a loan you took out to make a down payment on the business. But if you follow my advice you'll have no trouble obtaining a loan of up to $35,000 at simple interest rates with six years to pay off the loan. So, don't worry about capital; you're in good hands while you're reading this book. Remember:

> Plan your home business so it earns enough to pay off any loans you take out for it, plus a suitable income for yourself.

Business Travel Can Be Fun

Some home businesses require that you get out and travel—either in your local area, as with a newspaper, refuse-collection, computer-repair, or vending-machine route, or to distant cities, as with a sales route for home-manufactured products. Contrasted to these "travel" businesses is the home mail-order business where your longest trip is to the corner mailbox.

Don't become over-romantic about business travel. As an experienced business traveler who sometimes covers 100,000 miles per year, I warn you that travel for business purposes is hard work. Yet it can still be fun because you can:

(a) Have a relaxing dinner at the best restaurant in town
(b) Take in the newest show or movie
(c) Stay at an expensive hotel

All these activities are fun to many people. But you still must go to work the next day.

Despite the attractions of business travel, there are some people in this world who'd rather work in their own homes than on the road. Fine; all they need is the right home business. If you'd rather not travel for business, then take a clear look at each business you're thinking about. *Determine if its travel requirements will suit you.* If they don't, you'd better look for another business.

Employ as Little Labor as Possible

The most desirable home businesses require the least labor in terms of number of employees and the number of hours required to produce one unit of product or service. For example, you can run a Rent-a-Dog service in which you rent dogs to people who want protection or companionship. Typical rates are $35.00 per day for a Great Dane or Doberman Pinscher, $25.00 per day for a German Shepherd, $16.00 per day for a Malamute Husky. It's easy to see that your labor costs are nil while your dog is out on hire. In fact, the person hiring the dog does all the work related to the dog (feeding, cleaning, etc.) while the dog is on hire. Much the same is true for other popular rental services—TV sets, videocassettes, personal computers, tools, autos, boats, airplanes, etc. So:

> Avoid high labor content home businesses. Shun business requiring large labor forces to turn out the product, or lengthy production schedules for each product.

Don't Let Overhead Break You

You've probably heard the remark "Business is great, but the overhead is killing me!" What the person means when he or she says this is that fixed expenses—depreciation, supervisor's salaries, rent, a portion of electricity charge, etc.—are high. When he or she finishes paying variable expenses—material, labor, machine operating cost, etc.—so little is left that he or she can just about meet fixed expenses. Thus, they have little or not profit and the overhead, as they say, is "killing" them.

This doesn't mean that a high-overhead business is an unprofitable business. Instead, such a business can be highly profitable—if operated correctly. But to be as safe as possible, I recommend that you start with a low-overhead business (such as mail order, a delivery route, an advisory service, etc.). Once you gain some experience working in your own home you can then consider a high-overhead business, if you wish.

Use Professional Advice Sparingly

Steer clear of a home business requiring large amounts of professional advice (legal, medical, dental, accounting, etc.). The cost of professional advice can rise faster than the cost of living. If you have to pay for this advice you may be caught in a squeeze between the professional and your client. The result will be that you're a middleman who does little more than swap dollar bills.

So stay away from home businesses requiring constant professional attention—unless you have the professional qualifications to give your business the required attention. Thus, many lawyers operate rental real estate units (apartment houses, hotels, private homes, etc.) from their homes. Their legal training allows them to handle leases, deeds, and other documents with ease. If they had to pay for this advice, their profits would be much lower.

Steer Clear of Customer Complaints

This is the age of the complaining customer. Thousands of people buy something one day and return it the next. Large businesses can afford a liberal return policy. But a small business can go broke if returns are high.

Other areas where you can run into losses are repair of items you sell, replacement of damaged or broken parts, and free servicing of products you sell. So don't go into a complex business like personal computer or TV and VCR repair unless you know the entire technical side of the business. Choose a business with which you have some familiarity. Otherwise, customer complaints may drive you broke and batty.

Know Where You Like to Work

Some of us enjoy working indoors; we dislike spending long periods in the sun and wind. Others feel trapped when working indoors; they want to get outside where they can expand. Don't pick an outdoor business when you're the indoor type, and vice versa. You may find that your dislike of the work area leads to poor performance in your business.

Plot Your Money Future

The most successful home business operator I've met has one wall of his basement covered with simple charts showing

Monthly sales
Monthly expenses
Advertising results
Worker output
Cash reserves
Planned annual income

Whenever he has a question about where his income stands in relation to his plans, he simply glances at the wall to obtain a quick answer.

You don't need such an elaborate planning center when you first start your business. But if your income reaches $100,000 per year, as I most certainly hope it will, you may find such a planning area helpful.

How can you plot your money future? It's easy. Just follow these four steps:

1. Estimate annual sales in dollars and units
2. Figure your annual variable costs
3. Estimate your annual overhead
4. Compute your profit

Do this now for each year for the next five years. In business this is called a long-range forecast, while a one-year estimate is called a short-range forecast. If you have a personal computer you can easily put your estimates on a spreadsheet and print out the results for future reference and guidance.

You Can Figure Out Any Business

"But I'm going to open a Swedish massage salon in my basement," you say. "How can I possibly figure sales in dollars and units?"

"That's easy," I say. "What will you charge for a massage? Once you know this, guess at how many massages you'll give per day, per week, per month, and per year. Just remember that every business has its busy and slow periods. So if you estimate that you'll give eight massages a day during busy periods, reduce this to six, four, or two during your slow periods, depending on how much you think your business will fall off."

Your variable costs, as explained earlier in this book, are materials, supplies, labor and other items which increase with greater activity, decrease with less business. Use actual costs when you can obtain them; estimate those costs you cannot obtain. WARNING: *Be safe; when you must estimate costs, estimate on the high side, not the low side.* You can *always* reduce your selling price to reflect lower costs. But you cannot always increase your selling price to reflect increased costs and stay in business.

Overhead Never Goes Away

Your overhead, like taxes, will always be with you. Include your salary in the overhead. The United States Government, through the Small Business Administration (SBA) states that the profit a business shows is figured *only* after the owner's salary is deducted. Why is this approach used? Because *your* salary is a necessary overhead cost in the business. If you weren't working there, someone else would be, if the business stayed in existence. So don't neglect your salary when figuring the usual overhead items—rent, light, heat, general and administrative (G & A) costs. Incidentally, your salary is termed G & A. That makes you a real executive!

As with your variable costs, figure overhead on the high side. An attic book publisher who earns an excellent income amongst the eaves, applies a direct overhead charge to each copy of a book he sells. Thus, he makes every product carry its share of his overhead. You can do the same with any other product, if you wish.

And a 27-year-old advertising art director who founded his own ad agency in the living room of his parents' California home after losing his job with a big ad agency pays rent to his parents from each ad he designs. Three years after founding his home-based ad agency, it won a coveted award for some of the best ads of the year. Today his agency has an enormous backlog of work for new clients clamoring to use his services—all of which started from a low-overhead home living room!

Profit Is Your Business Goal

Working at home is stimulating fun open to everyone, be a person 9 or 90. But the fun soon wears off if your home business doesn't show an early profit. Certainly, there are some home businesses like raising pets—thoroughbred dogs, rabbits, tropical fish, white mice, etc.—in which your profit will be delayed by the life cycle of the animal. In such a business you will expect profits to begin a little later than in a quick turnover business like mail order, parking-lot operation, or invisible reweaving of garments.

Always keep in mind this important fact: *Profit is your goal.* Some people will say to me during my consulting sessions: "I'm only in this home business to pass the time. Profit really doesn't interest me. My kids are grown and married—my wife and I need only a few dollars to make ends meet."

Don't Work for Low Profits

When I hear remarks like these I nearly explode. Why? Because I believe that anything *worth* doing at all is worth doing *well.* Over the years I've noted that the man or woman who seeks an honest profit from his or her home business renders a better service to his customers. A profit-motivated businessman is more anxious to please his customers. People leaving his place of business feel satisfied that they're getting their money's worth.

So always work for a profit. Your business and customers will stimulate you more, you'll render better service, and your income will be higher.

What's more, I'm positive you'll find a use for the extra income. I've yet to meet a man or woman anywhere in this world who didn't need a slightly higher income. Plot your money future in terms of profits and you'll grow richer than you ever thought possible, much sooner than you think.

One excellent example of seeking high profits is the Business Funding Consultant who, working from home, earned a $72,000 commission on just *one* transaction! Sure, the deal took time. But the commission on just this one transaction was more than some people earn from a year's work.

By focusing on a big deal, this BWB was able to earn a larger commission than would have been due from several smaller, time-consuming deals.

You too can do the same. Just look for larger profits from your home-based efforts. Just because you work from home doesn't mean that you'll slave for a pittance! Just look for a larger income and it *will* come to you! (If you'd like to become a Business Funding Consultant, refer to the Kevin Clark Ultimate Cash Flow Funding System Kit listed at the back of this book.)

Recognize Low-Income Activities

No matter where you were born, no matter who your parents were, and no matter how little money you now have, you *do* have one thing in common with millionaires. What is that? You and the millionaires have the same number of hours, minutes, and seconds in each day. If you want to become a millionaire, or even half a millionaire in your own home business, you have to make full use of the time available to you.

One of the saddest situations I can imagine is the ambitious man or woman who works long hours at home at activities having a low-income potential. Why run a home telephone answering service for housewives that nets you $100 per month when a business telephone answering service run in your home can net you $10,000 per month, and more? You'll put in the same number of hours in each business, yet one nets you one-hundred times more than the other.

You can spot potentially low-income activities from these six characteristics:

- Excessive competition in your area
- Cheap substitutes readily available
- Unskilled labor can do the work
- Product or service appeals only to low-income people

- Very high labor hours per unit produced
- Demand for product or service is very small

Let's take a quick, close look at how you can avoid unprofitable, low-income activities.

Overcome Excessive Competition

Suppose you want to open a dog-grooming salon in your own home. If you live in a small farming town where most of the few dogs around are mongrel strays, your chances for a high income are almost nil. But if you live in a large city—Chicago, Dallas, Los Angeles, New York, etc.—you have an excellent chance to build a prosperous business because many people keep pets in large cities. And, luckily, this is a business in which there is only restricted competition because a person must have skill and training before he or she can go into it with much hope of success.

Avoid Cheap Products

You *can* make a fortune in your own home business if you sell ten million items at ten cents each—*if your operating costs are low enough.*

Your chances of hitting the big money are greater, however, if you try to sell fewer units at a higher profit per unit. Recently, at an expensive and exclusive dinner party in Stockholm, Sweden, the host, who sells Swedish furniture by mail order throughout the world, remarked to me "I keep my prices high because this policy keeps my problems low. Only the more desirable customers can afford the higher prices—these customers pay their bills with checks that don't bounce. Once you begin to sell cheap products, you get cheap customers. This leads to problems of all kinds—bouncing checks, merchandise returned in damaged condition, and so on."

Deal in better-quality products in any business and you eliminate the threat of cheap substitutes. Why? Because the cheap substitute can seldom provide the same results a better-quality product does.

Help Unskilled Workers

Unskilled labor can dig ditches, tar roofs, lug heavy loads, and perform similar tasks. Fortunately, unskilled labor isn't as big a threat to you, the intelligent home business owner, as it used to be. As the minimum wage required by law climbs, unskilled labor becomes less attractive to factory operators and business owners. Often a machine can do the same work at a lower cost and higher efficiency.

Avoid a home business in which you're at the mercy of part-time or unskilled workers, or both. Thus, a man I know of, Mal K., opened a catering business in his home in a university town. The students at the university form an excellent labor pool for waiters, busboys, dishwashers, etc. Mal's business prospered in all departments except one—the serving of drinks.

Mal noticed that he hardly ever had a call to cater an affair where drinks were served. Investigating, he learned that "every boy on this campus thinks he's the world's best bartender. These boys cater every cocktail party for fifty miles around here."

Check Out Business Facts

To be sure of his facts, Mal checked several upcoming cocktail parties. As reported, college boys were tending bar. To check further, Mal had himself invited to several cocktail parties. What he saw shocked him. "Why the boys didn't even know what a 'Rusty Nail' or 'Screwdriver' was, let alone know how to mix them," Mal laughed.

What to do? Mal wanted to reduce competition while offering better service. Musing about it one day while relaxing on a ski outing, Mal hit on the idea for a bartender's school. For a low cost—$50— he'd offer a complete course in bartending. With well-trained bartenders available to local hostesses, Mal was sure he'd win most of the cocktail-party catering jobs.

That's just what happened, except for one other success. Mal's bartending school is so popular that he opened the course to people who are not students at the university. These people—both men and women—pay a $350 tuition fee. Thus, Mal is able to reduce the competition from unskilled labor by offering them training at a nominal fee. He not only increases the volume of his catering business, he also improves the quality of his service while helping people increase their skills. This is an excellent way to solve the problem of competition from unskilled labor.

Aim at Middle-Income Markets

There are millions of underprivileged people in this world today. Yet their number is steadily decreasing. Why? Because nations everywhere are trying to improve the financial and social positions of their citizens.

Aim your home products at the middle-income market and you can't lose. "Prove it," you say. "Sure," I reply. "Here's your proof."

The middle-income group is the largest in the United States, the United Kingdom, Scandinavia, and western Europe. What the millions of people in this group go for—motorcycles, low-cost art works, development housing, sports cars, group travel, etc.—constitutes probably the largest market for sales in the world. And, happily for you, the tastes, desires, and needs of this enormous middle-income group are steadily improving and increasing. Thus, your market is constantly growing larger.

Joan A. was selling modern telephone equipment to a variety of businesses. While her customers were happy with the equipment she sold them, they often told her that their bills for telephone calls were higher *after* they got their new equipment than before.

This annoyed Joan because the new telephones were supposed to *reduce* bills, not increase them. Taking a batch of bills home, Joan studied them to see if she could find the cause of the increased charges.

To her amazement, many of the bills contained big errors, resulting in overcharges to the customer. This is why their bills for telephone calls were rising instead of falling.

Starting on a part-time basis, Joan started looking for corporate clients who would be glad to have their phone bills reduced by searching out errors. She charged half of what she saved her customers. Thus, if she saves $100,000 on a customer's phone bill, she keeps $50,000. Just 10 years after her business started—from home—she found some $5 million in errors. Today, of course, she has a nice office and a staff of assistants to help her.

Low Incomes Are Steadily Increasing

But what about the people with lower incomes? Why not develop and sell to them cheaper products especially developed for their needs? This is a good question. Cheap products for lower-income people won't appeal as strongly to them as more expensive products aimed at higher-income people. Everyone in this world dreams of getting ahead. One of the definitions of getting ahead used by lower-income people is the ability to buy the same products the middle-income people use.

Today, as you start your climb towards an income of $500,000 per year in your own home business, you may be driving a Ford or one of the other cars in the low-priced three. It may be new or old. But no matter what its condition is, the car won't satisfy you if you long for the rich, throaty purr of a well-tuned Cadillac, Mercedes, or Lexus. Just as you aspire to something better in your life, and I in mine, so too do lower-income people. There is, however, one big difference. The lower-income individual may have a much stronger drive for better things in life. He or she just has to have those middle-income products which you turn out. That's why you're sure to hit the big money if you aim your home-originated products at the enormous middle-income markets of the world.

Another positive aspect of this market is often overlooked. This is the conservative buying approach used by many wealthy people. Remembering when they had less money than they do now, or fearing worse times in the future, these people buy down—i.e. they buy items made for the middle-income group. So you capture the market both ways—people buying up *and* people buying down.

Shun High Labor Hours

Time is money is one of the basic truths of every home business. No matter what your product or service is, you're investing your time and, perhaps, some money in it. The longer it takes you to turn out one unit, be it a guitar, bottle of jam, letter of advice, etc., the higher your price for the unit must be. Why? Because as we noted earlier, we all have the same number of hours available to us in a day. If you want to generate a certain daily income with ease (and why make your home business a struggle?) aim at producing a unit of product or service quickly enough so you can price it for the middle-income market.

Some home business operators earn an excellent income catering to. the luxury trade. For instance, Joe M. runs a lucrative ($120,000 per year gross income) private limousine service from his home. But

Joe didn't start his business by catering solely to the wealthy. Instead, he started a small taxi service in his town. Gradually, however, Joe saw that he could earn more per hour by serving the rich people than the usual cab riders, so he slowly switched over to a private limousine service. The wealthy are willing to pay both a standby charge when a limousine is held waiting for them, as well as an hourly operating charge when the vehicle is in use. The combination of these two produced a much larger hourly income for Joe than his taxi service did. This, in effect, reduced the number of hours Joe had to work to earn any given level of income.

Be careful, when using this technique, not to turn down a low hourly income unless you're *sure* you can earn a higher income doing other work. It's better to take in $25 per hour in your home business than to take in no money at all while you look for a $100- or $200-per-hour activity. Do what Joe did. He kept one source of income going while he gradually switched over to a higher source.

Avoid Small-Demand Businesses

A small-demand business—i.e. a business having very few customers or small demands for its products can break you sooner than you think because

  (a) You spend many hours finding prospects
  (b) Sales are difficult to close
  (c) Complaints and repairs can be troublesome
  (d) Your chances for repeat business are low
  (e) There are few leads from one customer to another

Check the probable demand for your product or service *before* you go into business. Whenever I start a new business, or act as a consultant to someone starting one, I put on my "pessimist's hat." Too many people when starting a new business are misled by the thought of all the money they *think* they'll earn. "Gee," they say, "we'll be rich in a month."

"Before you spend all that money, let's figure how much money you may *not* make," I reply in the saddest tone I can use. This brings them up with a start. "You're looking at the upside of the business," I say, just as sadly. "I want to look at the downside. What'll happen if you can't sell as many products or services? Will you be ruined for life with an enormous debt? Or could you pay it off with just a little extra struggle, using income from another source?"

"But how do I check the demand?" you ask, somewhat discouraged. "I can't hire a researcher or consultant."

Here are six easy, inexpensive ways to check product or service demand. They work beautifully for my clients and myself. Up till now I've never revealed *all* these methods to one person at one time. This is the *first time* they've appeared in print. These methods can be worth thousands of dollars to you. A handy checklist included with the methods helps you evaluate the demand for any product or service.

Six Powerful Moneymaking Tips

(1) Use the *Yellow Pages* of your phone book. Are many (four or more) firms offering a similar product or service listed? If the answer is yes, there's a fair, or large, demand for your proposed product or service.

Yes ....   No ....

(2) Check the ads in the Business Opportunities section of a large-city newspaper (Los Angeles, Chicago, New York, Dallas, etc.). Are people trying to buy or sell a business like that you're thinking of? A yes answer is a good sign.

Yes ....   No ....

(3) Read the trade magazines serving the business you intend to start. There aren't any magazines serving the field? This *may* indicate that you'd be better off in another business. If there are magazines available, do they see a promising future for the business? Call the editor, if necessary, and ask him or her.

Yes ....   No ....

(4) Run a survey of your experience. Do you know of any other people earning big money in this or a similar business? Review your past life, from childhood on. Can you remember such a business?

Yes ....   No ....

(5) Conduct a survey amongst your friends. Have any of them heard of, seen, worked in, or been connected with such a business in any way? *Don't ask them for advice—just get the facts from them.*

Yes ....   No ....

(6) Put numbers on paper. List the number of products, number of units of product, or the number of customers you think you could sell to in your business. Take half the estimated number. Would the business still be attractive if you had only this many sales?

Yes .... No ....

Take Action Now

Use these six methods *now*. They won't cost you a cent, but I guarantee you that you'll learn plenty from them. You may even find, during your search of the *Yellow Pages*, newspapers, and magazines that there are other, more attractive home businesses you never thought of.

For example, one man who used these methods found that the home business he had in mind (exterminating services) was *too* popular. Competition with well-established and well-known insect exterminating firms in his area would probably be too intense for comfort. But he found that exterminators need information about new families moving into a neighborhood because these people are excellent prospects for exterminating services. So this man formed an information bureau which supplies data on new families to many businesses in his area. Where does he get data about new families? That, he says, is a business secret. (But I note that he's very friendly with real-estate agents, post office clerks, telephone installers, etc.)

Aim for the Big-Money Profits

Keep profits foremost in your mind whenever you choose a new home business. Why? Because a home business is so easy to form that you'll find that you may have several within a few months. This is excellent—the more experience you acquire early in your career, the better your business judgment becomes. With a mature, reliable approach to home businesses you can easily build a big income within a few years.

Aim for big-money profits in your home business. Don't settle for a dime when you can earn a dollar instead. By aiming for big-money profits you prepare yourself for periods of reduced income caused by conditions you can't control.

To aim for big-money profits, apply the various pointers given earlier in this chapter. Adopt an attitude of seeking out the best in every deal and you'll start a big and steady flow of income into your home business office.

Stimulate Your Thinking

Think—your future riches lie within your mind! Don't wander around in a muddled state, one incomplete thought chasing another through your mind. Direct your thinking towards the goals you want to reach. Thinking builds a drive for physical action which can put you into a profitable home business within a few weeks.

Home wealth builders are among the most creative people I've ever met. Like this BWB who told me, I made a sale the first time I tried to export. I saw an ad seeking 10,000 police billy clubs for an overseas country in *Worldwide Riches Opportunities* (see back of book for details). There's a firm that makes these clubs in this area; so I faxed the overseas country that I could supply the clubs. They bought 10,000. I'll make about $15,000 on the deal, with a letter of credit to my bank.

5-Step Master Wealth Planning Technique

1. Define your wealth problem. Do you want to buy or sell, start or end a business, take on a new product, etc.?

2. List, on paper, possible solutions to your wealth problems. These might be yes; no; next week; next month; next year, etc.

3. "Live through" each solution. Assume you've decided "go", "no-go," etc. Live, in your mind, and on paper, the solution. Figure out what you'll have to pay, where the money will come from, etc. Figure one, two, three, or even five years in advance, if necessary.

4. Evaluate your "living-through" results. List the advantages and disadvantages of each decision in separate, parallel columns. Try to weigh each decision by giving it a number between 1 and 10. Add up the numbers in each column. This will give you a rough measure of which side contains the best decision for you.

5. Make your decision; then get to work. Take as long as you need to make your decision. Don't allow anyone to pressure you into doing something you may later regret. But once you make up your mind, move ahead with speed and confidence.

Here's an example of how Jack J., a successful home wealth

builder, used this technique to solve an important business problem. Read it carefully to learn how you can use the technique on your problems.

Actionize Your Wealth Planning

Step 1: Should I go into a mail-order business in my own home? (This is Jack's definition of his wealth problem.)

Step 2: Possible solutions: (a) Buy a going mail-order business; (b) start a new mail-order business; (c) open a franchised mail-order business.

Step 3: (a) A good, going mail-order business will cost me $20,000. I'd have to pay $350 per month for it if I took seven years to pay it off. This is nearly $100 per week, which would be a heavy strain on my budget. With two children just starting their college education, I could really be in trouble if the business didn't earn its keep. (b) Starting a new mail-order business would be cheaper—I could do it for $500, or less. But if I didn't have the cash to carry on I might lose my entire investment—some new mail-order firms fail during their first year. (c) A franchised mail-order business involves the least investment—as little as $100. I can handle this amount and I'll have cash left over to move into wider distribution. Also, my franchiser can guide me over the initial rough spots.

Step 4: Alternative c, a franchised mail-order business, has many advantages—preprinted catalogs, helpful advice, low investment, etc. The only disadvantage is the possibility of failure but this exists in every business.

Step 5: I'll select franchised mail order. To begin I'll contact several franchise mail-order firms immediately.

Profit from the Right Associates

You can zoom your home business profits by spending your leisure time with people who can help you. This may sound boring but it really isn't. People with similar business interests often have more in common when it comes to relaxation. So you can network while you relax!

Betty D. got the idea for a circulating library of paintings which could be operated from her home. The idea came to her after she heard, at a party she attended, that many industrial concerns and individuals would like to display paintings in their premises but they didn't want to invest cash for ownership of the paintings.

Checking with art galleries and museums, Betty learned that many owners and some custodians would be delighted to rent their paintings for three-, six-, or twelve-month periods. Also, Betty found, painters would be happy to have their works hung in large or small companies and the homes of the well-to-do.

Betty immediately set out to meet company executives, artists, gallery owners, museum directors, and people interested in fine art. She joined the Rotary in her town, attended art exhibits, read art magazines and books, and began a small, but highly dignified mail-order advertising program directed at executives of large and small companies and prominent citizens. Soon she had more applications for painting rentals than she had paintings to rent. "That's a delightful situation," Betty says happily. "It's like having too much money. It can't hurt you."

Today, Betty's painting rental service is a booming business which she runs from her apartment. Monthly rental fees for the paintings range between about $25 and $250, depending on the artist, painting size, rental period, etc. Betty sees nothing but improvement in the future because she knows many of the key people in the art world and they recommend her service to people interested in renting paintings. She really profits from networking with the right associates.

Choose Your Home Wealth Business

You now have enough general data to choose your home wealth business. Make your choice, here and now, in the space provided. Six spaces are given below because, if you're really interested in earning *big* money at home, you'll probably choose two, or more, businesses. Fine! The more ideas you have, the greater your chances for success. Enter your choices now.

Home Business Choices

1. . . . .
2. . . . .

3. ....

4. ....

5. ....

6. ....

Once you've made your home business choice, you can take the steps needed to start bringing in the profits. Your next chapter shows you exactly how to begin with a profit from your very first day in business.

Start Your Business

for Maximum

Profits

Almost anyone can start a home business and *lose* money for the first three or four years. All you need is enough money and tenacity to hang on until you earn a profit.

But it takes true business talent to start with little or no capital and earn a profit the first year in a home business. This chapter shows you how to do just that. Use the many business secrets given you in this chapter and you'll be years ahead of your competitors.

Know How You Can Operate Your Home Business

There are three general forms in which you can operate your home business:

1. Sole proprietorship
2. Partnership
3. Corporation

The first two types are the easiest and quickest to form, and also are the most economical. For these reasons, most home fortune builders use either form 1 or 2 when starting their first home business.

If you can afford a lawyer's fee, spend a few dollars for advice *before* you pick the form for your business. While this book can give you general guides for forming your business, it can't give specific details for every city and town in which a reader might be thinking of starting a home business.

Consider a Sole Proprietorship or Partnership

In a sole proprietorship you are the only owner of the home business and you have the right to sign contracts, leases, bank checks, and other documents for the company. In some states you can operate a sole proprietorship in your own name without registering the business with your county or state. But if you use a company name, like Ajax Wake-Up Service, you must register the name with your county or state.

In a partnership you can have one or more partners who help you in your business or who supply capital. Any partner can sign checks, contracts, or other documents, if the other partners authorize him or her to do so.

As a general guide, try to run your home business by yourself—as a sole proprietorship. Partners can be helpful—if you have the *right* partners. But finding the right partner—like finding a good husband or wife—isn't easy. So I recommend that you steer clear of partners unless you are positively certain your prospective partner will definitely add some profit potential to your home business.

It's Easy to Form Your Business

For most *beginning* home businesses, either the sole proprietorship or partnership form of business is satisfactory. Either type of business can usually be formed without the help of an attorney. The usual procedure in forming either type of business is:

(1) Visit, or write, your local County Clerk's office
(2) Request an application for a business certificate
(3) Fill out the application

(4) Have the application notarized, if necessary
(5) Submit the application with the required fee (about $10 to $50)
(6) Display your endorsed business certificate in a frame in your home.

You May Want to Form a Corporation

If you wish to form a corporation for your home business, consult an attorney. He or she will also give you the advantages—and disadvantages—of corporations in your state. The cost of forming a corporation can vary from about $75 to $800, depending on the state in which you incorporate.

Some attorneys offer a reduced-price "package deal" on corporation formations. Shop around until you find such an attorney by calling the law firms listed in the *Yellow Pages* of your phone book. Most lawyers are understanding people and will give you a break on the price of forming a new corporation.

Hold your expenses to a minimum when starting your home business. Why? Because I guarantee you that you'll find other uses for the money in your new business.

Pick a Place to Work

Where do highly successful home fortune builders work at home? Everywhere. Such as, the

Attic	Garage	Closet
Basement	Kitchen	Bedroom
Backyard	Living room	Den

Home fortunes are made in apartments, rooming houses, furnished rooms, private homes, house trailers, boats, camps, hospitals, prisons, ships, etc. In fact, home fortunes are made in almost every place someone calls home. This proves that anyone with enough drive and ambition can earn a fortune in his or her home, no matter how humble it is.

For example, a 15-year-old high school student on the East Coast started an Internet access business in a spare room in his parent's home. Using his personal computer and phone lines, he's become a commercial provider for a slew of customers seeking faster access to Internet. He works at his high-tech home business after high school classes. Business is booming.

Your Work Place Can Be Beautiful

One successful portrait photographer does all his developing and printing work in a small closet in his three-room Los Angeles apartment. His living room serves as his studio. He counts his rather sizeable profits in the kitchen. Is he happy? He drives the biggest car on the block and owns a palatial summer home on a hill overlooking one of America's most beautiful harbors—Newport Beach, California. As he says, "I couldn't ask for more in life."

So don't worry about a place to work—no matter where you live. One highly successful writer uses his wife's breadboard as his desk. "That's the way I started selling big-money stories and that's the way I'll continue. The breadboard brings me good luck," he claims.

Don't invest in a big mahogany desk, expensive metal files, mainframe computers, etc., when you first start your home business. Instead, buy a $2.00 notebook; work on the kitchen table; or use a neat pile of discarded orange crates for your desk.

Then you'll be putting to work, in a small way, the recommendations of J. Paul Getty, said to have been one of America's richest men. Mr. Getty recommended that ambitious businesspeople adopt a cost-conscious and profit-minded outlook if they want to be successful. He called this the *Millionaire Mentality*. If you work at it, you can develop this important outlook.

Line Up Some Money Sources

You *can* get the money you need for your home business. However, I hope to get you started on as little money as possible—say less than $200. To line up your money sources where you need more than this amount:

(1) Buy a copy of *Business Capital Sources* published by IWS, Inc., available from Prima Publishing, P.O. Box 1260HB, Rocklin, CA 95677. It costs only $15 per copy yet it lists thousands of capital sources—some have as much as 100-million dollars to lend. You can use this list anywhere in the world—it's international in scope.

(2) Visit your local banks and collect from each the little folders called Business Loans; Personal Loans; Home Improvement Loans; and Emergency Loans. Study the range of loan amounts offered, the payoff period (12 to 60 months), the interest rate charged, etc. This will prepare you for the next step.

(3) Drop by to see the loan officer at a nearby bank during your lunch hour. Tell him or her you're thinking about taking out a loan and you'd like to learn how the bank works with its customers.

(4) Question the loan officer. DON'T BE AFRAID OF HIM OR HER. THEY NEED YOU to keep loan totals high. They want your business. Get to know them because they can be an invaluable friend.

(5) Meet the loan officers in *several* banks. Travel to the next town, if there's only one bank in your town. These visits will teach you that some loan officers are more ready to lend you money than others because they need the business to keep their loan totals up.

(6) Probe; experiment. Ask for a personal loan at one bank; a business loan at another. Keep a record of the results. Sometimes it's easier to get one type of loan than another. Remember this when you actually apply for a loan at a later date.

(7) Write to the various banks, brokers, and firms listed in *Business Capital Sources* mentioned in item (1), above. You can often arrange a loan by mail, simply by filling out an application. This is an ideal way to borrow money if you're confined to your home or if you dislike interviews with bank officials.

Remember—don't borrow any money yet. Right now you're like the baseball player taking several warmup swings with a couple of bats before you step into the batting box. Also remember—strikes during the warmup don't count. What does count is the hit you get when you're in the batter's box. Now we'll see how you can get that hit easily and surely—without working too hard.

Try This Valuable Tip

Many beginning home business operators think that they *must* invest several thousand dollars to start their business. If they don't make a big investment, they feel that they're only playing at being in business.

This is a silly attitude. I can show you hundreds of home business operators earning $10,000, $20,000, $100,000, or more, per year in their own homes who have hardly any investment in their business, other than time. And, if you're the typical beginning home wealth builder, similar to the many who call on me for advice, you have more time than money.

Fine! Let's see how you can turn that time into a golden downpour—a torrential deluge of crisp new money that will flood your bank account and pockets.

Here's Your Key Secret to Home Wealth

Your key secret to starting your home business for maximum profits is this:

> **Begin with the lowest cash investment and the lowest overhead possible. Aim at making profitable sales from the first moment you're in business.**

With a small or no cash investment, your fixed expenses for interest and debt repayments are lower, or nil. This means that there's more money left in each sales dollar for your profits after you pay your variable costs—labor, materials, shipping, etc. Let's see how this works in an actual home business.

Put Your Key Secret to Work

Bob Z. wanted to start a newsletter. His ideas for the name of the letter, its contents, and market were excellent. These ideas were so good I said to myself, "Gee, why didn't I think of that?"

But when it came to the business aspects of the newsletter, Bob's ideas were weak. He wanted to spend $12,000 for a printing press, hire a desktop publishing specialist, buy mailing and collating equipment costing $2,000, together with spending $8,000 for his initial advertising campaign. Thus Bob was planning to spend $22,000 before he got his first subscriber.

"Suppose," I said to Bob, "you don't get enough subscribers to pay off the $22,000 you want to invest? What happens then?"

"I guess I'll be out that money," Bob replied.

"Well, let's take a closer look at this," I suggested. We did. I showed Bob that he could have 100 pages of his newsletter printed by a commercial printer for 3.7¢ a page. If he printed it himself on the equipment he proposed to buy the cost would be 8.7¢ per page. The only advantage of owning a press was a slightly greater flexibility in getting the newsletter printed. Bob agreed to use a commercial printer.

Sell before You Spend

"Now that we have your production problems solved, Bob," I said, "I want to let you in on another very valuable secret."

"What's that?" he asked, his eyes bright.

"Just this—*sell before you spend*. I'll explain it in terms of your newsletter.

You've been planning to spend $8,000 on advertising for your newsletter before you have your first subscriber. Yet I'm sure, Bob, that with a little investigation you could easily find one or more ways to promote your newsletter free of high cost *before* you spend a cent for advertising. In fact, Bob, I don't think there's a product available today that can't be sold *before* you spend—if you use some ingenuity in your approach to the market. So our second money-generating secret is:

> Promote your product at the lowest cost possible before you spend any money on advertising, production, personnel, etc.

How to Get Free Publicity

The next big question, of course, is: How can *you* obtain low-cost publicity for a product or service? Your best method for most items and services is to use the New Product columns of the magazines serving the fields in which your product will be sold. For the cost of one sheet of paper, one envelope, and one stamp, you can obtain publicity worth thousands of dollars. You can even test-market a product this way. But let's get back to Bob.

Big Sales for a Pittance

"Bob," I said, "who'll buy and use your newsletter?"

"People interested in earning big money all over the world. That's why I call it *World Money News.*"

"What magazines do they read?"

Bob named several. "Fine," I said. "Now go to the local library and sit down with one copy each of the following two excellent references: *Business Publication Rates and Data* and *Consumer Magazine and Farm Publication Rates and Data*. Both are published by Standard Rate & Data Service, Inc. Copy from each of these publications the name and address of *every* magazine whose readers you think might be interested in subscribing to your newsletter. Then come back and see me."

Bob returned in a week, somewhat groggy-eyed. He had a list of more than 2,000 magazines.

I grinned at him. "Do you think you got every one?"

"Don't be funny," he groaned. "Now what do we do?"

How to Write Your News Releases

"You send a one-page, double-spaced typed news release to each magazine. Include in this news release the following:

* Name and address of the newsletter
* Typical topics the letter will discuss
* What benefits readers will get from the letter
* Annual subscription fee
* How to subscribe to the letter

"Be clear, concise, accurate, and to the point. Tell me what the results are."

Two months later Bob called. "It's great," he laughed over the phone. "I have a hundred subscribers already, and the inquiries are still coming in. Thanks for saving me twenty-two grand."

If you'd like to make home millions publishing a newsletter, see *How to Become Wealthy Publishing a Newsletter*, described at the back of this book.

A Technique for Any Business

No matter what kind of home fortune business you plan to run, you *can* generate big sales from a pittance. How? *Sell before you spend.* Do exactly as Bob did.

And, incidentally, for more ideas on selling before you spend, send $24 to Prima Publishing, P.O. Box 1260HB, Rocklin, CA 95677, for a one-year subscription to my publication, *International Wealth Success*. This pithy publication will give you thousands of marketing wealth ideas every year. With some easy work you should be able to turn these wealth ideas into a personal fortune for yourself.

Spend Time Instead of Money

Almost every home business operator gets started in a unique way. For example, Robert S., a police patrolman, invented and is manufacturing a writing clipboard that also serves as a bulletproof shield for police officers. The board is made of several layers of strong fiber glass which has withstood six straight shots from a .38-caliber revolver. Patrolman S. got his idea for the shield after reading about bulletproof fiber glass vests worn by soldiers. Since vests of this type would be expensive for police officers, Patrolman S. adapted the material to the clipboards police officers use in their patrol cars.

Today Patrolman S. spends about two hours per day in his basement riveting the necessary straps and clips to the board. Police throughout the world are interested in the board and orders are building up for it in Patrolman S.' basement.

Time Is Money

Earlier we said that most beginning home fortune builders have more time than money. So, when you first start, consider spending time instead of money. Patrolman S., for example, could perhaps have his product completely made in a factory. But it is probably more economical to do most of the work himself—at least at the start. Later, when there is a large volume of orders, he may turn the production work over to a factory.

Use this same technique yourself. When first starting your business:

* Do as much of your own work as possible
* Put in time instead of dollars
* Keep a tight fist on spending
* Learn, and perform, every step in the procedure

By following these four simple rules you'll increase your chances for success a hundredfold.

Five Keys to Low-Cost Sources

How can *you* develop low-cost sources for your business? Here are several keys to low-cost sources that many home wealth builders find are winners almost every time:

(1) Handicapped workers often work faster and for lower wages. Also, the quality of their work is usually excellent, reducing rejects.

(2) Overseas sources are often more economical than domestic. But don't assume that just because an item is made overseas that it's cheaper. Domestic prices can surprise you.

(3) Rebuilt, reclaimed, or remanufactured parts are often as good as new. They can sometimes be used when you do not claim your product is 100% new.

(4) Surplus, auction, and discontinued items are still new and can be sold as such. Keep an eye on special sales and similar chances to obtain good, new items at reduced cost. Get a copy of the IWS *Directory of High-Discount Merchandise Sources,* listed at the back of this book. It gives you thousands of low-cost items.

(5) Do it yourself. Instead of hiring someone to do work, do the job yourself. You'll probably do it (a) faster, (b) better, and (c) easier than anyone you hire. What's more, you'll do it right the first time and almost every time.

You *can* develop low-cost sources. Keep in mind the fact that you can do business on a shoestring *out of choice.* Your profits will be higher and you'll get more fun out of your home business. Try it and see!

How One Fortune Builder Keeps Costs Low

Allan Swallow, owner of the publishing house named after himself, published an average of 30 books a year in his home. Each year he shipped some 70,000 books from his garage and house. All the editing, designing, packaging, addressing, and shipping were done by Dr. Swallow in his home. Today his firm is called one of the biggest little publishing houses in America. And it all began as a spare-time, minimum-capital venture in Dr. Swallow's home.

One of Dr. Swallow's profit-generating secrets was low-cost labor sources—in this case himself. That is, Dr. Swallow did most of the necessary work himself instead of hiring and paying someone else to do it. This is one of the smartest ways to keep your costs down and keep your profits high.

Emphasize Your Profit Builders

No matter what home business you open—from hairstyling for thoroughbred dogs to manuscript typing, certain activities in your business will always be more profitable than others. The usual home fortune builder reacts in a strange way to this common situation.

Says he or she: "My profit on product A is 20%; on product B it's 5%. Why aren't the profits on the two products almost equal? They should be."

Time passes and both products continue to sell but the profit percentages remain about the same. Our home business operator decides to do something about the difference in profits between the two products. "Product A is returning a nice profit," he or she says. "It continues to sell well. So I'll ignore it for awhile and concentrate on making product B more profitable."

Why Home Profits Can Fall

A few months later this home fortune builder's profits from both products are suddenly lower. He's puzzled and worried. Why? Because he can't figure out why his profits are lower, and he thinks he may soon be operating at a loss.

I can tell you why his profits are lower. They're lower because he ignored his *most* profitable product to concentrate on his *least* profitable product. In the typical small, restricted-capital home business such tactics can ruin you. To avoid financial disaster, apply the following marvelous secret for zooming your home business profits:

> **Concentrate on your most profitable items until your income is high enough to employ someone to do this for you. Then, and only then, get to work on building the profits of your slower-moving items.**

Profitable Bill Collecting

Gary K. runs a bill collecting firm for local businesses from his home. He collects most of the bills by mail. Some of the more difficult bills require personal attention on Gary's part and he uses, where possible, his telephone. In especially tough cases Gary will visit the delinquent bill payer personally. But he doesn't have to do this too often.

Gary came to me for advice on how he might increase his income. His most profitable bill collecting, we found, was by mail. Why? Because use of the mails allowed Gary to work anywhere, at any time. Thus, he could put in more hours of work. He wasn't dependent on the telephone, answering machine, computer, or doorbell.

We developed a plan to emphasize Gary's profit builders. This plan covered such items as better collection letters, greater mailing frequency, and more detailed records. Within the first year Gary's net profits jumped by $20,000. Recently he told me that in the second year he hopes his profits will be $37,000 higher. If Gary had emphasized his less profitable lines—telephoning and personal visits —he might have neglected his lucrative mail-order business and lost money.

You Can Start with No Money

Most people have a few dollars—say $100 to $300 to spend when starting their home business. But some people have very little money—less than $100—to spend. What should such people do when starting their home business for maximum profits? Here's one technique that could be worth at least a million dollars to you.

> Start with any readily available no-cost source of funds and build it up to produce all, or part, of the money you need.

"Give me some examples of readily available no-cost sources of funds," you say? Sure. Here are six.

Six No-Cost Fund Sources

You can obtain no-cost funds these easy ways.

1. Collect, and sell, scrap metals or other materials
2. Sell what you find in attics, basements, etc.

3. Take products on consignment (speculation); sell them
4. Accept a temporary spare-time job; save your pay
5. Become a consultant; use word-of-mouth advertising
6. Attend a paid-while-training course given by a school or firm

Other Sources of Business Funds

There are many other sources of funds available to you when you start your home business. With most of these sources you must pay interest on the money you obtain from them.

For example, you can, if you have a good credit rating, borrow from banks. If a bank turns you down, apply to the Small Business Administration (SBA). Many friends of mine find the SBA is a ready source of capital for starting a business.

If you have a personal computer with a modem, you can get lots of business information free of charge from SBA. Just tap into *SBA Online* from any location, and you can download data on SBA loans and programs. You can also get information on SBA publications and services available to small businesses.

You can access *SBA Online* at 1-800-859-4636 (1200/2400 Baud) or 1-800-697-4636 (9600 Baud). SBA also has mailboxes and computer online meetings for people in small business. (*NOTE:* Should either of these numbers be out of service, contact your local SBA office—listed under U.S. Government in your local phone book—for alternate numbers and services.)

Other BWBs use their own methods and sources to borrow money for their home business. Here are two who told me of their experiences in borrowing money. "I read two of your books on borrowing and decided to try the ideas. In just 9 months I've borrowed $250,000, starting with no cash of my own." The other BWB stated, "We started our business with no cash on hand. It took us 3 weeks to find a bank that would lend us $2,000 to buy a few tools, etc. Since then there has been no looking back. Last year we grossed $234,000."

Should You Borrow Some Starting Capital?

Recently, during a reception in one of London's exclusive and private dining clubs, a beginning British home wealth builder asked me if I thought he should borrow 100 pounds (about $150) to start his business. Standing in the group when the question was asked were several successful businessmen and psychoanalysts. Since they all agreed with the answer I gave, I'd like to give you the answer to this question now because, if we would ever meet, I'm fairly certain some of you might ask me the same question. The answer is:

> **Don't borrow money to start a home business if you can earn the money in another way—preferably from some type of home business.**

Why should you avoid borrowing money to start your home business? Because, to some people, borrowing is not as great an incentive as earning money is. So if you're one of these people, actually working will spur you on to much greater efforts than borrowing will.

Tom D., a successful art dealer in his own home, borrows money from one bank after another. Then he works like mad to earn enough to repay the loans in half the time the bank gave him. Thus, if he borrows for a 24-month period, he tries to repay in 12 months. To Tom, borrowing is an incentive. But I don't recommend this procedure for most people. Why? You can get yourself into trouble by borrowing beyond your means.

Think Positively and Win

Your mind is a treasure house of valuable moneymaking ideas, if you think positively about your future income. Recognize this fact and you're well on your way to a fortune in your own home. But if you think negatively about your future income, there is hardly anything you can do to make wealth come your way.

Believe you can build wealth quickly in your own home, and you will build this wealth. Be calm, confident, and secure. Though the outside world may be cold and hostile, in the warmth and snugness of your home you will be outstandingly successful. Within a short while you will grow richer than you ever thought possible.

Where do I get the right to tell you this? How do I come by my facts? Why am I so sure *you* can earn what you want to in your own home? Let's take these questions up one at a time.

Experience Is a Good Teacher

My right to tell you these facts comes from long personal experience in many businesses which I run in my own home. The income from these businesses exceeds $100,000 per year, yet I spend only a few hours a week working at them. I lead an otherwise normal life—I have three nice kids, a contented wife, a well-maintained home. I go to parties, swim, dance, go to the theatre and opera regularly, jet to Europe twice a year, spend a winter vacation in the Caribbean, fly a small private airplane, own a beautiful, spanking new 50-foot yacht, etc. At the same time, I hold a top executive job with one of America's largest financial and lending firms.

Could the income from these home businesses be increased? Yes; it certainly could. But, for the present at least, I prefer to spend less than ten hours per week on the businesses so I'll have time for other things in life.

Facts Can Help You

How do I come by my facts? In several ways. From my own experiences; from the experiences of people I advise; from analysis and study. I fly to Washington, D.C. at least four times a year to talk to high government officials about the fate of small business in the United States. While there, I buy for later study, all the newest government publications prepared for small businesspeople.

Why am I so sure *you* can earn what you want to in your own home? I'm sure because I've experienced in my own life the power of thinking positively about business, the future, and success. Thousands of others are doing the same and are hitting the big money. You can, too, if you:

(1) Decide how much you want to earn at home — $10,000, $50,000, $100,000, or $500,000 per year

(2) Choose, after reading this book, the way you'll earn your home income

(3) Start your business using the hints given here for high-profit starts

(4) Operate your business as this book recommends

(5) Maintain high enthusiasm and complete confidence that you will succeed

(6) Be positive and determined in everything you do for your home business

(7) Believe in yourself, your skills, and in the brighter future you can build for yourself and your loved ones

Use the Magic Riches Checklist

To know where you're going in life you must have some way of checking your progress. You already know, from Chapter 5, what kind of home business you'd like to operate. The present chapter points out many ways you can use to start your business for maximum profits. Now here's your Magic Riches Checklist which you can use to check your progress towards home riches.

Magic Riches Checklist

	Yes	No	*If* NO, *I will by* (*Date*)	*Done by* (*Date*)
1. I have selected my home business	....	....	....	....
2. Business legal details finished	....	....	....	....
3. I picked a place to work	....	....	....	....
4. I lined up several money sources	....	....	....	....
5. I am ready to begin with low cash	....	....	....	....
6. I will invest time instead of money	....	....	....	....
7. I can sell before I spend	....	....	....	....
8. I have publicity plans for my business	....	....	....	....
9. I have checked low-cost product sources	....	....	....	....
10. I will do all the work by myself, where possible	....	....	....	....
11. I am emphasizing my profit builders	....	....	....	....
12. I think positively about my home business	....	....	....	....

Complete this checklist today. Refer to it again in a month. See how many dates appear in the last column. Keep working until there *is* a date in the last column for every item listed. Once you've accomplished everything on this list you'll see why it's called a Magic Riches Checklist. The money will flow into your home in a "five-foot high river of checks," as one delighted home fortune builder remarked to me.

Six Outstanding Fortune Builders

Do people really earn large incomes at home? Let's take a look at the record, as lawyers so often say.

One of the world's most popular and loved orchestra leaders works on many projects at an inn he owns. These projects include inventions—a useful food blender—music publishing, choral teaching, song writing, and several others.

Elsie and John Masterton run the famous Blueberry Hill Restaurant and Blueberry Hill Farm in Vermont. As part of their activities they have written several books, including the *Blueberry Hill Cookbook, Blueberry Hill Kitchen Notebook,* which are best sellers.

Arthur W. Brown, the well-known magazine illustrator and caricaturist, does his famous drawings in his home studio. During his long and successful career he has drawn the illustrations for stories by many famous authors.

Captain Cal Yellott, a New York harbor ship's pilot, turns out beautiful furnishings based on parts of ships—wheels, binnacles, lights, etc.—in his home workshop. Some of his home-produced products carry retail prices of $2,000. Besides the pleasure of his shopwork, Captain Young relaxes by traveling the seaboard to collect running lights, whistles, compasses, and other ship parts which he converts to furniture, bookends, tables, etc.

Two brothers, Ralph and Henry Feld, started a vending-machine business by operating from a garage. They soon had to move because their business reached the high volume they sought. Today the Feld brothers have a modern new plant from which they control the 50,000 vending machines they have in the United States and Canada. The steady flow of pennies, nickels, dimes, and quarters has built a profitable business from gum balls, charms, cards, etc.

Samuel Mendelsohn is an inventor who's busy developing worthwhile items for modern life. He's the inventor of synchronized flash photography and holds numerous patents for various types of electronic equipment. He works on many of his inventions at home.

Thus, there are many activities which can be turned into profit in your own home. With proper planning you can start your business for maximum profits and go on from there to greater income. So start today because you have a great and profitable future! You'll find that many of the Kits described at the back of this book will give you an excellent start in a home business of your choice—such as export-import, mail order, financial brokerage, real estate, leasing, etc. Be sure to refer to the list of Kits because you may find one or more that can put you into your own profitable home business quickly and easily.

7

Earn Enormous Income from Good Products

You live in an age of tremendous demand for good products. Everyone in the world—you, me, our friends, children, the natives of Africa, the citizens of Moscow—all want one or more good products at this very moment. The product can vary from a cheap plastic comb to a multimillion dollar private jet airplane—someone, somewhere needs and wants that product.

Take a moment now to think about people and how universal their demands for good products are. No matter what political system a person believes in, he or she still has certain fundamental needs—such as combing his or her hair. And people need a comb no matter where they live, what religion they practice, the color of their skin, or the length of their hair. The only person who doesn't need a comb is a totally bald one—and if you look far enough you can find a product you can sell at a good profit to bald men.

Classify Product Needs

In your life you probably have two kinds of product needs—(1) necessities, and (2) luxuries. The necessities are needed by most of us. They include products like combs, toothbrushes, socks, shoes, etc. Luxuries are products we'd *like* to have but don't really need. Yachts, private airplanes, backyard swimming pools, ivory back scratchers, and fur-lined coats for pet dogs are a few of the luxuries people seek these days.

Some people regard luxuries as necessities. "It's good for my ego," they say of a luxury. "Just knowing that I own it makes me feel good—more successful. So it really helps me earn more money. Therefore, it isn't a luxury—it's a necessity."

You may or may not agree with this way of thinking. But since luxuries are almost always products, you should at least recognize that this outlook is popular today. This luxury = necessity attitude will certainly help you sell some products. Also, you may want to buy yourself one luxury you've always yearned for, calling it a necessity. Unless I misjudge my readers, I think you'll enjoy your luxury *without* guilt feelings. In fact, you may soon be preaching that there's no such thing as a luxury—all needs are necessities!

Pick Your Type of Product

Which would you rather handle, a common item nearly everyone needs (shoes, soap, socks, etc.) or unusual items that appeal to the few? Big, glittering home fortunes are made on both types of products. When you handle the commonly needed item you can expect: (1) stiff competition, (2) problems with wholesalers, (3) small profits per unit sale, and (4) the need for a large volume of business to generate a suitable profit.

Unusual items give you problems, too. Thus, when you handle unusual items—that is, items having a somewhat specialized market —you can expect: (1) a constant search for customers, (2) slow payment of bills by some customers, (3) product complaints because customers tend to be more particular, and (4) widely varying business activity with busy and slow periods alternating.

How Widely Used Products Pay Off

Yet either type of product can put you into the big money faster than you think. For example, Jared K. wanted to start a home business selling a commonly used product. He heard of a franchised line of greeting cards and sales racks for the cards.

Checking into the business potential, Jared found he could obtain three racks and a selection of cards for less than $100. Jared installed the racks in three local stores, servicing them from his home. Business boomed. Within a year Jared was netting $5,000 per month from his card racks. He expects to double this soon.

Unusual Products Find Their Market

Frank Hanighen wanted to start a conservative newsletter. Working in the bedroom of his home in Washington, D.C., Hanighen founded his newsletter which he called *Human Events*. This four-page weekly newsletter grew steadily to a circulation of 8,000 copies per week. Greatly expanded today, and published as a newspaper, *Human Events* is the largest conservative organ in the country, having a circulation of more than 80,000 copies a week. Thus, Frank Hanighen took an idea for an uncommon product and turned it into a winner.

Jacqueline W., mother of two children in Albuquerque, NM, saw a large need for stuffed animals that parents can make for kids. Since many mothers enjoy sewing, Jacqueline decided to sell paper patterns for the stuffed animals. These patterns are lightweight and easy to mail. Starting her home business by running ads in craft and children's magazines, she soon had a slew of orders. Today her business, still run from a spare room in her home, is booming. Besides patterns she also sells cloth, stuffing, threads, and other accessories. All her sales are by mail or telephone orders. She accepts major credit cards for her orders because many mothers want to pay for their purchases later.

Which Is Your Best Product?

If we could meet for an hour I could tell you the best product for *you* to sell. But it's impossible to meet every reader of this book. So I devised a short checklist to help you decide which kind of product is best for you. Use the checklist right now—I think you'll find it's fun, while being useful and interesting.

Product Sales Checklist

	Yes	No
1. Do you enjoy going to the theatre?	....	....
2. Have you ever sold against tough competition?	....	....
3. Are you a lover of fine music?	....	....
4. Do repetitive tasks bore you?	....	....
5. Are most people interesting to you?	....	....
6. Is your favorite hobby one in which you associate with other people?	....	....
7. Do you strongly "want to get away from it all"?	....	....
8. Are you a person who prefers working alone?	....	....

Score yourself this way: If your answers to questions 1, 3, 4, 5, and 6 are *yes,* you will probably make more money selling the uncommon product. A *no* answer to questions 2, 7, and 8 reinforces this result.

No answers to questions 1, 3 ,4, 7, and 8 indicate that you'd make more money selling the commonly needed product. *Yes* answers to the other questions reinforce this result.

Where to Find Profitable Products

You now know which type of product will earn the most money for you. "Fine," you say "now where do I find a suitable product?" We'll show you, right now. But before spending a cent on a product, apply this riches-making rule:

> **Never invest in a product or a campaign to sell it until after you have carefully determined how large a need exists for the product in your area.**

So—remembering that you're still just looking and that you haven't yet invested a cent, other than some spare time—we're ready to start. Here are seven valuable leads to finding suitable products for home preparation (i.e. cultivation, manufacture, assembly, etc.).

(1) Study the *Business Opportunities* and *Auction Offerings*

columns of your local newspaper. You may find a number of products listed there.

(2) Read a big-city newspaper (*New York Times, Los Angeles Times, Chicago Tribune,* etc.) for three months. Pick the most respected newspaper in the nearest large city. Study its business columns and business ads every day.

(3) Read the *Wall Street Journal* regularly, paying particular attention to the advertisements.

(4) Study the classified and display ads in *Popular Mechanics, Popular Science, Science and Mechanics, Modern Franchising, Income Opportunities,* and similar magazines.

(5) Read the new-product columns of every magazine serving your field of interest. Many of these new products may be available to you on a discount, distributor, or franchise basis.

(6) Be alert to every new development in your field of interest. When you see or hear of a new product, check it out immediately.

(7) Read *International Wealth Success,* the newsletter mentioned in earlier chapters. This newsletter will give you many valuable product leads.

(8) Use the IWS *Directory of High-Discount Merchandise Sources* described at the back of this book.

Looking for profitable products can really pay off in big profits to you, as this reader told us: "I made several million dollars exporting oilfield equipment. It all grew out of the lead I got from your publication for exporting handcuffs to police departments around the world, selling to their government departments." You really never know how profitable it can be until you try getting useful information about profitable products.

Evaluate Available Products

Suppose you find several potentially profitable products using the above sources of information. What do you do next? That's easy; you evaluate the available products.

"How," you ask, "can I evaluate products I may have never seen, have certainly never sold, and know nothing about?" "That's easy," I reply, "you just use some common sense and the checklist given here."

Product Marketing Checklist

	Yes	No
1. Do people *need* this product?	....	....
2. Is this product consumed during use?	....	....
3. Can you sell the product at a reasonable price?	....	....
4. Is there much competition in selling this product?	....	....
5. Are cheap substitutes for this product available?	....	....
6. Would *you* buy this product for your own use?	....	....
7. Can you resell the product to the same customer?	....	....
8. Is the product of good quality?	....	....
9. Will the supplier meet your sales needs?	....	....
10. Could you put your brand name on the product?	....	....
11. Will you have to advertise the product?	....	....
12. Will sale of this product lead to other sales?	....	....

For a potentially profitable product you should have *yes* answers to questions 1, 3, 6, 8, 9, and 12. *Yes* answers to the other questions are also desirable but not absolutely necessary.

But what can you do if you can't find a suitable product? You can develop your own! A good real-life example of this is the woman model who couldn't find a hair wig she liked. So she went into the wig business, starting in her own home. Four years later her business is grossing $6 million a year!

Plan Your Marketing

How will you sell your product to the market? There are many ways, a few of which are:

(1) Mail-order sales
(2) Door-to-door selling
(3) Open a store
(4) Sell to distributors
(5) Establish franchise outlets
(6) Sell to stores

Let's take a quick look at each of these ways you can use to sell your products. Hopefully, you'll find that *your* products can be sold in several ways.

USE MAIL ORDER

(1) *Mail-order sales* are important for any widely used or specialty product because they open the door to millions and millions of potential customers. In fact, mail order is so important to you as a home fortune builder that I've devoted an entire chapter to it later in the book. So if you're confined to your home, dislike face-to-face selling, or can't get around too readily, consider mail-order selling for your products. Today many home wealth builders combine mail order with telephone sales using a toll-free 800 number. This gets orders to you faster, increasing your cash flow. With an 800 number, you must also accept credit-card charges.

NEIGHBORHOOD SALES CAN PAY OFF

(2) *Door-to-door selling* in your neighborhood can get you started on building your home fortune. If your products are quickly accepted you might want to expand your sales territory into other neighborhoods using a staff of part-time or full-time salesmen or saleswomen.

Bertha K. started to sell knitted-to-order dresses by selling door-to-door in her neighborhood. Soon Bertha had so many orders that she had to stop selling to go home to knit the dresses. While working at home she became annoyed thinking of all the profitable sales she was losing. Yet she had to knit the dresses to fill the orders she had on hand. Then she hit on the idea of getting other women at home to knit the dresses while she made sales calls.

Checking with her friends, Bertha found that those who could knit would be delighted to work in their homes. For awhile Bertha had more workers than orders to keep them busy. But she soon changed that. Today Bertha has a large staff of happy women busily knitting in their homes. Meanwhile, Bertha concentrates on door-to-door selling.

BECOME A WEALTHY SHOPKEEPER

(3) *Open a store* in, or near, your home. I consider a store that is very near your home to be a home business because it has all the characteristics of a home business, as we discussed them in Chapter 1. Must the business be only a store? No; you might open a school, manufacturing company, or any other type of organization in your home. Thus, the forerunner of one of America's giant aluminum

companies was organized in the parlor of a home on Shady Lane in Pittsburgh, Pa. Where you're selling products manufactured by yourself or others, a store in your home is often an excellent way to begin marketing your products at a profit.

MOVE YOUR PRODUCTS THROUGH DISTRIBUTORS

(4) *Sell to distributors* the products you build, carve, sew, assemble, or otherwise create in your own home. Selling to distributors is much easier than selling to the general public because (a) distributors are businesspeople interested in earning a profit on your products, (b) distributors aren't emotionally involved with your product—hence you'll have fewer complaints, (c) you can often deal with distributors by mail or phone, bypassing face-to-face deals.

While selling to distributors has these and other advantages, there is one slight disadvantage—the profit you earn on each sale to a distributor will usually be lower than on the same sale made to the general public. But many home wealth builders are willing to skip this extra profit in order to have the greater ease of doing business with distributors.

SET UP YOUR OWN FRANCHISE SYSTEM

(5) *Establish franchise outlets.* You can become a franchisor if (a) you have a product or service others can sell (b) you've developed a marketing approach that is easy for others to follow (c) you can instruct others in the ways to promote, advertise, and sell your product. As a franchisor you receive a payment—usually a flat fee—from the persons you instruct in the sale of your product. You may also derive a profit on the sale of your product to your franchisees.

As a franchisor you have several advantages—fewer people to deal with, larger cash flow, and fewer contacts with the public. But there are certain disadvantages—higher advertising costs, fewer outlets, and greater dependence upon your dealers. Use the *Franchise Riches Success Kit,* described at the back of this book, to start building *your* wealth in franchising today.

USE DEPARTMENT-STORE OUTLETS

(6) *Sell to stores.* Large department, discount, supermarket, specialty, bargain, and auto-supply stores are hungrily looking for new

products and services to sell to their customers. If you have a product or service these stores want and need, the welcome mat is out. How do I know? Because I've sold a number of home-produced products to a variety of stores.

How do *you* make such sales? Just go to the store and ask for the buyer who handles the type of product you want to sell. The buyer may see you immediately or he or she may ask you to come back in a few days. If so, be certain to arrive on time.

When dealing with store buyers, be sure you:

(1) Prepare your sales pitch in advance
(2) Give your pitch quickly, accurately
(3) Know the discounts you can offer
(4) Have your order pad and pencil ready
(5) Leave as soon as you get the order

Keep in mind the fact that most store buyers are busy people. The more you respect a buyer's time, the greater your chances for a sale. As one buyer said to me recently "Your products sell nicely and I'm glad to handle them. But even if they sold slowly, I'd still handle them. You make it so easy to place an order that I enjoy doing business with you."

So if you ever feel dejected because a buyer slighted you, just remember this simple fact of business life:

> Buyers are your key to success when you sell to stores. Treat every buyer with respect and remember that they're busy people.

Four Whose Products Hit It Big

CHOCOLATE CANDY AND ANTIQUES

Carl F. has two big loves in his life—chocolate candy and antiques. The chocolate candy he mixes in his kitchen is so popular that Carl runs a prosperous home business in which he makes and sells his candy. This candy retails for $10 to $25 per pound. And if you want a special antique arrangement of your pound of candy in an attractive bowl for some special event, Carl's price is $200. "You'd be surprised at how many $200 candy bowls I sell," Carl laughs. "It really keeps me in Cadillacs." Carl also sells his candy by mail order and has a steadily growing customer list.

OVERSEAS NEWSPAPERS

Gerald A. runs a business whose products are overseas newspapers. For an annual fee, Gerald will send you, once a week, a copy of an English-language newspaper published in a foreign country—England, Scotland, Ireland, France, Holland, Germany, Switzerland, etc. By reading this paper you can get an excellent idea of what the overseas press is saying about various important issues. Also, businesspeople and immigrants have greater use for and interest in overseas news of all kinds. Gerald runs his business entirely by mail order—finding his customers and obtaining his products by mail. As interest in overseas affairs expands, so does Gerald's home business income.

BOARD FOR LOVABLE PETS

Paul Z. started his pet boarding business in his garage. There he built comfortable cages for cats, dogs, birds, hamsters, rabbits, etc. To advertise his boarding service for pets, Paul had local shopkeepers put notices in their windows. His service was so well received that Paul now has signs throughout his local area. He pays each shopkeeper a nominal monthly fee for keeping the sign in the window. Today Paul has a separate building for boarding nearly one hundred pets. His reputation for good care, proper feeding, and adequate exercise for every pet continues to spread while the profits roll in.

TAPED MUSIC FOR BUSINESSES

Ben F. started his home business in what is probably the smallest place available to a man in his home—a clothes closet. In this closet Ben installed a tape recorder to play soft music which he "piped"—i.e. wired into local restaurants, factories, hotels, department stores, and gasoline service stations. Ben quickly outgrew the closet and had to install more equipment in the bedroom. But when Ben announced to his wife that the next new player would be installed in the living room, she let out a yell of dismay. That's when Ben moved all his equipment to a modern building. Today Ben's "pipe dream" is the second largest piped music company in the world. And it all started in a spare clothes closet at home!

How to Finance Your New Products

When the beginning home wealth builder is starting the new business he or she usually has one major problem which is succinctly summarized by one five-letter word—MONEY. This typical wealth builder needs money for at least three items:

1. Purchase of products to sell
2. Advertising and promotion for the products
3. Necessary business items—stationery, postage, etc.

Usually, the money needed to purchase products is one of the largest investments you'll have to make when starting your business. If you're making your own products, you'll spend money for materials instead of for the products themselves. Either way, however, you'll have to spend some money. The usual problem is that the products or materials cost more than the beginning home wealth builder wants to spend from savings, or has readily available.

You *can* obtain the money for your new home business no matter how small your bank account, no matter how stretched your credit rating may be, and no matter how many problems you may have had in the past. Please understand that I'm not saying or implying that *you* have these problems. I'm just setting up the worst possible situation *I* can imagine. Then I'll show you the secret, magic, powerful, and profitable ways to finance your products, advertising, promotion, and other business expenses. If you use my techniques, and work hard, you can soon earn $100,000 to $500,000 or more per year in your own home. Once your income reaches those levels, you're on your own!

Seven Powerful Financing Techniques

Here, for the first time that I know of, are the seven most powerful and profitable financing techniques ever used by successful home fortune builders. I have checked thousands of businesspeople throughout the world and they all tell me that this is probably the first time these golden secrets were ever published in a book for home wealth builders.

Here are the seven secret techniques that will rocket your income to a glorious new high:

(1) Know who has money to lend
(2) Use your supplier's extended-pay plan
(3) Try an SBA loan
(4) Have your customers finance your products
(5) Sell franchised products
(6) Obtain loans from your state or city
(7) Use a factor to finance your products

Let's take a quick look at each so you can decide which one, or ones, you want to use to build your home fortune by the sale of products.

KNOW WHO HAS MONEY TO LEND

Many beginning home fortune builders call me and complain "Nobody wants to lend me any money. I went to a bank today and the man laughed at me. What am I to do?"

My first answer is a question "How many banks did you apply at?"

"Only one," the new home fortune builder usually groans.

"And you're ready to give up already?" I ask.

"Well, more or less," is the usual reply.

Then I tell them about Roland and Janet C. who wanted to buy an old Chicago brownstone house to convert it into a home, a dress store, fitting rooms, and a workroom. Roland and Janet applied to 73 banks, mortgage brokers, and real estate agents before they found someone willing to lend them the $35,000 they needed to start a business in their own home. Today they have one of the most successful dress houses in the country—their income tops the $500,000-per-year mark.

Roland and Janet got the money they needed the hard way—they tramped around until they found someone who was willing to take a risk and lend them the money. You don't have to do the same. Why? Because there's an easy, quick, and inexpensive way to find out who has money to lend throughout the United States and the world.

All you need do is subscribe to the monthly newsletter, *Interna-*

tional Wealth Success, available from Prima Publishing, P.O. Box 1260HB, Rocklin, CA 95677. Costing only $24 per year for twelve issues, this valuable newsletter annually lists hundreds of organizations, banks, and individuals who are actively seeking companies and people to whom they can lend $1,000 to $5,000,000, or more, for business use. Send $24 to this newsletter for your annual subscription. One issue, which contains many other useful ideas—such as 100% financing for businesses, mail-order loans, finder's fee opportunities, real-estate mortgages, profitable franchises, etc.—could make you rich for life. What's more, you'll save time and energy because most of the deals it lists can be worked out by mail. You never have to leave the warm comfort of your living room to use the facilities of this excellent newsletter. Knowing who's in the market to lend money can put you way ahead of the crowd.

USE YOUR SUPPLIERS' EXTENDED-PAY PLANS

Many suppliers will give you up to 180 days (six months) to pay for the products you buy from them. This means that once you establish your business (see Chapter 6), you have six months during which you can sell your products without paying a cent for them.

Some manufacturers will go even further—they'll allow you a one-year free return privilege. This means that you can keep their products on your shelves for a year. If you don't sell the products, return them for a full refund or credit. All you'll be out is a small postage fee.

Two yachtsmen—Ben P. and Allen K., decided to sell high-grade marine paints to other yachtsmen by mail order. Using the membership lists of several yacht clubs which they obtained free of charge, Ben and Allen spent $48.33 on a mailing to 100 members. They received orders for $435 worth of paint. Their net profit on the orders was $208.80, after subtracting the cost of the paint and the mailing. This is 9 times their investment in the mailing. Yet they hadn't spent a cent on the products they were selling because they used their supplier's 180-day delayed-payment plan.

Today Ben and Allen run the largest mail-order marine paint business in the country from Ben's basement. Both men, by the way, own sparkling new yachts, purchased from their paint business profits.

Now here's another dollar-laden profit secret you can put to use this very moment.

When two suppliers offer competitive products, pit one against the other to obtain the longest delayed-pay plan.

Suppose you're planning to sell jigsaw puzzles from your home. Please don't laugh—jigsaw puzzles are a big business. Puzzles sell at retail from as little as $1.00 to as high as $2,000, or more. Some jigsaw puzzles have only ten pieces—others have up to 10,000 pieces. There are many suppliers of jigsaw puzzles. By talking to the salesmen from several companies you can get competitive prices and delayed-pay plans.

Let's say one salesman offers you 30 days delayed-pay; another offers you 60 days. When the third salesman calls and offers you 45 days, you calmly and politely say "I have a much better offer than that." If he asks you how much better, you reply "I don't reveal competitive information—but I *can* tell you this—the offer is *much* better than yours." The third salesman might reply "I'm so sure my puzzles will really move out of your shop that I'll go the limit—180 days extended-pay."

Thus, without investing a cent, and without misleading anyone, you've tripled your delayed-pay period. This means you can sell for three times longer before you have to pay out a cent. Can you find a better deal than this with which to build your home fortune?

TRY AN SBA LOAN

The best loan interest rates in the world are offered by SBA—Small Business Administration—an organization operated by the United States Government for folks just like yourself. You can borrow money at lower rates for longer periods from SBA, or with an SBA guarantee, than from any other organization I know of. While some firms may, under special conditions, allow you a longer payoff period, their rates are considerably higher.

SBA recently introduced its Microloan Program for business loans of less than $100,000. This program uses a one-page simplified loan application that can be filled out quickly and easily by any BWB. These loans are handled by the staff at some 14 one-stop SBA centers. The number of these centers will ultimately be expanded to 60 throughout the nation. Truly, the SBA is the friendliest, most understanding lender you can deal with. Try them and see for yourself!

Figure 3 shows some of the excellent business finance programs available from SBA. And remember—All SBA programs are extended on a non-discriminatory basis. So it doesn't matter what your color, religion, or ethnic background is—you're eligible to apply to SBA for business finance help. Give your local SBA office a call today and learn more about the help awaiting you.

Fig. 3: SBA business finance programs

7(a) General Loan Program—Represents 90 percent of the agency's total loan effort. Promotes small business formation and growth by guarantees of up to 90 percent of amount provided by commercial lenders. Between 1980 and 1990, SBA provided guarantees for 180,000 loans worth more than $31 billion. A recent study by Price Waterhouse reports that businesses which get these loan guarantees show higher growth than comparable businesses.

504/503 Development Company Loan Program—Uses public/private partnerships to finance fixed assets. Has produced over $5 billion in investments and more than 301,000 jobs since its beginning in 1980.

The Small Business Investment Company (SBIC) Program—Private capital combined with SBA-guaranteed funds provides venture capital for start-up and growth. SBICs have invested nearly $11 billion in more than 70,000 small businesses.

The Microloan Program—Small loans help entrepreneurs in inner-city and rural areas form small, often home-based enterprises.

Export Finance—Normal and specialized loan-guarantee programs offer working capital and longer-term financing to promote exporting.

Disaster Loans—Low-interest loans help individuals, homeowners and businesses rebuild after a disaster.

The 8(a) Program—Helps socially and economically disadvantaged individuals enter the economic mainstream, partly through access to federal contracts.

Procurement Assistance—Ensures maximum competition by encouraging contracts for small businesses. Saved taxpayers $230 million in 1991.

The Surety Bond Guarantee

Program—More than 236,000 surety guarantees for $19 billion in contracts since 1976, helping businesses win government construction contracts.

SBA'S BUSINESS DEVELOPMENT PROGRAMS serve as the catalyst for today's small business development and growth, providing marketing and training information. Programs focus on management training, international trade, veterans affairs, women's initiatives and resource partnerships.

Business Initiatives, Education and Training—Produces a broad range of management and technical assistance publications and audiovisual materials. In 1991, SBA distributed more than three million SBA publications and videotapes.

International Trade—Information, advice and export financing help, prepare businesses to take advantage of the new world market, particularly in Mexico, the Pacific Rim, Canada and Europe.

Veterans Affairs—Business management and technical training, and counseling. About 1,200 training conferences were held for prospective and established veteran business owners in FY 1991.

Women's Business Ownership—Mentoring programs, and training and counseling centers for women nationwide. More than 119,000 women counseled and more than 184,000 trained in 1990. Sponsors "Women Going International."

Small Business Innovation and Research—Competitive opportunities to win federal research and development contracts.

Resource Partners—Service Corps of Retired Executives (SCORE), Small Business Institutes (SBIs), and Small Business Development Centers (SBDCs) handled more than 116,000 counseling cases during the first quarter of FY 1992. Over 800,000 business owners were counseled or trained in FY 1991.

If you live in a large city—Los Angeles, San Diego, San Francisco, Denver, Dallas, Houston, Chicago, Cleveland, Atlanta, Miami, Washington, New York, etc.—there's a local SBA office to serve you. Just look in the phone book, under U.S. Government. The same is true of many smaller cities. If you live in a very small town write to the Small Business Administration, Washington, D.C. 20402, asking for a loan application and the address of the nearest office. At the same time, request a list of SBA publications. They're well worth the nominal prices the SBA charges for them.

An engineer friend of mine recently borrowed $15,000 for six years from the SBA at an extremely low rate of interest. He is using the money to form a corporation in the space communications field. SBA was delighted to lend him the money. In general, you too can get a loan from SBA for any worthwhile business purpose. SBA is guaranteeing more loans than ever before, especially for women and minorities. These guarantees make it much easier for small businesses of many types to get the business loan they need.

HAVE YOUR CUSTOMERS FINANCE YOUR PRODUCTS

How? There are many ways. Here are a few.

(1) Collect down payments from your customers *before* you deliver the products. Use the down payment to pay, in whole or in part, for the products, or materials for the products, you sell to your customers. If you can arrange for your suppliers to accept partial payment, then you're having both your customers and your suppliers finance your products.

(2) Offer your customers an inducement for complete prepayment prior to delivery of their purchases. Thus, you might offer free delivery, free installation, free checkups, etc. if your customer pays or finances in advance of delivery. With the customer's cash in your hand you can often negotiate a much higher discount from your supplier (increasing your profit) because you are ready to pay cash to your supplier. Also, with cash on hand you can, if you wish, finance the purchase of other products, expanding your profit opportunities.

You can pyramid advance cash payments into more goods to sell the same way that Steven K. does. He sells fireplace screens, pokers, and wood from his basement in the winter and garden supplies, tools, and equipment from his backyard in the summer. Since part of Steve's success depends on having exactly *what* the customer wants, *when* he wants it, Steve must carry a big inventory. He does this by collecting advance and budget payments for fireplace wood in the summer and for lawn supplies in the winter. Recently Steve whispered some details of his home income to me. Although he works at home only in his spare time and holds down a full-time executive job, his home business profit in a recent year was $36,000! And all of this resulted from pyramiding advance payments into saleable products.

SELL FRANCHISED PRODUCTS

Some franchisors will finance you, or obtain financing for you, when you first go into business. Please note that I said *some* franchisors— not all. Why do I use an extra few sentences to point this out? Because other franchisors insist that you have the needed cash—$500 to $30,000—in hand when you apply for a franchise. Their theory is that if you have the needed cash you have a certain amount of business ability because you must have done something right to accumulate the cash. This is excellent, and makes plenty of sense.

But suppose you're like Carl M. who came out of the Navy with $200 in his pocket and a burning desire to open a billiard room. The most economical franchise he could obtain cost $30,000. What's more, most of the franchisors wouldn't listen to Carl because the spot he picked had an apartment in the rear where he could live. Carl finally got the franchise from a small, aggressive billiard firm looking for young men who would work hard. Carl's billiard room is booming and the franchisor has been able to open other rooms in nearby towns.

So if you're short of cash, look for a franchise which includes financing. You'll get a quicker start than if you wait to save the money you need for the franchise. Profits will start sooner and, before you know it, you'll be a 100 per cent owner of your franchise, its equipment, and inventory.

OBTAIN A CITY OR STATE LOAN

Home wealth builders often overlook a major source of business loans—their city or state business agencies. The names of these agencies vary from one city and state to another—perhaps that's why home wealth builders make so little use of them.

In some states these agencies are called Industrial Development Commission; in others Chamber of Commerce. The city names are similar. You might also find the name State Commerce Commission used. When checking on city and state agencies that make business loans, don't overlook subagencies. Thus, in one state the Job Development Authority, an arm of the State Commerce Department, makes loans to firms that develop new jobs for people.

Three recent state loans I know of are: (1) $63,000 for 10 years at 3.75 per cent interest; (b) $37,000 for 10 years at 3.75 per cent interest; (c) $150,000 for 15 years at 3.75 per cent interest. Each of these loans improved the job opportunities in the state in which the loan was granted. With such a loan, the home wealth builder can easily finance the new firm or products.

USE A FACTOR TO FINANCE YOUR PRODUCTS

A factor lends you money while collecting the money people owe you for the products you sold them. Thus, the factor finances your purchase of new products to sell to your customers.

You must make some sales *before* you use a factor. Hence, for your first few sales you must use extended-pay, a loan, or any of the other methods listed above to finance your products. Once you've made a few sales you can go to a factor for further financing.

Most factors prefer to collect from companies instead of individuals. Some small factors will, however, collect from individuals. The fee you are charged may be a trifle higher than for collections from companies. But the fees that factors charge are so modest that you'll hardly notice the difference.

Factoring—placing your accounts receivable with someone else for collection—was once considered to indicate that a firm was in a shaky financial condition. This is no longer so. Some of the best and biggest firms use factoring today. You can join them by using a factor to finance your products.

Bill N. began to sell small, portable fire extinguishers from his home in his spare time. Why? Because Bill has ten kids and he needs every extra cent he can get his hands on. Bill's business expanded almost explosively. The first month his total business was $26; the second month $1,012; the third month $5,118.

When Bill came to me for advice he had a frantic, hunted look on his face. "What am I going to do?" he groaned. "I've got so many orders for so many different fire extinguishers that I can't keep up with them."

I suggested a factor who would bill and record each transaction and furnish capital as needed. "Check the *Yellow Pages* of your phone book for the names of factors," I suggested. Bill did. Today his monthly sales volume is close to $150,000, allowing Bill to show a net profit of $500,000 per year in his home business.

Send for any one, or more, of the many wealth-building publications listed at the back of this book to get help in financing, expanding, or improving your home business. Once you have any book, newsletter, or Kit in hand, I'll be glad to answer whatever questions you may have. Just give me a call—I answer on the first ring!

You *can* get the funding you need for your home-based business, if you work at it. Two readers say: "Thanks—I negotiated a $100,000 loan through an ad I ran in IWS." And "The idea of offering a finder's fee (including a cosigner's fee) to raise money is outstanding. I raised $50,000 for a corporate loan by offering a potential investor a finder's fee which included a cosigner fee."

Make Your Fortune Selling Products

You can do as well as or better than the various businesspeople cited in this chapter. Just follow the many hints given here; work hard; don't give up easily. And remember that you can apply these hints to all kinds of products—new, used, surplus, scrap, etc. As long as a product is available and someone else wants it, you have a potential home business. Every moment of your life is a new start. Begin *now!* People don't fail; they just stop trying.

8

Become Incredibly Rich
with
These Mail-Order Secrets

Y ou can make more money today
in mail order than you could at any other time in history. Why?
There are several reasons. You can summarize these reasons in six
words—people, products, prosperity, promotion, publicity, and
profits.

Why Mail Order Is Booming

Today mail order is a multi-billion-dollar business because the six
factors listed above are on the rise. Thus:

- People willing to buy by mail are greater in number. It's
  "respectable" to buy anything by mail today.
- Products are more numerous. The buyer has a wider choice
  of things to buy. Hence, he or she is inclined to buy more.
- Prosperity is spreading throughout the world. People have

more money to spend on more products. The mail-order person is certain to benefit.

- Promotion of mail-order products is easier and cheaper today because more publications have special pages devoted to mail-order items.
- Publicity for mail-order products is easier to get because many more publications have new-product columns which welcome news about your newest items. What's more, they'll print it free of charge.
- Profits in mail order are greater today because people are willing to pay higher prices for the products they buy through the mail. This means you'll earn more each hour you work, especially if you accept orders using a credit card charge for payment. (Later in this chapter we show you how to get a Merchant Account so you can accept credit-card orders.)

Mail Order Is the Ideal Home Business

You can't beat mail order when it comes to making a fortune in your own home. Why? Because

1. You can start in your spare time
2. Little capital is needed
3. You can work anywhere, anytime
4. It's easy to expand your income
5. Profits can be very high
6. Labor costs are low
7. Your income can go on for years
8. You can sell many different products

More important than any of the items listed above is what I call the *psychological aspect* of mail order. This is the daily impetus the mail-order operator receives from the checks, cash, and orders that arrive in his or her mailbox. To see the psychological aspect at work, come with me on my mail-order rounds.

A Day in the Life of a Mail-Order Man

It's a Saturday morning, about 8:30 A.M. Before we leave we'll have a leisurely cup of coffee in the dining room. Both of us glance at the financial pages of the *New York Times* to see what new products were patented during the week. There may be some good mail-order items in the list. If so, we'll write the inventor immediately, asking for an option on the product for mail sales.

A Fortune in Your Mailbox

About 9:00 A.M. we hop into the station wagon and drive to the post office where I rent a large mail box for $48 per year. Through the glass door of the box we see that it is jammed full of envelopes and postcards. I spin the dial of the combination lock and open the box door.

"You take the mail out," I say. "I want you to experience every thrill of the mail-order businessperson."

You take out a thick wad of envelopes and postcards. The envelopes are all sizes, colors, and shapes. You reach into the box for the last few pieces of mail and find a card at the bottom of the box. It says: "Call at the Window for More Mail."

We go over to the window, tell the clerk the box number, and receive another thick wad of mail. As we jump into the station wagon to drive home I notice that you're quickly flipping through the mail, neatly arranging it according to size and type. When I see you hold an impressive-looking envelope up to the light to see if it contains a check, I laugh. "The bug has bit," I say, and I think you understand.

What the Mails Bring You

At home you can hardly wait to get the letter opener into your hands. "Be systematic—open all the envelopes but don't take anything out yet," I advise. You nod and get to work.

You open one envelope after another. They come from all parts of the world. Some are gaily colored air-mail envelopes; others are neatly printed personal stationery; some are scrawled in big bold writing; others have the neat script of a lady; some have the word URGENT! printed across the bottom; others contain PLEASE RUSH! at the side.

Keep Simple Records of Orders

"Count the checks and mark on the outside of the envelope the amount and the product," I tell you. There's a gleam in your eye as you extract check after check from the envelopes. When you pull several $20 bills from the envelopes you whistle with delight.

"I thought you weren't supposed to send cash through the mail," you say.

"You're not," I reply, "but people do it all the time. As I say to my wife, 'Don't argue, honey, as long as it's honest money.'"

After opening the last of the many envelopes, you have a neat pile of checks and cash. You don't have to be told what to do next—you take a pencil and add up the income. When you're finished you look at me with amazement. "The total is six thousand and fifty-two dollars," you say.

"That's just about right," I reply. "I figured we should do six thousand to seven thousand dollars this week."

You sit back in your chair. "I need another cup of coffee," you mumble.

During the next hour I show you how to make a few entries in the simple mail-order record system I devised. Then we address some labels, stick them on the prepackaged products, and add the pre-figured number of stamps. I make out the bank deposit slip, endorse the checks with a rubber stamp, and put them in an envelope for depositing in the bank. We also address labels for inquiries about products and prices, attach them to our standard catalogs, and we're finished. "Now," I say, "let's go fishing. I'll deposit the cash in the bank Monday."

On the way to the boat we drop our products and catalogs into a local mailbox. By noon you've caught your first fluke. "This is great," you say. "I'm thinking of that money piling up in the post office box while I sit here fishing. There's nothing greater!"

"That," I reply, "is the psychological aspect of mail order. Just the thought of the money rolling in every day of the week will keep you young forever!"

"I'm starting my own mail-order business tonight," you grin as you hook into a big fish.

How to Start Your Mail-Order Business

The first step in starting any mail-order business is to decide which you prefer: (1) to be in the mail-order business as your main source of income, or (2) to use mail order as another means to promote your products or services. This decision is important because it will influence many of your future actions. Since I want this book to be as useful to as many people as possible, both types of mail order activities are covered in this chapter. First we'll look at how *you* can build a home fortune just through mail order.

Seven Magic Steps to Mail-Order Success

Here are seven mail-order steps that are outstandingly successful for the students in my wealth-building course, and for myself:

(1) Find a suitable mail-order product
(2) Determine product cost for various quantities
(3) Choose publications suitable for advertising
(4) Determine advertising cost
(5) Run an ad in a chosen publication
(6) Tabulate results
(7) Compute profits

Where mailing lists are used instead of, or in addition to, advertisements for sale of the product or service, the expert terms this method *direct mail* as opposed to mail order which uses only ads. The first two steps are the same. Then, however, you must:

(3) Choose the types of mailing lists suitable for the product
(4) Determine the cost of the list rental
(5) Make a test mailing
(6) Tabulate the results
(7) Compute profits

How to Start with a Smaller Investment

You can start your mail-order business with a smaller investment if you use mailing lists instead of ads in national magazines. But you won't reach anywhere as large a market with the mailings unless you spend a very large sum of money. Feel discouraged? Don't, because I'm about to reveal my first mail-order secret. But before I do I want to show you how this secret developed.

All my life I've done things in small bits. For example, I write about 500 words a day. In 160 days—about seven months' working time because I write only five days a week—I have a book, such as the one you're now reading. The same is true of my other income sources. For example, I give a 40-minute speech and receive a $1,000 payment. And I go right on working at something else after I give the speech. In fact, though I've never revealed this to anyone before, I think the reason for my outstanding financial success is *doing many things in small bits.*

You can do the same in mail order. How? Here's a secret that could be worth one million dollars to you:

> Sell a mail-order product that will give you a good profit per unit sale and a suitable income on an easily attainable sales volume.

Volume Doesn't Always Mean Profit

Some mail-order beginners insist on seeing an enormous volume potential before they'll invest in a product. What these beginners fail to understand is that volume doesn't always mean profit. You can spend yourself into financial disaster seeking volume and have little or no profit to show for your investment.

You will often find it easier to sell 1,000 special wrenches to a list of 50,000 plumbers than it is to sell 1,000 toothbrushes to a list of 50,000 people with real teeth. When mail-order beginners have a product for Mr. Everyman they think their fortune is made. Yet when they go out to look for Mr. Everyman via the mails he seems to have run away, so far as sales are concerned. Why? The answer is in your first secret, above, and the second one, below.

> Sell a mail-order product to a clearly defined audience whenever you can because, in general, your sales costs will be lower, and your profits higher.

What's more, specialized mailing lists can usually be rented at a nominal cost from list brokers. A few of the larger list brokers are:

American List Counsel, 88 Orchard Rd., Princeton NJ 08543
The Coolidge Co., Inc., 25 W 43rd St, New York NY 10036
Alan Drey Co., Inc., 333 N Michigan Av, Chicago IL 60601
IC Direct, 17 Paul Dr, Suite 202, San Rafael CA 94903
Market Share, 5726 Cortez Rd W, Suite 303, Bradenton FL 34210
World Innovators Inc., 72 Park St, New Canaan CT 06840
Write to these brokers for their general catalog showing which lists
are available and the cost of each.

How to Make Mailing Lists Pay Off

Let's say that a list costs $75 per thousand names to rent, including
the addressing, insertion, and placement of the envelopes in the post
office. You pay, we'll say, $105 per thousand to have your circular and
envelopes printed. Postage for the one thousand circulars is $220.
Hence, your total out-of-pocket expenses are $75 + $105 + $220, or
$400. What sales volume should this mailing generate to be profitable
to you?

A quick rule of thumb for a product you manufacture or have
manufactured for your exclusive sale is:

**Each mailing on a product you manufacture should
produce three dollars in sales for every dollar spent
on the mailing.**

Thus, if you spend $400 on a mailing to a list of 1,000 names you
should receive at least $1200 worth of orders to make your mailing
profitable. Out of this minimum of $1200 you must pay $400 for the
mailing cost, leaving $800 to pay for the cost of manufacturing the
product, mailing it, billing the customer, and paying you a profit. The
first three are direct costs which you can usually identify accurately
and with ease.

Know Your Indirect Costs

In almost every mail-order operation there are indirect costs
which are difficult to predict in advance. Typical of such costs are

damages to your products in the mail, products returned by the buyer in unusable condition, bad debts—i.e. people who fail to pay for the product or service, correspondence explaining how to use, repair, or maintain the product, etc.

Some mail-order dealers allow a fixed percentage, based on past experience, to cover indirect costs. Thus, one dealer might allow 5 per cent of every sales dollar to cover his or her fixed expenses. Other dealers might use higher or lower percentages, depending on their specific experience. You can, however, take the 5 per cent as a good starting point if you haven't had any previous experience.

Which Mail-Order Product for You?

You can sell almost any product or service by mail. Probably one of the smallest items sold by mail today is a diamond; the largest is an automobile or boat. If you're already in business selling a product through other outlets and just want to use mail order as another market, you have little or no choice in the product you offer for sale. But if you are just starting and do not yet have a product to sell, you have a full range of products available to you.

My experience in mail order and direct mail indicates that the products which have the longest sales life are those you create or "dream up" yourself. Why is this? Because your product will probably be completely unique, or have unique features the competition lacks. This uniqueness keeps it on the market longer than when the product is competing with ten identical items. So if you're just starting in mail order

> Consider creating your own product or your own approach to solving a common problem. A unique product can give you an exclusive corner on the market.

Find, or Develop, a Unique Product

Bob C. enjoys investing in the stock market. When he first started investing, Bob didn't have too many free dollars. Yet he wanted to invest like a professional. So he subscribed to an expensive ($720 per year) stock advisory service. Soon he began to wonder if the recommendations of another advisory service weren't better. By the end of two years Bob was subscribing to eight different stock advisory services.

One night Bob sat down to write the checks to renew his subscriptions to these various advisory services. Though he didn't realize it at the time, this evening was a momentous one in his life. As he wrote one check after another, Bob began to ponder. "This is foolish. Why do I subscribe to *eight* of these services. Why can't I subscribe to *one* service which will give me the recommendations of these eight and all the other major advisory services?"

Sometimes You Must Research New Products

Bob stopped writing checks and spent the remainder of the evening looking for information about a stock advisory service that summarized the findings of other services. He was unable to find one. Nor could his friends name one when he asked them the next day. But he did discover two valuable facts while talking to his friends: (1) most of them subscribed to two or more advisory services (2) most of his friends said that they thought that a summary of recommendations was a great idea and that they'd be glad to subscribe to such a service.

Bob spent the next few weeks figuring the costs of starting and running a summary advisory service. For example, he'd have to subscribe to some seventy-odd advisory services; he'd have to run ads for his summary in the various newspapers featuring good financial news; he'd also have to advertise, at a later date, in the better financial magazines. Other direct costs would be preparation of the weekly advisory letter (typing, printing, etc.), postage, envelopes, etc. When he totalled all his costs, including allowances for bad debts, bank charges, and overhead, Bob found that he could earn a worthwhile profit after he reached the break-even point.

Test Your Product in the Market Place

As a test, Bob ran his first ad. True, it was a small ad, but he ran it in the best newspaper in a large city. "The results were fantastic," Bob says. "Within a week I went from zero subscribers to eight hundred. The volume of mail was so enormous that I couldn't get it into the basement where I worked on the advisory letter. I had mailbags piled up in the living room. My wife was good about this for awhile but then she began to ask for her living room back."

Bob had problems with this many subscribers. But they were sweet problems because almost every letter contained a check or money order covering the cost of an annual subscription to the advisory service.

Today Bob is on top of the world. His unique product, which he sometimes calls the *Reader's Digest* of the investment advisory world, is booming. Though he still writes the weekly contents of his service in his basement, his print order is so large that it must be handled by a commercial printer. Bob works only two or three days a week from about eight to noon; the rest of the week he swims, golfs, plays cards, or reads. With a unique mail-order product *you* could do the same.

Another example of a unique product is given by this reader who says, "Using many IWS ideas we started a new magazine; eight months ago we took in $200 for the month. Last month we grossed over $5,000 from our home; this month will be even better."

Market a Unique Service by Mail Order

Some people, myself included, have trouble trying to dream up a new *product*. Why this is so I can't explain and I don't have the time to try to figure it out. I'm too busy earning money from *services* that I do dream up.

June K., a librarian, was a worried young woman when she called me at home one night. "I've tried and tried to develop a 'unique' product," she wailed. "But I can't think of any."

"What about a service?" I asked. "You're a librarian. Isn't there some kind of service that libraries need that you could provide?"

"I'll think about it and call you back," June replied.

A Service Should Help People

It took six weeks before June called back. But when she did she was bubbling over. "I *have* the service; I have it," she said excitedly. "It's in the technical-book line," she continued, without giving me a chance to say a word.

June's mail-order service business idea was this: Every month she'd mail news about the newest technical books to libraries of all kinds, but particularly company libraries—i.e. libraries run for employees of large corporations. All the librarian has to do is check off the books she wants, return the list to June, and she ships the books, bills the library, etc.

Mail-Order Service in the Living Room

Recently I stopped at June's house to see how her mail-order book business was doing. June was typing labels, using a portable computer on a card table in her living room. Two youngsters romped in a playpen close to the card table. In the dining room another woman was busily at work typing bills on a laptop computer.

"How's the technical book business?" I asked.

"Great," June laughed. "We're really booming along. This month we've been in business exactly one year. And just last night I was adding up the income. We grossed $250,000 in sales in our first year—and almost all of that was through mail order. Isn't that great!"

"It sure is," I said, "particularly since you can work at home at your convenience."

June, I might add, should net at least 20 per cent on her gross business income. Thus, her first-year, before-taxes income should be $50,000 on a $250,000 gross. This is the magic of mail order. And, incidentally, June never sees the books she sells. After receiving an order in the mail she has the publisher ship the book directly to the customer. This is called *drop shipping* and can save the mail-order man or woman much time and effort. Check into the possibilities of drop shipment in all your mail-order activities.

Your Quick Guide to Mail-Order Millions

In my experience most people who are considering mail order or direct mail have a number of questions they want answered immediately. Once they have their questions answered, these people are ready to weigh the information they have and make a decision. Here are the usual questions people ask, and the practical, moneymaking answers they receive from me. I'm certain you'll find these questions and answers useful. Many other people have.

Q. What is the difference between mail order and direct mail?

A. Very little, really. However, some purists insist that the term *mail order* be used only when a product or service is sold by running a display, classified, or other type of ad in a publication. People send in a coupon or write directly to the address given in the ad. In *direct mail* you send, by mail, circulars, catalogs, or other advertising material to a selected list of people. These people send you an order for the product or service if they want it. In both mail order and direct mail you're trying to do the same thing—that is, sell products by using the mails. Many mail-order ads are designed primarily to produce inquiries about a product or service. The direct-mail promotion material sent as an answer to the inquiry is relied on to do the actual selling of the product or service to the customer.

Q. What are good mail-order products which I might sell?

A. Typical products that sell well by mail are specialty foods (cheese, fruit cake, jams, etc.), home needs and novelties (furniture, mailboxes, pillows, etc.), gifts (letter paper, bottle openers, serving dishes, etc.), pet products (blankets, doghouses, food, fish tanks, etc.), courses of instruction (in electronics, jiu jitsu, printing, auto repair, etc.), business cards, shoes, pants, uniforms, gloves, auto parts, greeting cards, watches, computers, electrical and electronic equipment, books, magazines, tools, and hundreds of others. Lastly, don't overlook industrial products—those you can sell to large and small companies.

Q. How much may I have to spend on advertising to get an order for a product?

A. The typical maximum advertising cost of getting one order of a product you sell by mail order is: for a $10 product, 10% or $1.00; for a $25 product, 25% or $6.25; for a $75 product, 40% or $30. This is the usual way of stating the cost of getting an order—that is, as a percentage of the sales price of the product or service. If you can get an order at a cost less than that listed above, you're doing great.

Q. How can I consistently make money in mail order?

A. Aim at obtaining orders from each ad or mailing that amount to at least three times the cost of the ad or mailing. Thus, an ad or mailing costing $500 should bring in at least $1500 in business. At this 3-to-1, sales-to-cost ratio almost every mail-order business can show a good profit, particularly if you operate in your own home.

Q. What total costs must I pay to market a product by mail order?

A. The total costs you must pay will vary with the product you are selling but they *must* include:

Ad or mailing cost	Order-handling cost
Product cost	Overhead cost
Package cost	Refunds cost
Label cost	Bank cost
Postage cost	Instruction-sheet cost

To make money on a product or service having a $10.00 selling price, your total costs — that is, the sum of all the above costs — should be less than $3.00.

Q. What refunds, guarantees, C.O.D., free examination, approval plans, etc. should I offer?

A. NONE! If you want to live a peaceful life in mail order, avoid all these gimmicks. True, you'll get a few less orders. But you'll have fewer problems with damaged merchandise, false claims, and long letters complaining about your products. Find and market a reliable product or service; write accurate ads and promotion; package the product carefully; insist on cash, check, or money order with the order. I run several mail-order activities on this basis and they are outstandingly successful. You can do the same, or better.

Q. What can I do about bad checks?

A. Very little, except to figure your losses from bad checks as a part of the cost of doing business. Some banks will charge you $10 to $15 for every check you deposit that bounces. And checks *do* bounce in the mail-order business. Many mail-order operators add a 3 per cent check-bouncing cost—that is 3¢ for every dollar of product or service list price—into their product cost. This protects them from excessive bad-check losses.

As a further protection for yourself, use my simple rule: NEVER SHIP A PRODUCT UNTIL THE CHECK PAYING FOR IT CLEARS. Speak to your bank official to determine the typical clearance time for checks from different localities.

Q. How long should I run a small ad?

A. As long as it earns a profit. Some mail-order men and women live by a series of complex rules concerning how long to run an ad, when *not* to advertise, etc. I scrapped all these rules in my own activities and substituted just one, which anyone can understand. That rule? RUN AN AD OR MAILING UNTIL IT STOPS PRODUCING A PROFIT. THEN REPLACE IT WITH ONE THAT DOES MAKE A PROFIT. Would you believe that a 1-inch ad could produce $3-million in mail-order business? One such ad did, over a 25-year period. Yet the cost of running this ad was only one-tenth the business it produced. The ad, incidentally, is still running.

Is Mail-Order Training Worth the Money?

Some people hit it big in mail order without ever taking extensive training. For instance:

- A mail-order dealer who sells an expandable clothes rack for cars grosses $100,000 per year.
- A young couple placed a $100 ad for printing personal stationery. Within a few weeks they were flooded with orders worth $30,000.
- A fireman ran an ad for a unique set of corncob holders. A month later he had orders worth $25,000.
- A lawn sprinkler that does an excellent watering job grossed $1-million in one year for its mail-order seller.

I could go on for page after page with similar stories. These are the BIG hits, the once-in-a-lifetime home run that wins a World Series. But what about these:

Sally K., a housewife, nets $150 per week selling pretty paper flowers by mail. How many hours does she work each week? Ten—in the privacy of her own home.

Bruce L. nets $500 per week selling spark plugs by mail order to sports-car buffs. How many hours does he work each week? Twenty—in his basement while his hi-fi set plays soft music.

Should you take mail-order training? It all depends on your previous business experience. If your only business experience is in a job having nothing to do with mail order, you will probably profit from mail-order training. But if you've done mail order or direct mail as part of your work for someone else, mail-order training may not help you. One good source of training which won't cost you much is my Kit, *Mail Order Riches Success Kit,* described at the back of this book. It will really give you the information you need to run a highly successful mail-order business!

What Will Mail-Order Training Teach Me?

Good mail-order training will give you answers to the important questions you'll meet in your business, such as:

Q. How much should I pay for a mail-order product?

A. Never pay more than 60% of your mail-order selling price—i.e. $3.00 for a product that sells at $5.00; $6.00 for a product that sells at $10.00. This is a 40% discount. Better yet—try to get a 50% discount. Then you'll really earn a BIG profit. But you can't make a worthwhile profit on a discount of less than 40%. Incidentally, most mail-order pros aim for a much higher discount—60% or more.

Q. What is a test ad or test mailing?

A. Test ads and test mailings are small, low-cost ads or mailings that you make to see what kind of a market there is for your product. If the ad or mailing pays off—i.e. brings in three or more times its cost, you "extend" it. To extend an ad, you run it in more magazines. To extend a mailing, you mail to a larger list containing the same kind of names as your first mailing. The usual test mailing contains 1,000 names. You extend it to 10,000, 100,000, or 500,000 names, depending on the amount of money you have on hand, and your estimate of the potential market for your product.

Q. What are important characteristics of a mail-order product?

A. Here are just a few characteristics you should always consider before deciding to market a given product:

- Is the product too heavy to mail?
- Is the product too fragile to mail?
- Is the price of the product too high?
- Is the price of the product too low?
- Is the product dangerous to people?
- Is the product useful to its buyers?

If you answer yes to any of the first five questions you may have a troublesome product on your hands. This is where good mail-order training can come to your help.

Where Can I Get Mail-Order Training?

There are a few successful mail-order dealers who will train you for a nominal fee. The monthly newsletter, *International Wealth*

Success, available from Prima Publishing, P.O. Box 1260HB, Rocklin, CA 95677, periodically lists mail-order dealers who offer training. It also lists the few schools of mail order that are operating today. The annual subscription fee for this newsletter is $24.

Some of the direct-marketing and mail-order newspapers and magazines such as *DM News, Income Opportunities, Spare Time, Moneymaking Opportunities*, and *Home Business News* contain ads of mail-order dealers who will train you. Obtain several copies of each magazine and write to the dealers and schools that interest you. Take a course, if you think you would benefit from it.

Talking about training for business success, the best and most comprehensive plan that I know of is The International Wealth Success Fortune Builder's Program. This is a complete, supervised action program which shows you, step-by-step, how to build a quick, sizeable fortune in:

* Your spare time
* Mail order and direct mail
* Your own home business
* Rental real estate
* Specialized consulting
* Venture capital
* Export-import
* Finder's fees
* Financial brokerage
* Ventures using 100% financing
* Unusual businesses

The Fortune Builder's Program is a no-nonsense, hard-work plan to put money into your pocket. While the cost of the Program—$300 complete—may seem small, the results can be enormous. So if you're really serious about earning a fortune in any kind of business of your own, enroll in The Fortune Builder's Program. You can obtain full details on this Program from Prima Publishing, P.O. Box 1260HB, Rocklin, CA 95677.

Is Mail-Order Drop Shipping Profitable?

Some mail-order firms print catalogs which contain photos, descriptions, and prices of merchandise stored in a central warehouse.

To go into the mail-order business, you purchase a supply of catalogs imprinted with the name of your organization. You mail these catalogs to a list of prospects of your choice.

When you receive orders for items in the catalog, you forward the order and the wholesale price of the item to the warehouse. The warehouse ships the item to your customer, and furnishes you with a receipt showing when and to whom the item was shipped. Thus, you are freed of warehousing, packaging, and shipping problems. This means you can concentrate on the profitable aspects of the business—finding the customer and making the sale.

Can drop shipping be profitable? One man, Paul Z., working in his kitchen, manages to net $40,000 per year from drop shipping. This is his second year in business and Paul hopes to net $100,000 per year in his fourth year. He truly believes that mail order will make him a millionaire. Though Paul can afford a new kitchen table he refuses to sell his old one because he believes it brings him good luck.

Ask Paul Z. his secret for mail-order drop shipping success and he'll answer, "Lists—you have to get good lists of prospective buyers. Sure, you can rent these lists. But I never had much luck with them. So I develop my own mailing lists from every source I can think of—club membership lists, people I meet, etc. Sure, it's hard work. But I'm earning at least four times as much as the 'smart' guys who laughed at me when I said I was going into a home-operated mail-order business. Next year I hope to increase my net by at least $150,000. The 'smart' guys *may* get a $3,000 per year raise."

Drop shipping may be your answer to home wealth through mail order. Think over your chances for coming up with lists of prospective buyers. If you can find 10,000 or more names on your own, you can probably hit it big with drop-ship mail order.

You can sell the financial and home-business products produced by my firm, IWS, Inc., if you're our Executive Representative. We drop-ship all our products at no cost to you or your customer for regular delivery. You earn a 40% commission on the first $2,000 in sales; then your commission rises to 50% for life. See the Executive Representative Plan at the back of this book for full details.

Work through Mail-Order Dealers

Up till now we've been talking about *you* being a mail-order dealer. You write the ads, or hire an ad agency to write them, wrap the product, address the label, keep the records, etc. You do all the work and earn all the profit.

But suppose you don't want to get involved with all the details of mail order (and there are many details). What then, particularly if you have a good mail-order product? Well, you can give away a little of your profit by using mail-order dealers. What do you gain when you give up some of your profit this way? Plenty.

What Mail-Order Dealers Do

Mail-order dealers will advertise and promote your product if they think it has a market. Thus, you are relieved of the advertising burdens and details. Since there are thousands of mail-order dealers in the United States, you can usually find one who will be glad to handle your product on mutually satisfactory terms.

Sometimes a mail-order dealer can give you the sweetest kinds of problems. Jerry C. invented a handy clothes hook for closets. He had 500 hooks made up and sent them to a group of mail-order dealers, after we discussed how the hook should be marketed. Several dealers agreed to market the hook on a non-exclusive basis.

Successful Dealer Product Promotion

I called Jerry about two weeks after the first three dealers started their ad campaigns on the hook.

"Get right over here, you scoundrel," he growled good-naturedly over the phone.

A few minutes later I scrambled down the backyard steps leading to Jerry's basement. When I opened the door I spied him in the middle of a sea of white paper spread around the entire basement floor.

"Look what you did to me," he groaned. "Every one of these pieces of paper is an order for clothes hooks. What am I gonna do?"

It took some doing to get Jerry out of "trouble." We had to get three manufacturers to handle the enormous number of orders. But, as people say, Jerry "cried all the way to the bank."

Today Jerry has a booming business devoted to finding and

developing new products for his many happy mail-order dealers. As Jerry remarked to me recently, "Now the mail-order dealers plead with me to handle my products. In the beginning it was different; I had to plead with them."

To obtain what I think is the best available information on mail-order dealers, buy a copy of *Mail Order Business Directory* from IWS, Inc., POB 186, Merrick NY 11566-0186. Priced at $75.00, it lists some 10,000 mail order catalog dealers who might be willing to sell your product for you. This list can be a real profit builder for you if you have a few good mail-order products.

You Have a BIG Mail-Order Future

If mail order interests you, there's a multi-billion-dollar market open to you. I know of no pleasanter or more suitable way to millionize your income by starting at home, either spare time or full time.

And the beauty of mail order is that you can make it as simple or complex as you wish. Are you the easy-going, relaxed type who enjoys freedom from worries and responsibilities? Then run a small, loosely organized mail-order business in your home. You'll welcome the stimulation the business offers you. Further, the extra income will improve your standard of living immensely.

Do you enjoy figuring averages, percentages, costs, etc.? Then mail order is the business for you. You can figure more things in mail order than in almost any other business. But you don't have to figure, if you'd prefer to operate free and easy.

Mail order is here to stay. If you're interested in mail order or direct mail you have a BIG, BIG future ahead of you. Just be sure you approach mail order and direct mail as sound and profitable ways of doing business. If you do, I'm certain you'll have a good chance to earn a profit. And if you persevere, you may even reach the magical goal of $500,000 per year in your own home business!

Social changes throughout the world—with more women working to help support their children and home—make your future in mail-order/direct-marketing bright! Everyone, it seems, has less time to shop. So the typical working mother or harried father, calls an 800 number to order children's clothing, home equipment, gardening supplies, hobby items, educational materials, etc., from a mail-order catalog using a credit card to pay the bill.

This trend in direct shopping will continue to expand, especially with the Information Superhighway offering 500 TV channels. Many channels will feature home shopping via satellite—again with an 800-number and a credit card. So you can expect nothing but greater sales and profits for yourself in the world of mail-order/direct-marketing—the world's greatest business!

And if you'd like to accept major credit cards in your business, buy a copy of my *Business Merchant Account Kit* listed at the back of this book. It shows you how, and where, to get a merchant account for your business to accept credit-card customers. Much of the Kit concentrates on getting a merchant account for a home-based mail-order/direct-mail or telemarketing business. This Kit will really help you get *your* business merchant account!

9

Get Rich Fast in Home Service

Nearly everyone complains today about the lack of good craftspeople in almost every occupation. Try to have something in your home fixed on a weekend or during the evening. You'll be lucky if you can talk to the craftsperson instead of an answering service. Or try to have a complicated repair made on an appliance, personal computer, auto, lawn mower, or some other item. Most craftspeople today will recommend that you junk an item instead of repairing it. "It's cheaper in the long run," they say.

People Hunger for Good Service

Most people don't want to junk valuable or treasured possessions. Instead, they'd like to have them repaired, when necessary, for a nominal fee. Some people even say "I'd pay anything, just *any* price if I could find a reliable mechanic who'd show up on time and do a good job when he gets here. I've been waiting two weeks for a plumber who's made, and broken, four appointments to come to my home."

As our appliances and other products become more complicated, we can do fewer of the needed repairs ourselves. Also, almost everyone seems to have less time to spend on these tasks. For these, and many other reasons, people long for good service. You can easily get rich supplying this kind of service from your own home. Provide reliable service and I assure you that you'll have so many customers so anxious to put you to work that there will be many times when you'll wish they'd stop pushing money into your hand and go away.

One reader who believes in good service for his customers says, "Your books inspired me to start a part-time carpet cleaning business. It has been much more successful than I thought it would be—and it may develop into a full-time business for me."

What Type of Service Business for You?

If you've read every page of the book up to this point, you're probably a dedicated home wealth builder. And if you haven't yet selected the way you want to build your home fortune, then a home service business may be the answer. And I'm determined to put you into the right business—one that will make you wealthy.

Claude C. was anxious to build his fortune in a service-type business he could run from his own home. "But I couldn't get started," Claude told me while we lunched at the Overseas Press Club, "because I didn't know what kind of service to offer. But one night at a local gathering some women began to bend my ear about the difficulties they were having in getting maids to work in their homes. Later that night, while I was half asleep, the idea, which I now call *my great idea*, came to me. Why couldn't I start a maid service? I lay awake half the night thinking about it."

Today Claude runs a booming business out of his home. He supplies a number of cleaning services for homes, offices, and industrial plants. Claude also runs an employment agency for domestic help. His business is so big now that he owns more than a dozen cleaning trucks. "I'll have to build my own plant," he told me with a grin. "But my profits are so high I can easily afford it. Boy, am I glad I heard those women complaining about their lack of maids!"

Three Important Types of Service Businesses

CRAFTSPERSON'S SKILLS PAY OFF

(1) Your home service business can be based mostly on your skill

as a craftsperson. Thus, typical home service businesses of this type are:

Auto tune-up	Cesspool cleaning
Piano tuning	Oil burner maintenance
Home repair	Emergency repairs of all types
Lawn care	TV and computer repair

To conduct any type of business based on your skills, you must have some knowledge to start with. But you can easily acquire this knowledge in a few hours. For example, you can learn 85 to 90 per cent of what you need to know about TV and computer repair from one good book in about three hours.

So don't be discouraged because you think you lack knowledge. Today we all lack information in one area or another. But fortunately for us, the many excellent books that are available in free public libraries or from the publishers make it easy for anyone to acquire new information quickly and efficiently. You can also rent, or buy, a number of helpful videos that show you how to repair a variety of popular home, industrial, and commercial items. A video has the advantage of showing action, where needed.

BRAIN SKILLS BRING BIG INCOME

(2) Your home service business can be based on your brain skills. Thus, typical home service businesses of this type are:

Music teacher
Accountant for small businesses
Tax adviser
Tutor for students
Author of books and articles
Computer and software instruction
Computer repair

You must spend more time preparing for a brain-skill type service business. But if you were good at some subject in school, or you've kept up another skill like music, you should be able to start your home business quickly.

"But how can I make $100,000 per year teaching music at home?" you ask. My reply is: "You probably can't, unless you expand your business until it becomes a school with several teachers offering lessons in piano, violin, accordion, trumpet, guitar, etc. Then, even after you pay your assistants a percentage of the fees, you might make

$100,000 per year. Of course, you'll be earning money all the time while you're building up to that $100,000 level. And I have the feeling that if, as a result of reading this book, you build your home income to only $80,000 or $90,000 per year, you won't ask for your money back."

One music teacher, Sarah C., who began giving piano lessons in her living room, soon had to expand into the dining room, basement, and attic, hiring several assistant teachers. When she had to convert the two-car garage to a waiting room and three practice rooms, she decided to move into another home. Today, her two-building music school, with a faculty of seven assistants, gives her a net income of close to $100,000 per year.

Her secret? She started her school in an area of many small homes inhabited by young families with lots of growing children. She aims her advertising directly at this big market. By charging nominal fees for her lessons, and by offering lessons for a variety of instruments, Sarah C. has built a highly profitable home business.

SALES ABILITIES ARE WORTH PLENTY

(3) Your home service business can be based on your sales abilities. Thus, typical home service businesses of this type are:

> Door-to-door selling
> Real-estate selling
> Mail-order selling
> Specialty selling

Rose M. uses her sales abilities in a unique and highly profitable business requiring only a telephone, a pencil, and a pad of paper. Here's how Rose earns more than $100,000 per year while working two hours, or less, per day.

Rose rents about 100 luxury apartments in a large city. In the lease for each apartment is a clause which allows Rose to sublet the apartment, if she wishes. And that's exactly what Rose does. She sublets her apartments to top executives, embassy officials, and other desirable tenants for short or long periods—from one month to a year, or longer.

Rose earns a profit on each apartment she rents. For instance, let's take an apartment Rose rents from the building owner at $1,000 per month. When Rose subleases this same apartment for one year she will probably charge $1,400 per month for it. Thus, her gross profit on this apartment is $1,400 − $1,000 = $400 per month. When renting the same apartment for a shorter period, let's say 6 months, Rose would probably charge $1,500 per month. Why? Because she has double the amount of work to keep the place rented.

How can Rose earn such a large annual income with so little work? What is she doing that rates her such a large income?

Rose can earn so large an income with so little work because she uses her sales ability to convince people that her home service business is dependable and worth paying for. In renting the 100-odd apartments Rose is taking a risk. If she can't sublease the apartments, Rose has to pay the rent out of her own funds. To date, she has managed to keep every apartment rented every month. So, just like every other business, the business of subleasing real estate has its risks.

You Have a Good Friend Near You

While reading this book you have a friend near you. Why? I'm so interested in helping you earn a big income at home that I'll do anything to get you started right, guide you, listen to your troubles, and try to advise you—if you're seeking advice. Many of my readers write or call me and I meet them at a mutually convenient place. They tell me what they're trying to do. I try to give them some useful ideas. Incidentally, I have never charged a fee of more than $50 for such a meeting if the person is a one-year, or longer, subscriber to our newsletter, *International Wealth Success*. Actually, I usually wind up paying for the lunch or dinner we share.

But it isn't necessary that we meet. This book contains everything you need to know to start and run a successful home business. But if you have any questions, just call me on the phone. I answer on the first ring and I will try to help you with any questions you may have. Let's now turn to getting *you* started.

How to Pick Your Home Service Business

What three home service businesses do you think you would *like* to run in your neighborhood? Enter them in these spaces.

1. ....

2. ....

3. ....

What equipment, facilities, tools, and other special units do you need to earn a profit in this business? List them here.

1. ....

2. ....

3. ....

How much money do you need to start, or buy, the home service businesses that interest you? Enter the amount for each business here.

1. ....

2. ....

3. ....

"But," a beginning home wealth builder might say, "I don't know how much I'll need to start. I don't have any experience in business and no one wants to help me."

This is a fairly common experience. To overcome it, don't let the hopeless feeling you may have, win out. *Do something!* Guess at how much money you'll need. Go to the library and borrow some books on the business that interests you. Ask the librarian to help you locate the information you seek. Most librarians will be delighted to help.

Lastly, list the three most needed service businesses in your local area. Use the form below.

1. ....

2. ....

3. ....

Make Your Choice Now

You now have four items listed: (1) the three service businesses you think could run in your area, (2) the equipment needed for each, (3) the money needed for each, and (4) the three businesses your neighborhood needs.

Study these lists. Does the same business appear on lists (1) and (4)? If it does, you're on the right track. Can you afford, after some financial stretching, the equipment or investment in (2) and (3)? If your answer is yes, then choose the business listed in both items (1) and (4). Why? Because this is a business you like and your area needs.

Suppose, however, that all your answers are no. What then? Should you give up? No! *Never give up*.

Take the word of your good friend, the author of this book, that you should never, never give up your search for the right home business for yourself. You may change your goals, but you should never give up your search for home wealth until you achieve it. And even after you've hit the big money in the right home business, you'll get so much joy from working at home that you'll go right on looking for other profitable businesses. The only change you'll make in your work schedule after you hit the big money is that you'll take longer, and probably more expensive, vacations.

How to Try Again

But *your* answers are no. What should you do? Try again. Go back and list three other businesses you think you would like to run in your area. Check each against the needed list. As a general guide, try to pick a business which you like and which coincides with the area's needs. Don't try, at least in your first business, to force your likes on the public. Rather, see if your likes coincide with the public's needs. So keep trying to find one of your own interests or likes which jibes with the needs of the public in your home area.

Remember—to make a study like this you need only pencil and paper. Thus, it's a low-cost way to find the best home service business for yourself.

Three Examples of Success

To show how this system works, I'd like to tell you about some successful home wealth builders. Here, briefly, are their stories.

HANDICAPPED PERSON CONQUERS

Ben C. is physically handicapped. He's confined to a wheel chair. Yet Ben is ambitious, hopeful, and wants to get ahead. He tried working at a local electronics company for a few years. Ben did an excellent job but he wasn't completely happy. He wanted to work at something that was all *his;* something he could do at home that people *wanted* done.

Ben explored his own skills and needs. Because of his handicap, he decided that he'd have to work at something that people brought *to* him, or came *to* him for. Ben considered a number of businesses—computer repair, shoe repair, article writing, addressing envelopes, etc.

While computer repair interested him, two stores already in the local area provided all the computer repair service the residents needed. So Ben discarded this idea, even though it appealed strongly to him. "Why try to sell a sun lamp in the Sahara Desert?" Ben laughs when telling how he started his local home business. "Turning my back on what *I* wanted to do was a smart move," he continues. "Three other computer repair stores later opened in this area. Each thought it could compete with the existing stores. But the three new ones failed."

Ben finally chose article writing as his home service business because several local weekly newspapers and monthly magazines needed articles with strong local color. While Ben hadn't written much since his high-school days, he was sure he could write the kinds of articles the editors wanted. Further, the equipment needed —typewriter, desk, paper, etc.—would cost only about $200. Lastly, Ben could do all the work at home.

Ben started his article-writing business in his spare time while he was still working in the electronics factory. His articles were quickly accepted and within six months his writing income was greater than his salary in the electronics factory. That's when Ben decided to quit his job and concentrate on writing. Today Ben regularly writes for about 100 newspapers and magazines. His income is soaring and Ben sees a greater future need for the kinds of articles he writes.

YOUNG WIDOW FINDS SUCCESS

Ann R., a young widow, wanted to start a home business so she could be with her three small children. When Ann sat down to try to decide which business she'd like to run in her area she was partial to real estate. The trouble was that Ann lives in the center of a large city where land is very expensive. With land and buildings costing so much, Ann decided, rightly so, that real estate should be left to the professionals.

Looking further, Ann found that her area didn't have a really good dress shop. She decided that what her area needed was a completely modern boutique—a dress shop selling specialty items at relatively high prices.

Checking her fixture and money needs, Ann found that she could get started for a nominal investment—about $500. In the beginning she would take dresses on consignment—that is she wouldn't have to pay for them until *after* the dresses were sold. This method of obtaining her inventory wasn't perfect because she had to accept some dresses which didn't, in Ann's opinion, have too much sales appeal. But it certainly was better than making an investment of several thousand dollars (which Ann didn't have) in inventory. By taking products on consignment Ann could start her home dress business owing very little money to anyone except herself. Few people starting a new business can say that.

Ann opened her boutique in the first-floor front parlor of a brownstone house in a good neighborhood. She took an option on the back rooms "just in case I'm lucky," she said.

Ann was lucky—her business boomed instantly. Women from the many apartment houses and residential hotels in the area crowded into Ann's boutique. Within a month Ann exercised her option on the back rooms and rented the remainder of the brownstone—basement, second, and third floors.

Today Ann owns this brownstone and several others. "I got into real estate through a boutique," Ann laughs. "But the boutique income is what made me rich. What's more important, though, was being able to be near my children when they needed me most."

CORRESPONDENCE COURSE PAYS OFF

Arnold F. wanted to run a photography business in his own home. When he surveyed his neighborhood he found that the area was well-supplied with photo studios. So instead of opening a business immediately, Arnold wisely decided to take a correspondence course in photography.

As part of this course, Arnold learned much about the photography business. One important aspect which Arnold had previously overlooked was free-lance photography—working for himself and selling his photos to the top bidder.

When Arnold finished his course he began to free lance in his spare time. One of the photos Arnold took was an ole' swimmin' hole type, showing a number of boys gleefully swimming in a small pond. "That one photo," Arnold proudly told me "has earned me more than $10,000 in fees. Yet I composed and shot the photo in seconds."

Today Arnold works out of his home on all kinds of free-lance photo assignments. His income is now more than $350,000 per year, and he has high hopes of reaching $500,000 soon. "Taking that course was the best decision I ever made," Arnold says. "The guys in these neighborhood shops are just scraping by. I'm really living while they're just existing."

Start Small; Grow Big—Fast

Some beginning home wealth builders dream of starting with an income of a million dollars their first year in business. This is a pleasant dream and I'm the first person who'd work with you and for you to make it come true. But for various reasons it's difficult to build your income this fast, unless you buy a healthy, booming business. And when you do this you have an enormous investment you must pay off.

So for most of us, the best way to get our home business going is to start small; grow big—fast. This way you have a chance to learn the business while it's growing. If you make mistakes—and almost everyone does—the chances are that the mistakes won't be too costly. That's why I usually tell people to start their home wealth hunt in their spare time, without giving up their present job.

HIGH PROFITS FROM RENTALS

Bert F. started a rental real estate business as small as anyone I've ever met. He called me and asked if we could have lunch. I agreed to meet him in the Pierre au Tunnel Restaurant on 46th Street in New York. This is where I often dine with readers of my books.

"I want to go into rental real estate," Bert said soon after we sat down. "I'd like to buy a one-hundred unit apartment house."

"How much cash do you have?" I asked him.

"About two hundred dollars," he replied.

"Bert, I hate to tell you this, but that wouldn't buy you the front door of the building," I said, feeling sorry for him.

We talked for half an hour, exploring Bert's skills and interests. During our conversation I learned that Bert:

(a) Is a good handyman
(b) Enjoys working with people
(c) Drives a car
(d) Wants to be a property owner

I was turning these four items over in my mind as Bert talked on. Suddenly I had an idea. "Bert, I have just the business for you," I said. "It fits you perfectly."

"What is it?" he asked excitedly.

"Bert," I said, "you don't have much money. So you have to start small; grow big—fast. Now here's how you can do just that."

"There's a type of single-family home for sale today that's called a 'repossession.' What that means is that the person who originally bought the house didn't make his or her monthly mortgage payments. So the bank 'repossessed' the house—that is they took it back from the owner. Often, a bank will offer these repossessed homes to anyone with a good credit rating. The usual offer the bank makes is very attractive—*No Cash Down; No Closing Fees.*"

"You, Bert, have all you need to take over a string of such houses. You're a handyman; you can drive from one house to the next; you enjoy working with people; you want to be a property owner."

"How do I get started?" Bert asked.

"All you have to do is watch the real-estate ads in your local area and pick the houses that interest you."

"But I want to warn you about one aspect of single-family property ownership, Bert. You can go broke quickly if you own just one or two houses. To make one-family repossessions pay off you must own at least ten houses. The reason for this is that you must have some way to cover your expenses if you lose a tenant in one or more homes."

Bert took over thirty one-family houses without investing a cent, except for the money he spent on gas to drive around to inspect the houses before taking them over. Today he has 200 houses giving him a monthly profit of close to $20,000. Thus, Bert is earning nearly $240,000 per year working out of his own home. He hopes to reach $500,000 per year very soon.

Know Your Risks

Most real-estate investors shy away from one-family properties. Why? "It's a feast or famine business," says one experienced operator. "The house is either rented or vacant. In a multi-family building, such as an apartment house, you're never completely vacant—you always have a few tenants to help you pay the bills."

Yet the one-family repossession is one of the best examples of a technique that has made me fortunes in several different businesses. I call this the *little-bit technique*. That's not a very fancy name but if it adds another $100,000 to $500,000 to your income, who cares what the name is?

Use the Little-Bit Technique

To use this technique,

> **Make do with little bits of income, time, energy, knowledge, strength. Don't wait for the day when you have everything you need—time, money, strength —for success because that day will never come.**

Watch any building while it's being constructed. It rises brick by brick. One workman can lift a brick but the same workman could not lift the wall he built of the bricks he lifted.

The same applies to you when you're building your home fortune. Don't wait for the day when you have hours and hours to think about your future home business. Think about it the next time you have one minute to spare.

The Little-Bit Technique Really Works

Many people ask me how I could write and publish eleven books in eleven years while holding a big executive job and running several profitable businesses on the side. My answer always is "Little bits of time and energy. If you write one thousand words a day you have a 70,000-word book in 70 days. Nothing could be easier."

Bert, the real-estate man we mentioned above, used little bits of income to put together a big income. Did you ever stop to think that ten $100 checks each month give you a monthly income of $1,000? Increasing the number of $100 checks to fifty will give you an income of $5,000 per month. That's all it takes—little bits of income and time and you soon have a big income—$500,000 per year, or more, if you want.

And the lady mentioned in an earlier chapter who's building a fortune in computer repair is doing it one little circuit board at a time! Her real-life story shows that you *can* succeed using the little-bit technique.

Know Where You Want to Go

During many talks with beginning home wealth builders one fact I've noticed over and over again is that many lack a plan in life. Planning is a nuisance because it requires us to think ahead. And for some people thinking is painful, particularly when it involves thinking about things that haven't happened, and may never happen. Yet without a plan which shows

1. What you intend to accomplish
2. How you will reach your goal
3. When you will reach your goal

most people are lost. They drift, like a ship without a rudder. Wind pushes the rudderless ship first in one direction, then in another. Temporary or passing enthusiasm push the person without a plan. These people wind up chasing rainbows without ever reaching the pot of gold at the end of the rainbow.

Remember that every moment is a new start. So begin now to do what all successful home wealth builders do—*plan*. Remember that the best years of your life are *now*. And time is like money—you can spend it only once. With a good plan that fits *your* situation you can move ahead ten times faster.

What Is Planning?

Planning is little more than deciding three things

1. What you want to do to earn money at home
2. How you'll reach your goal
3. When you'll reach your goal

You can become an expert planner without previous training, experience, or interest. All you need do is make some plans, carry them out, and watch the results.

Harry F. couldn't spell the word planning when he first came to me. "Harry, I'll not only teach you how to plan, I'll show you how to earn money at the same time."

"Great!" he said. "When do I start?"

"Sit down and figure out the what, how, and when of your home business. *Put your plans on paper.* Just the act of writing out your plans will make them clearer to you and will reinforce your desire to reach your goals. And to learn about planning while you have an actual project in the works, observe very carefully such items as these:

1. Time spent in planning
2. Inactivity after planning
3. Start of action
4. Speed of business growth
5. Relation between planned and actual outcome

Once you do this you'll be a competent planner."

Harry F. did what I told him to. He planned an auto tune-up shop that he could run in the backyard of his home. Though he had only $12 with which to start his business, Harry carefully thought through the what, how, and when of his future business. When I saw his plans I was impressed and delighted. "Harry," I said, "these plans are prepared so well you could safely spend twelve million dollars on this business."

To prepare a professional business plan, be sure to use the *Business Plan Kit* mentioned at the back of this book. It gives you full details on preparing a professional business plan you can use to raise money in the form of loans or grants.

Put Your Plans into Action

Harry put his plans into action and carefully watched and recorded the results. Here's what he found.

(1) **Planning takes time.** You can't make good, realistic plans in a few minutes. Hours are required.

(2) **Planning is work.** You can't sit back in your easy chair and expect plans to fall out of the air into your mind. Instead, you must sit down at a desk with pencil and paper and work at your plans.

(3) **You may be inactive after finishing your plans.** Once your plans are finished you'll usually have to wait a few days or weeks before you can put them into action. This waiting period can be

torturous when you're anxious to move ahead.

(4) **Action usually starts slowly.** When you begin action on your plans, things move slowly. You're impatient to move ahead and start the money rolling in. But most new activities start slowly.

(5) **Activities can speed up quickly.** Your plans may move along slowly for awhile. Suddenly, your business multiplies within days. You're running so fast your feet hardly touch the ground. But the money pours into your business so fast you hardly know what to do with it.

(6) **Actual results often differ from your plans.** When you plan, you're trying to peer into the future to determine what it will be. Few planners can predict the future exactly. So results usually *seem* different from what was planned. But even if results are a little different, you have done something you wouldn't have done if you neglected planning.

Valuable Planning Guide for Your Business

Here's the guide Harry used to plan his successful home business. Use it in your planning and you'll save time and energy.

Master Planning Guide

1. What I plan to accomplish ....
....

2. How I will accomplish item (1) ....
....

3. Date by which item (1) will be achieved ....

4. Troubles I might meet in my business:

(A) ....   (D) ....

(B) ....   (E) ....

(C) ....   (F) ....

5. Master plans for overcoming each trouble:

(A) ....   (D) ....

(B) ....   (E) ....

(C) ....   (F) ....

6. Sources of help I shouldn't forget:

(A) ....

(B) ....

(C) ....

(D) ....

If you have a personal computer you can put your plans up on it and print them out. Then you can carry a few sheets of paper with you to check on your progress as you work along toward your goals.

Other Profitable Aids

You can get lots of ideas free of charge if you use the six profitable aids listed below. They are brought together in this chapter because they are particularly useful in a home service business. But you can use them in any and every home business.

MAKE YOUR IMAGINATION EARN YOUR FORTUNE

(1) **Use your imagination.** Picture yourself in your home service business *successfully* rendering your service, selling your products, or helping your clients. Emphasize in your mental pictures the success you plan for you yourself and your business.

(2) **Make definite plans for your business.** Put your plans on paper, in writing. Use the master planning guide above. Be specific in your plans. List every major step you'll take. Estimate the time you'll need for each step. Enter this time on your list.

(3) **Picturize your plans.** Put your imagination to work again. This time concentrate on *successfully* beginning and completing each step. Try to imagine the problems you'll face in putting your plans into action. See yourself successfully overcoming each problem, after you've figured out the solution to the problem. Experience, in your imagination, the satisfaction you'll get after you successfully solve each problem.

(4) **Choose your financial and personal goals.** Put into writing *your* financial goals for your business. Thus, your goal for your business may be an income of $2,000 per week. Next, translate this money goal into a more personal goal—i.e. the principal things you want to do with your money. Thus, you may want a big car, a larger home, a vacation cottage in the mountains, etc.

(5) **Picture how you'll achieve your goals.** Work, in your imagination, at each step in your program for reaching your financial goal. Go through, in your mind, every element of each step on the way to your goal. Don't give up after imagining just the beginning of a step—carry it through to completion.

(6) **Live with your personal goals.** See yourself driving that big car, enjoying the surge of its powerful engine. Hear the quiet putter

of its exhaust, the rich thump when you close the door. Use your mind to see yourself as capable, rich, and successful and that is exactly what you'll be.

Home Service Wealth Can Be Yours

If you've read this far in the book you've shown me that you have the stamina to build a fortune at home. And you will build that fortune if you put to work the ideas you're getting here. Or, change these ideas to suit your situation—and get to work making your dreams come true. Remember—the toughest problems are easy to solve when you work on them in small bits, taking a little at a time.

There's a *great* future for you in the home service business, be it a travel consultant business, a child-care facility, an appliance repair center, a catering business, etc. People need and want thousands of different services today. Earn your home fortune by providing one or more of these services. Start today to build *your* home fortune. See the back of this book for many helpful guides and kits for your home business success.

10

Build Your
Daily Income
to the Maximum

Working at home is one of the greatest joys a person can experience, particularly when the money pours in in a steady stream. But working at home requires that you carefully plan your time. Also, you must be able to resist the temptation to "take it easy for just one day" because the days quickly slip into weeks.

Follow a Regular Schedule

As a successful home worker with many years experience I think I can be a big help to beginning home workers. For I too faced, and overcame, the temptations every home worker faces.

Follow a regular schedule in your work activities. This needn't be a 9-to-5 schedule. Instead, choose any hours that appeal to you. Thus, one writer works from midnight to about 6 A.M. A furniture repairman works from 8 A.M. to 3 P.M., while a music teacher works only in the evening—7 P.M. to 11 P.M. The key point here is that you must choose a work schedule and *stick to it*.

Inform your family and friends of your work schedule. Tell them you don't want to be interrupted by nonbusiness matters during your working hours. For instance, some wives will interrupt their husbands several times during the working day to fix this, move that, etc. If you want to produce the maximum possible daily income you must be able to work steadily, free of nonbusiness interruptions.

One reader who avoids all nonbusiness interruptions says, "I've helped my small business clients raise almost $2 million in loans and investments in the last 12 months. Methods I learned from your books and courses were responsible for most of that success."

Work at a Steady Pace

At home there isn't any boss to watch over you, to prod you on when you slow down. *You're the boss* and you must keep an eye on your output. That's why it's important that you work at a steady pace.

In your own home it's very easy to linger over beakfast, have an extra cup of coffee, dally with the newspaper, etc. Before you know it, the clock shows 10 A.M. and you haven't done anything yet to earn your day's income. Soon it will be lunchtime and the day will be half over.

Ten Rules for a Big Income

To avoid this situation, follow, for at least the first two years you work at home, the ten rules given below. They are based on the long experience of many successful home workers. These rules are:

    (1) Start work at the same time each day
    (2) Work without pauses or breaks for two hours
    (3) Take a short break (10 to 15 min.)
    (4) Return to work promptly at the break's end
    (5) Allow just one hour—no more—for lunch
    (6) Take only one ten-minute afternoon break
    (7) Stop work in time for some relaxation before dinner

(8) Work after dinner, if you need the income
(9) Maintain this schedule six days per week
(10) Work seven days a week when you need the income

If you work during the night instead of the day, alter the time in the above rules to suit *your* schedule. *But follow the rules!* I regularly earned up to $2,000 per week working at home when I followed these rules. Since you're just as smart, or smarter than I am, you can do the same.

Find an Easy Income Measure

To build a big income in your home business you must develop a quick, easy way to measure your daily income. Thus, a man who uses his big backyard near a commuter railroad station as a parking lot simply counts the cars in the lot. He immediately knows his day's income because he just multiplies the number of cars by the daily parking fee he charges. And a woman who bakes special birthday cakes at home counts the number of cakes she delivers. Since she knows the average price of her cakes, it's easy for her to estimate her day's income. And, I'll add, it's usually high!

And a man I know *rents* a field which he uses as a parking lot. Thus, his only expense is the field rental, since the land owner must pay the taxes.

Other easy income measures you might use are:

Business	Good Income Measure
Writing articles	Completed words or pages
Animal training	Number of training contracts
Mail order	Cash received
Auto tuning	Number of cars processed
Specialized food sales	Number of units sold

Be careful, when developing your income measure to use a yardstick which truly reflects your daily income. Thus, if you're selling special foods and you have both high- and low-priced items, don't figure your sales as all high-priced units. Instead, figure the typical mix of high- and low-priced items and use that.

Keep a Daily Record of Your Work

Buy a daily diary that appeals to you and that's large enough for you to make detailed entries about your business. Be sure your diary contains a full page for each day of the year.

Enter on each daily page of your diary the following:

(1) Time you started on a job
(2) Time the job was finished
(3) Probable income from each job
(4) Total income for the day

Since most daily diaries have the time printed on each page it is easy to enter your starting and finishing time. With the job time and income entered for each job, it will be easy for you to figure your gross income in dollars per hour.

"But," you say, "my home business is the kind where I'm continually making small sales. I couldn't possibly keep a record of the time spent on each job."

Fine. Just adopt another convenient scheme—keep a record of the income during the morning, afternoon, or evening.

Why Income Records Are Important

"Why should I bother with all this paperwork?" you ask. "All I want to do is make a lot of money, in a hurry, at home."

Your paper work is important for several reasons. A carefully kept work record:

(1) Gives you better control of your business
(2) Makes excellent tax evidence
(3) Shows you exactly how close you are to your income goals

Without a daily income record you don't have the degree of control of your business that you should have. Weekly and monthly records, while helpful, are not as powerful for controlling your business.

Keep Other Business Records

Does your home business depend on warm weather, cold weather, rain, snow, etc.? Some businesses are seasonal; others have a steady year-round income.

Keep a record of the weather, if it is an important factor in your business. Then you'll be able to compare one type of day with another. You might even learn that there are some days such as 100-degree summer scorchers when you're better off playing golf than working because customers just go elsewhere than to your place of business. So take the hot days off—that's one of the joys of working at home in your own business.

Other business records you might want to keep include annual rainfall, snowfall, temperature, degree days, etc.

How Records Can Pay Off

Jake M. took my advice when he opened his own home printing business. However, Jake went far beyond my simple recommendation and built a thick file of weather data throughout the country. Weather is one of Jake's hobbies so he enjoyed keeping the records.

Jake's printing business progressed nicely and he soon had over one hundred steady customers. One day Jake decided that a collection of weather information about the local area might interest his customers. So he included a brief one-page flyer called *Local Weather Notes*, with each order.

Within a day Jake was beseiged with orders for hundreds of copies of the flyer. Some of his customers asked Jake to print their name on the flyer so they could distribute it to *their* customers. Being an alert businessman, Jake quickly filled the smaller requests free of charge. Also, he set up a price list for the larger orders.

But Jake's weather flyer grew far beyond anything Jake or I could foresee. As he made larger printings of the flyer Jake began to get calls from businessmen in other parts of the country. They wanted a flyer covering *their* area. And they wanted a flyer that was published regularly. Jake quickly expanded his coverage and the size of his flyer. Today Jake has several thousand subscribers to his weather newsletter who each pays $36 per year. So what started as a collection of records for customers of Jake's printing business is now a larger, and steadier, source of income than the printing business itself. In the world of home business you never know how valuable a good idea will be.

Take a Regular Day Off

Up till now we've been talking about working because, after all, it's work that produces income—and it's income we're thinking about in this book. But you can't work seven days a week (as many beginning home wealth builders do) forever. You need a rest, a change of outlook to rebuild your enthusiasm for working at home. Not only that, how and when will you spend the money you earn, if you don't take a day off?

Many new home fortune builders find that it's best to keep their business open on weekends and take a weekday off. Why? There are several reasons why it might be profitable for you to stay open on weekends:

(1) Your customers may want weekend service
(2) Weekend service may help you beat the competition
(3) You can raise some prices for weekend service

Besides the income advantages of staying open on weekends, there are certain personal advantages in having a weekday off instead of the weekend. These include:

(1) You can usually get more done on a weekday off
(2) Recreational facilities are less crowded
(3) You will enjoy yourself more when you're off while others are working
(4) Greater fun on your day off will build your enthusiasm for your home business

Time Off Can Increase Your Income

"How," you ask, "is the time I take off related to building my daily income to the maximum?"

Time off is linked to a maximum daily income by enthusiasm. While you're away from your home business, relaxing, you're rebuilding your enthusiasm and energy. When you return to work you're rarin' to go and you give your work the maximum attention.

Result—you do better work.

A real-estate man who works out of his own home takes every other day off. During his time off he plays golf with friends. If the weather is bad he stays at home or goes to the library to read. His regular reading includes the best real estate magazines, such as *National Real Estate Investor*. "People often laugh at my reading habits," this real-estate man remarks. "But I've closed many deals as a result of my real-estate reading. One deal alone was for more than two million dollars."

So while people laugh, this smart home wealth builder makes trips to the bank to deposit his big fees. Compared with the people who laugh at him, he works half as long each week, earns four or five times as much, and doesn't have to travel to and from work. No wonder the laughter doesn't seem to bother him at all!

Travel and Entertain for Business

I operate several lucrative and successful home businesses. The long experience I've had in the home business field has taught me many valuable lessons. To make you as rich as possible, I'd like you to learn from my mistakes. Then you'll get richer, sooner. That, after all, is why you're reading this book.

When people work at home and the money starts to roll in, there's a tendency to say "Gee, this is great. The more hours I put in, the more I'll earn. So I might as well work every night instead of watching TV. After all, money is very important in everyone's life."

"Fine attitude," I reply. "But you can't go on working sixteen hours a day forever. Especially when you can earn all you need in six hours."

One home fortune builder got so enthused with his home business (running a health salon in his basement) that he worked for three years without taking a day off. The money just gushed in but when I met this home fortune builder I could tell he had the cooped-up, trapped, restricted feeling that comes from too much work and not enough play.

"Charlie," I said to him, "you're a great guy. I really admire and, in a way, envy your great success. But, at the same time I think you're a trifle nuts!"

"Why?" he asked.

"Didn't you ever hear that the more you spend, the more you earn?"

"No."

"Well, Charlie," I said, "you're working too hard. You have to take some time off to enjoy the piles of money you're earning. Take a trip to Europe; entertain some of your customers overseas; enjoy yourself. Live a little."

Charlie wasn't convinced. I had to spend several more sessions with him before he finally agreed to take a few days off. At one point I even offered to run his health salon for him, if he'd only take a day off. Charlie finally hired a young assistant to spell him on his days off and during his vacation trips.

Now Charlie makes two trips to Europe each year and takes several of his customers with him. He runs a contest to select the customers who'll travel with him. The contest increased Charlie's business so much that he had to move out of his basement into a specially built health salon.

Today Charlie works only four days a week in his health salon. He has many hobbies but he's beginning to worry me again because he's talking about starting another home business to keep himself busy while he has time off from the health salon!

Use Your Legitimate Deductions

As a businessman or woman, you're entitled to travel and entertain, at company expense, if such travel and entertainment produces more business income. Thus, if you have business reasons for going to Europe you can do so at company expense.

Barbara M. runs a costume jewelry business from her home. She imports her major jewelry products from all over the world. So each year Barbara spends three months on a round-the-world trip during which she buys products for her upcoming jewelry line. Her home business pays all the trip costs. And these costs are deductible on the tax return for Barbara's business.

Also, Barbara enjoys entertaining her business associates throughout the world. The cost of this entertainment is tax deductible. Thus, Barbara lives a "dream life" visiting Paris, London, Berlin, Moscow, Bombay, Hong Kong, Singapore, Manila, etc. As Barbara recently remarked, "I can travel at any time of the year. I usually plan my trips so I'm in the warm countries during the winter. That way I avoid the snow and slush at home."

You can deduct legitimate travel and entertainment expenses from your business income, thus reducing your taxes. Just think—in your own home business you can travel throughout the world for business purposes and enjoy tax savings. Could you ask for anything more in a business you run in your own home?

Be Willing to Do Anything Honest

Were you to visit me in my office you would, I believe, be impressed by it. Why? Well, the office has a nice rug, leather chairs, oil paintings on the wall, etc. Thus, it's a typical well-furnished executive office. Yet in my home businesses I gladly

(1) Act as a delivery boy
(2) Type letters
(3) Stuff circulars in envelopes
(4) Moisten and apply postage stamps
(5) Write advertising copy
(6) Handle complaints
(7) Run errands

Why do I perform all these duties? Why, you ask, don't I hire someone to do these jobs for me? After all, you're a big executive—you shouldn't have to deliver packages, moisten stamps, etc., in a home business.

That may be true for some people, but not for me. I perform all these tasks in my various home businesses for several important reasons:

(1) To keep costs low
(2) To know what's going on
(3) To be sure the work is done

Because I perform these tasks myself, each of these businesses returns me more than $1,000 per week net income for little more than one hour's work.

So learn from my experience—be ready and willing to do anything honest in your home business. Then you'll have better control over your costs, you'll know what's going on, and you'll be sure that each of your customers is serviced properly. If you approach your home business with this attitude you will prosper far beyond your rosiest dreams.

Never Refuse Honest Income

Some people in this life feel they can't be bothered with small matters—such as the sale of a product for five or ten dollars. These people refuse to do anything until they find something "worth their while." Time, of course, passes for these people, just as it does for the rest of us. Before they realize it, ten years have slipped by and these people have made no progress towards their goal. And time, remember, is like money; you can only use it once; then it's gone forever.

Many home fortunes have been made selling low-cost items. Thus, people have made millions of dollars at home selling

Books	Labels
Gadgets	Rubber stamps
Razor blades	Hose nozzles
Belts	Key holders
Calculators	Software

and thousands of other items for less than ten dollars each. What those who "watch and wait" fail to recognize is that one million items sold at one dollar each brings in one million dollars.

So never refuse honest income—no matter how small it may be. Use this gold-laden rule in every home business:

> **If you have the choice of working for very small pay, or doing nothing, always work, no matter how small the pay.**

When you first start your home business you may work for as little as fifty cents an hour. So who cares? You're

Earning something
Gaining experience
Building for the future
Making the best use of your time

As long as what you're doing is honest and legal, keep working. Your fortune will come to you eventually.

Pyramid Your Working Time

Often, in a home business, you will be able to earn money from two or more sources at the same time. Let's see how you might do this.

Let's say you own a three-family house, such as home wealth builder Louis J. does. Louis rents out two of the three apartments in the house, and lives in the third one with his family. He also rents out two of the three garages the house has.

But Louis J. isn't satisfied with his rental income. He wants, and needs, more to build his home fortune. So he has a writing room in his basement where he writes articles for trade journals. His income from his trade-journal articles is more than $2,000 per month. (Later in this chapter I'll tell you how Louis J. learned to write salable articles.)

As a hobby, Louis J. raises rare tropical fish in his basement. When the fish are big enough he sells them at a nice profit. Thus, Louis J. pyramids his home income in three ways:

Rental property
Article writing
Tropical fish breeding

As Louis J. says, "Men don't fail; they just stop trying. Don't give up trying to pyramid your working time. For when you pyramid your time, you increase your income. As the number of jobs you do in an hour increases, so does your income. And, incidentally, so do your legitimate home tax deductions rise with the number of jobs."

Developing a Home-Business Skill

Earlier I promised to tell you where Louis J. learned how to write salable trade-journal articles. We have now reached the point where I can tell you.

Each year I personally train by correspondence a select group of my book readers in the art of successful nonfiction writing. Louis J. heard about this correspondence course and he applied for admission. Though the fee for the course—$300—seemed to stop him for a few moments, he was impressed by my guarantee that he would sell an article within two years of registering for the ten-lesson course, or his entire fee would be refunded.

Louis J. took the course and sold his first article within three months. Before he finished the course he sold over $2,000 worth of articles. "The three hundred dollars I invested in your article-writing correspondence course was the best investment I ever made," Louis J. told me. "But when I first heard that the course cost three hundred dollars I was frightened. I'm glad I decided to take the plunge and invest in myself and my future. My wife feels the same way about it."

How to Double Your Hourly Income

Take the case of a well-known and successful self-employed wealth builder who works in his home as an industrial consultant. He charges some of his clients by the day. If a client doesn't give him enough work for a full day, this home fortune builder turns to another client's work. He charges both clients for the time spent because the first is on a per diem (per day) basis while the second is on an hourly basis. To ensure pyramiding his time, this consultant wisely signs up both types of clients. Then when the work from one type runs out, he can easily turn to work for the other type. This arrangement ensures double income for him throughout most of the year.

Are you afraid you couldn't do this? Don't be frightened. Remember: *Whatever is unknown is magnified.* Use the tips in this book and you can overcome most business problems. The biggest of problems are easy when you take them on a little at a time.

Be Wary of Partnerships

Let me make a few predictions for you, based on long experience in home businesses. These predictions are:

(1) When you first talk about going into a home business, many people will laugh at you, including those closest to you—your wife, husband, etc.

(2) Once you begin to make big money those who laughed at you will suddenly become friendly.

(3) After your business is reasonably well-established the laughers and critics will come to you and ask that they be allowed to become your partner—for a slice of the profits, of course.

As a general guide, apply the following pointer which works well for almost every successful home businessperson. This pointer is:

> **Don't take a partner into an established home business unless there is a positive advantage to you, and unless you continue to receive most of the profits from the business.**

Note that you can start a home business with a partner and profit handsomely because two heads are sometimes better than one. But my observation of many home wealth builders is that most of them are happier and just as successful if they're the loner type. Perhaps, though, I'm a trifle biased because I'm a loner myself. Yet the less successful people come out on my 50-foot yacht and enjoy my refreshments. So maybe my bias is valid—at least I have achieved success.

Avoid partnerships with undependable people—be they relatives or friends. The partnerships that succeed are those based on equivalent contributions of time, energy, money, or skill by each member. You will rarely have a successful partnership where one member does all the work and the other does nothing.

So, as a general guide, be wary of partnerships. To be wary doesn't mean you should shun them altogether. Just be careful and don't rush into an arrangement you may later regret. A smooth-working partnership can make you a fortune at home within a few years. But a poorly conceived, badly run partnership can ruin you a lot faster. Look before you leap.

Read Widely in Your Business Field

No matter what business you choose to build your fortune at home, there is a magazine, book, pamphlet, report, learned-society journal, or another type of publication discussing the business. Your first task, even before you start earning money from your business, is to read as many publications about it as you can find. And your second task is to *never* stop regular reading about your business.

John L. opened a contracting business with an investment of only

$3,000. To reduce his expenses he lived in the back room of the building housing his business. Within one year John built his home business to the point where he was grossing $70,000 per year. And not too many years later his business grossed over $600 million per year.

Asked how he did it, John L. replies: "I read everything I could on the contracting business. It made no difference to me how new or how old a book or magazine was. If it had something about contracting in it I *read* the publication. As I read, my world expanded. I soon learned to have confidence in myself because I saw that if I did a small thing well, I could also do a big thing well. Why I even studied used correspondence courses, I was so hungry for knowledge."

You never lose when you read about your home business. Reading is the next best activity to actual experience. When you read you acquire information based on the experience of others. This increases *your* ability to earn a big income in your own home business. So never stop reading.

Keep Tight Control of All Costs

When you start your first home business you will almost always be short of money. In technical terms you are under-financed. The only way to overcome your cash shortage is to keep tight control of all costs. There's a right way and a wrong way to control costs.

Maggie L., a retired schoolteacher, wanted something to do at home that would earn her some income while keeping her interested in life. She decided to prepare and sell plasticized school-subject review cards for high school and college students. Maggie prepared the material for several cards, had it printed on the cards, and then had the cards laminated in plastic. The production process was simple and low-cost, except for the laminating. This step cost ten times as much as the rest of the job.

Maggie investigated ways to cut costs. In any manufacturing operation you can usually cut costs if you

> Manufacture a larger quantity at one time
> Manufacture at a faster rate
> Reduce labor costs
> Reduce material costs
> Reduce overhead costs

Maggie studied the laminating problem further and learned that she could reduce costs, if she bought her own laminating machine, installed it in her home, and ran it herself. Taking this step would reduce labor, material, and overhead costs. There was just one catch—a laminating machine would cost $10,000, and Maggie didn't have that much cash. Yet the fact that she could reduce the laminating cost spectacularly—from 25¢ to 5¢ per card—kept haunting her. The 20¢ saving she'd make on each card would soon make her rich, she thought.

Pushed by her desire to save money, Maggie placed an order for a $10,000 laminating machine. Then she sat down to figure out how she could pay for it. "If I save 20¢ on each card, I'll have to sell $10,000 divided by 20¢, or 50,000 cards to pay for the machine," she reasoned.

That's when Maggie got a cold shock. She hadn't sold 500 cards yet. How long it would take to sell 50,000 she didn't know, but it was longer than she wanted to spend paying off a debt. She cancelled her order for the machine and, fortunately, received a full refund of her deposit.

Solving Cost-Control Problems

To solve her problem, Maggie decided to sell as many cards as possible until she could see a sales pattern developing. Then, if sales seemed to justify a machine she would buy one. Two years later she bought her machine. Today she says: "I'm very glad I waited to buy the machine. Saving for those two years really taught me how to control costs in my business. I've made a lot more money since I learned to control costs."

To control costs in any home business take these general steps:

(1) Know what every item will cost *before* you buy
(2) Look at your costs regularly—daily, weekly, or monthly
(3) Pay a little more, if the extra pennies save thousands of dollars
(4) Keep accurate cost records of every business expense
(5) Do as much as you can yourself
(6) Never spend until you receive income
(7) Don't be afraid of debts but pay them off quickly
(8) Be tight-fisted rather than a big spender

Build Your Home Fortune with Will Power

You need will power to control costs in your business. Haven't you noticed many times in your life that it's much easier to spend money than to save it? Money is so easy to put to work on the things we all want. To save money is a different story, particularly when the money begins to flood into your home. Every successful home wealth builder learns early in his or her career how to say NO! to temptation to spend and spend.

Strengthen your will power by deciding right now how much of your home income profits you will save. The most successful home wealth builders save at least 70 per cent of their profits for the first few years they are in business. Thus, if you were saving this amount, you'd put seventy cents of every profit dollar into the bank. What would you use this money for? Many things. You could:

(1) Buy new equipment for your business
(2) Advertise your products or services
(3) Hire an assistant
(4) Open a branch office
(5) Improve the quality of your service

Note, however, that you'd only do these things *after* you saved enough to be able to afford them. This is how Harry B. became a millionaire in his own home business in less than ten years.

Harry B. was called a failure at forty by his friends. At fifty these same friends came to Harry's 100-acre estate to admire and, in a few cases, admit they'd judged Harry wrong ten years earlier. How could any man go from poverty to wealth in less than ten years? Listen to Harry as he briefly sketches his story.

"I Willed My Way to Home Wealth"

This is the way Harry always begins his story. "At forty I was a failure. I'd drifted from one job to another after flunking out of high school. On my fortieth birthday I came face to face with my lack of success. I was earning two-hundred dollars a week and living in a furnished room. If anyone had a drab life, I did.

"When I awoke on my fortieth birthday I felt miserable. My only future seemed to be a series of lowly jobs, furnished rooms, and hamburger joints.

"As I looked at myself in the mirror, I resolved that I would be a success. I would claw my way up, crawl through mud if necessary, but I would be a success.

"A new power surged through me. I felt almost superhuman. For the first time in my life I felt that I could succeed. Though I didn't know it I was proving to myself that those who can command themselves can command others.

"I looked at the HELP WANTED section of the newspaper. An ad, 'Earn Money At Home' caught my eye. 'Address envelopes and earn extra income,' the ad said. 'Handwritten envelopes acceptable.' Great, I said to myself. I'll start right now.

"I called the number listed and dashed down to the agency. Soon I was back in the furnished room with 10,000 envelopes ready to be addressed. I worked like mad that day and all night. My fingers were so sore they seemed like they would fall off.

"For the next six weeks I addressed thousands and thousands of envelopes. I saved every penny I could, resisting the temptation to spend my new-found income. When I had enough extra money I bought a typewriter. Within two weeks I taught myself to type while earning money addressing envelopes.

Ideas Make a Business Grow

"The agency owner told me he could give me all the addressing work I could handle. This gave me an idea. Why couldn't I 'farm' some of my work out to housewives interested in earning some extra cash?

"I ran ads in several local church papers and was swamped with replies. Soon I had ten housewives working for me. I earned a little on each envelope they addressed. In a few months I was selling each housewife a typewriter and earning a commission on the sale. I lived as cheaply as possible, and saved every penny I could.

"My big break came when I suddenly noticed that I was addressing envelopes to the same people over and over again. I asked the agency owner about it and he told me these were direct mail lists which he rented out to people who wanted to sell their products by mail. 'Why,' I asked myself, 'couldn't I build my own mailing lists to rent out?'

"This is exactly what I did. I developed a large list of names by advertising a low-cost mail-order product. I broke even on the sale of the mail-order product but made money renting out the names of the buyers over and over again.

"Today I net about $20 on each one thousand names I rent out. I have about half a million names on computer which I rent out ten times a year. This gives me a net income of $100,000 per year. I also run an addressing service for my clients which nets me another $25,000 per year. My business is no longer run in a furnished room— but I'll always remember how, in that dismal furnished room I re-solved to will myself to a home fortune. I did—and today I'm the happiest guy in the world. Every day of the year I will myself to the maximum income possible. This constant drive has made me a mil-lionaire in a fully computerized mailing-list business."

You need not work alone in building your wealth. You can get lots of help, as this reader did who told us, "I recruited 48 brokers through the free ads you ran for me in IWS. I was able to quit my 9-to-5 job to devote myself full time to this business."

Build Your Daily Income to the Maximum

Regardless of how you start your home business—as a full-time or a spare-time activity—make every moment count. Use the hints in this chapter to lead you to enormous wealth that will put you on easy street forever. Why work for one dollar when, with a little planning and thought, you can earn ten, twenty, or one hundred dollars?

Here, in capsule form, are the lucky eleven steps you can follow to build each day's income to a record level:

(1) Follow a regular schedule every day
(2) Work at a steady pace
(3) Use a reliable income measure
(4) Keep daily work records
(5) Take a regular day off
(6) Do anything honest for money
(7) Never refuse honest income
(8) Pyramid your working time
(9) Read widely in your business field
(10) Keep tight control of ALL your expenses
(11) Use your will power to build your wealth

Take these steps today and your wealth will grow and grow. Soon you'll be ready to pyramid your riches by expanding your business. The next chapter shows you how to do just that.

Pyramid Riches by Expanding Your Business

A home business has many advantages over a routine job. One of the biggest advantages you'll enjoy when you have your own home business is that you can expand it any time you want to raise your income. On a job the only way you can increase your income is to get a raise or a promotion. But to obtain either you must depend on someone else. And that's where the trouble usually begins.

Why Pyramiding Builds Wealth

Some home wealth builders are content with a modest income—$10,000, $20,000, or $30,000 per year. Others want to reach a level of $100,000, or more, per year. They achieve this high an income, or a higher one, by using their current income to create greater and greater wealth.

In pyramiding you use two powerful forces to drive your income skyward. These forces are cash flow and other people's money (OPM). When you use these two wonderful forces you climb aboard the secret rocket used by the most successful home wealth builders in the world today. Pyramiding builds your wealth because you use the marvelous power that money has to make money for you.

Tie Your Wealth Growth to Cash Flow

Once you establish your home business you will have an income from the sales you make or services you render. This income may be steady, or it may vary widely, depending on the type of business you operate. But either way you'll have a flow of cash into your business.

Your cash inflow is useful for many purposes, including paying your bills, paying your salary, and most important of all, paying the expenses involved in expanding your home business. Let's take a look at cash flow at work in your home business.

Cash Flow Builds Income Pyramids

Let's say your home business provides you with an average income of $500 per week. This income is in the form of checks, money orders, and a small amount of cash. We'll call it all *cash flow*, even though most of it is not in direct cash form, but it is easily converted to cash.

Your weekly expenses are:

(1)	Materials and supplies	$125
(2)	Labor (other than yourself)	50
(3)	Home expense for business	30
(4)	Advertising and promotion	35
	Total	$240

Thus, you have a free cash flow of $500 − $240 = $260 per week before you pay your own salary. You've decided you want to pyramid your riches by expanding your income. To do this you are willing to use all, or part of your $260 per week cash flow. Let's see how you can put this powerful tool of cash flow to work to expand your business by pyramiding.

With this $260 per week you can:

(1) Buy another business like, or related to, your own
(2) Borrow money for more production equipment
(3) Hire more help to sell products or perform services
(4) Purchase better materials which will allow you to charge higher prices for your product or service
(5) Advertise more to bring in a higher income
(6) Run contests to increase your income
(7) Buy give-aways to increase your business
(8) Give bonuses to your employees for increasing their sales or service
(9) Enter new markets for your product or service
(10) Set up a franchise system

So you see, there are many ways you can use your cash flow to pyramid your riches by expanding your business. In pyramiding with cash flow you are using this important rule:

> **Up to a certain point in a home business you can increase your income by working harder or longer. Beyond this point you must use money to earn more money. Your cash flow provides this extra money.**

Cash flow is the secret pyramiding rule used by thousands of richly successful home fortune builders who want to expand their income. Consider using this important rule in *your* home business when you want to double, triple, or quadruple your home income.

Use OPM to Pyramid Your Riches

There are times when you may not want to disturb your cash flow. Thus, you may be aiming at a cash reserve goal you've set for your business. For example, some home wealth builders like to have a cash "cushion" behind them of $10,000, $30,000, or $60,000 in the bank. So they let their cash flow accumulate in the bank until their savings reach the desired level.

To pyramid riches while you're building a cash cushion, you can use OPM. Here's why.

> **With a sizeable cash flow—say $200 or more per week—you can use the cash as collateral for a loan without disturbing**

your cash reserve. Money you borrow this way is at a very
low net interest rate.

Using this collateral technique, known as a passbook loan, gives
you the best of two worlds—cash accumulation and low borrowing
charges at a bank, factor, or commercial finance company.

Recognize here and now that *you can use money to make money*.
Since money is such a powerful force in our world today, a modest
investment can pyramid riches at a rate one thousand times that at
which *you* can work for money. Recognize this fact now and you never
need worry about money as long as you live. Now let's look at specific
pyramiding techniques which use either OPM or cash flow.

Buy Another Profitable Business

As a successful home business operator you're in an ideal position
to buy another profitable business. Why? Because you

    (a) Have time to study other businesses
    (b) Have the necessary cash flow
    (c) Are not in a hurry to close a deal
    (d) Can negotiate as long as needed
    (e) Can check out any claims made by the seller

These all add up to *time and money*—the ingredients needed to
be an outstanding success in any business. Very few people, except
home wealth builders, have these advantages. They're either short
of time or money, or both. This can force them into poor business
decisions.

Paul R. opened a Do-Anything-Legal business in his own home.
As Paul's client you can call him to find a magician for a party, have
yourself driven around town in a 1902 automobile, be serenaded
by a folk singer in a language of your choice, etc. Paul can provide
the unusual, the rare, or the unique any time or any place.

To provide this service, Paul charges his clients a monthly subscription fee, and an hourly fee while the service is being used. He
also charges the one-hundred odd specialists—chefs, acrobats,
magicians, drivers, writers, etc.—on his list a nominal monthly fee.
Paul also receives a 15 per cent commission on all work they do.

After building this home business from nothing to a level where it paid him $50,000 per year, Paul decided to look around for another home business that would really pay him big money. He decided that the best kind of business was one that would feed cash into his present business.

Paul studied the clients of his present business. They were mostly apartment dwellers in a big city. Every time one of his clients called he asked the client "What's your biggest problem in life other than what you're calling me about?" Client after client answered: "Getting a reliable maid." This gave Paul the lead he was looking for.

Investigating the field, Paul found he could:

(1) Open, or buy, a maid service
(2) Open, or buy, a maid's employment agency
(3) Open, or buy, a home-cleaning service

After much study, Paul decided to buy a home-cleaning service in which he could use both men and women cleaners. Clients preferred either men or women cleaners, depending on their previous experience with cleaning services. By being able to offer either men or women cleaners who are fast and efficient, Paul had a most attractive service for his clients and prospects.

Paul bought a failing home-cleaning service for a very small amount of borrowed OPM. To date, he has been able to sell his home service to eighty per cent of his Do-Anything-Legal clients. Thus, one business feeds cash into the other and Paul is profiting handsomely.

Or you may want to buy several other profitable businesses as this reader told us he did. "Thanks to your advice and ideas I did this in 2 years—(1) Acquired a retail clothing store with no money down, grossing $150,000 yearly, with a potential of $500,000 in 3 years; (2) Acquired a restaurant, convenience store, parking lot, and office complex with very little money down—present yearly sales $123,000; potential $180,000."

Expand Your Production Equipment

As a general guide, I recommend that you keep your investment in production equipment as low as possible in your home business. Why? Because with only a small, or no, investment in production equipment you are freer to change from one business to another. Also, you don't have a heavy debt to pay off when you first go into your home business.

Some home businesses—such as rug weaving, mail order, tutoring, etc.—require only a very small investment for production equipment. In these and similar businesses you can increase your income enormously with only a modest expansion of your production facilities. If your business is this type, you should consider the profitability of expanding your production equipment. Here's a good example of how to use this technique.

Rhoda C. operates a rubber-stamp business from her basement. Every evening after her three children are safely tucked into bed, Rhoda goes down to the basement and manufactures the rubber stamps which were ordered during the day. Most of Rhoda's rubber-stamp orders are phoned into her as a result of the ads she runs in the local papers and fraternal magazines.

When Rhoda started her rubber-stamp business she purchased a small stamp molding machine. This had a limited stamp size capacity and Rhoda had to turn down orders for large stamps on which she'd earn a good profit. Rhoda wanted to buy a larger molding machine and the related equipment when she first went into business. But she didn't have enough capital so she decided to wait until her cash flow was large enough to pay for the machine.

Rhoda accumulated a backlog of orders for large stamps as her cash flow built up. These orders were placed by firms and people whose rubber-stamp needs were not immediate. When she had enough money to purchase the machine, Rhoda asked her supplier to deliver it. Since she had ordered the machine earlier, the supplier was able to deliver it the next day.

As soon as she received her new machine, Rhoda began production on her backlog of orders for large stamps. Within a few weeks the cash flow from these orders replaced the money Rhoda spent on the machine. Today Rhoda has a full line of machines and she can supply any kind of rubber stamp her customers require. Her business is booming—for two or three hours work in her basement, Rhoda earns more than her husband does in eight hours. She now has a credit card merchant account so she can accept credit-card orders. This has increased Rhoda's business by more than 35 percent!

Hire More Help to Increase Your Profits

The day your home business reaches the level where you can earn money from the work of others is the day your riches will begin to pile up. Why? Because you can accomplish only so much by yourself. Beyond this you need the help of others.

You must, however, be careful when using others to pyramid your riches. For instance, you'll soon go broke if you pay a person $50 per day to work for you and he or she earns only $45 per day for your business. If you have twenty people working for you and you lose $5 per day on each you'll soon have little left other than an empty purse.

So be sure each person you hire at least earns his keep. Better yet, follow the advice of Paul L., a brilliantly successful home hair stylist. Paul helps restyle women's hair, advises them on the style of clothes that make them look their best, and offers guidance on other aspects of good grooming.

"When my business became so large I couldn't handle it by myself, I began looking for help," Paul recalls. "As I analyzed the job that I wanted to fill I realized that I'd have to train the person, watch his work closely for the first few weeks, pay extra payroll taxes, etc. In other words, the new person would have to earn for me more than his salary because it would cost me money just to have him on the payroll. This was the best decision I ever made.

"As a pure guess I told myself that each person I hired must earn at least twice as much for my company as I would pay him. Thus, a man being paid $400 per week had to bring in no less than $800 per week in business. The extra $400 per week goes towards payroll taxes, benefits, and *my* profit on the person's work. After all, I should receive some return for providing the job, taking the risk, etc.

"I learned, as I hired more people, that my 'two-times' figure was a little low. I should have made it two and one-half times. Also, I learned that some large companies use about the same two-times-salary figure; others use a four-times figure. This is an important way of taking care of overhead—that is all the costs you have to pay just to stay in business."

One of the best ways to pyramid your riches is by hiring more people for your business. Just be sure you understand, and use, the two-times or better rule for covering overhead and you'll solve most of the problems new home fortune builders face.

Don't Overlook Employment Laws

When you hire new people, be certain that you conform to all the state and local laws governing employees. These laws can be complicated. If you haven't had any previous experience with hiring people, consult your state and city employment service representatives. They'll be delighted to help you, completely free of charge.

Use Better Materials in Your Business

There's no substitute for high quality. All of us learn this at sometime during our lives. But quality, like everything else good in life, costs money. You, as a supplier of goods or services, must pay higher prices for quality materials. Your customers, in turn, must also pay a higher price for the quality goods or services you provide.

Karen B. runs a women's dress shop in a small shed on the grounds of her home. To promote sales she places ads in the local newspapers, ladies' club bulletins, church papers, etc. Since these ads attract a wide range of clientele, Karen decided, soon after opening her shop, to pyramid her income by expanding her business. Her approach to this problem was to use better materials in some dresses than in others. This gave her a line of dresses ranging from the low-cost to the high-cost.

Today any woman can walk into Karen's tree-shaded dress shop and find a dress priced to meet her budget. Thus, a young woman who must conserve her income can find a low-priced item she can afford. A society matron, able to afford the best, can also find the quality she seeks because Karen uses the best materials in her high-priced dresses. This policy keeps a steady stream of customers flowing into Karen's home business. Higher quality materials have expanded Karen's market and increased her income.

Another woman, Louise S., lost her job. Just a few days later her husband lost *his* job. Without any income, but with lots of ideas for a business of her own, Louise decided to sell teddy bears from a local flea market near her home. Starting in the lowest cost booth with little more than a folding table and a few teddy bears, Louise "grew" her business from nothing to an annual gross of $400,000. Though people laughed at her when she started, Louise today has a full line of cuddly, lovable teddy bears. And she's expanding her product line to include handmade dolls. Today Louise markets throughout the world using mail order to Europe and the Far East.

Advertise Your Business More

Throughout this book you've read of many instances of home wealth builders advertising their products or services. If you want to pyramid your income to enormous riches, remember this important fact:

> **There is no substitute for advertising when you are selling products or a service to the public. Carefully planned advertising pays for itself over and over.**

Why does advertising pay for itself? There are a number of reasons:

(1) Advertising keeps your name before the public
(2) Carefully worded ads convey a good business image
(3) Mail-order ads can generate extra sales
(4) Direct-mail advertising can increase your customer list

When you open your home business you may find that you have very little money for advertising. Don't be discouraged. This is a common problem and shouldn't worry you. Instead, you ought to look for low-cost ways you can spend what little money you have for advertising. Be sure to look into these low-cost advertising possibilities:

(1) Club and fraternal publications
(2) Religious publications
(3) Free ad space for new products and services

Many home wealth builders continue to use these low-cost advertising media long after beginning their business. Why? Because if any advertising medium is paying for itself—i.e. paying its cost by producing product or service sales several times greater than the ad cost, it should be continued. If you stop advertising in a certain magazine or newspaper that has produced good sales, you may lose future sales. So don't stop advertising in one medium until you find a much better one.

You can learn much about advertising by talking to the advertising managers of several publications you are considering for your business. Items that are important to you which you should know about include: advertising page rates (i.e. cost per page), frequency discounts, type size that can be used, color rules, etc. Once you have these facts clear you can begin choosing media.

As general guides to advertising costs, be sure to refer to the *Standard Rate and Data* publications. Copies of these are available in most large public libraries.

And don't overlook the *free* bulletin boards for ads in your local shopping mall, stores, and other outlets. You can often get started completely free of charge (other than the cost of a 3″ x 5″ card) using bulletin boards to promote your products and services.

Where your product or service has a wide market, consider using a computer bulletin board. Such services are low-cost and can get your message before a wide audience. Our newsletter, *International Wealth Success,* is covered on such a bulletin board and gets much wider circulation that way. The cost is small; yet we get information on our products to a completely new world of prospects!

Run Contests to Increase Your Income

Contests can be important sources of new business to you because contests

(1) Attract attention to a business
(2) Appeal to the something-for-nothing motive
(3) Can be related to product or service sales
(4) Are useful as eye-catching ads

Before planning a contest for your business, check the local laws in your state or community. You may find that contests are outlawed. If so, check what substitutes, if any, are allowed.

To plan an effective contest, start at the end—i.e. the prizes—and work back from there. When choosing prizes, aim at the popular interests of people. These are:

(a) Free foreign travel, trips, vacations
(b) Large awards—autos, boats, furniture, etc.
(c) Cash awards of large sums
(d) Common needs—food, clothing, housing, etc.

Don't make the mistake of assuming that because you are planning a contest everyone will become interested in your product or service. While you can often offer your product or service as one of the prizes, consider offering other prizes as well.

Herman Z., a successful home dance-school owner, decided to run a contest to promote business throughout his state. His first choice of prizes was a series of free dance lessons. Luckily, however, he checked with some of his customers before promoting the contest. He soon learned that most people thought they knew how to dance. They told Herman that they'd be more interested in other prizes like free trips to foreign lands, new clothing, an automobile, laptop computer, etc. On learning this, Herman immediately changed his concept of the contest because he saw that it would cost him much more than he originally anticipated.

To be sure he was planning his contest properly, Herman engaged an organization specializing in this work. For a nominal fee, this group undertook the organizaton and promotion of a statewide contest for Herman's home dance school. Prizes known to appeal to prospective dance-lesson customers were chosen, advertising media were selected, and the timing of the contest was planned.

When the contest was held it was a complete success. Herman's business increased to the level where he had to turn customers away. Today he has school branches throughout the state. Most of these branches were opened as a result of the business developed by the contest.

Use Give-Aways to Increase Business

Most people enjoy getting something for nothing. Inexpensive give-aways—like coin banks, ballpoint pens, calendars, diaries, software, etc.—are a profitable investment. Design your give-aways to carry an advertising message or your business slogan. This message can include items like:

> Business name, address, telephone number
> Hours business is open
> Typical products or services
> Brand names carried
> Motto or slogan

Check the classified pages of your phone book for the names of firms manufacturing give-aways. You'll find that effective give-aways are often available in lots of a thousand for much less than $100. Investing in one or more give-aways is a low-cost means of securing good local advertising and promotion for almost any home business.

Give Bonuses to Improve Sales

People work for many reasons but the main reason is to earn money. This is the reason why people get out of bed on a cold morning when they'd rather turn off the alarm and go back to sleep. You can turn your employees' desire to earn money for themselves to good use in your home business. How? By paying bonuses to your employees for greater sales.

When offering a bonus you appeal to the almost-universal desire people have to increase their income. A bonus gives a man or woman the chance to earn more money to pay for a new car, better clothes, a college education for a child, etc. It has been proven many times in all types of home businesses that well-planned employee bonuses can raise both the owner's and worker's income.

How do you plan a bonus? Base your bonus plan on the key measure of your business income. This might be

> Gross sales in dollars
> Number of product units sold
> Very large sales (dollars or units)
> New customers obtained
> Solving difficult problems
> Finding new products

Base the employee's bonus on him or her bringing in more business than you normally expect from him or her. Thus, many home business operators expect each employee to bring in business worth two to four times their annual pay. If you use the rule of twice the annual pay, then you might pay an employee a bonus on any business greater than this that he or she finds and brings in.

Before announcing any bonus plan to your employees, be sure that you'll earn a profit on the *extra* income the employees will bring in. Then be certain you don't give the employee all the extra income, unless you feel you could motivate him or her to bring in more business by doing so. Never forget that as owner of the business you are entitled to your share of the *extra* income. If you give away your share without a good reason for doing so, your employees will lose respect for you.

Relate your bonus plan to the extra profits the new business earns. Thus, you might give the employee ten to forty cents of each additional profit dollar he or she brings in over the normal profit you expect from him or her.

Before putting any bonus plan into action, carefully explain it to each employee involved. Be sure that the employee (a) understands the plan, (b) favors the plan, and (c) is willing to give the plan a try. You'll find that some employees are enthusiastic about bonus plans; others only go along reluctantly. But when they see the extra money in their paychecks, most people happily embrace the plan.

Enter New Markets

When most people start their home business their major interest is income. Thus, when Ian B. started a bicycle rental and repair shop in his basement, he had a goal of earning $500 per week from his home business. Within eight months after starting his business Ian was earning over $750 per week from the bicycle shop. That's when Ian started to do some thinking.

Looking around, Ian could see that the income from his shop might rise to $1,500 a week in another year. But he couldn't see it going much higher because by then he'd have reached the limit of the market in his area. So he decided to explore new markets.

Most of Ian's bicycle customers were exercise enthusiasts—they rode bicycles because they enjoyed the healthful exercise. But Ian detected that some of his bicycle customers were becoming interested in motor bikes because they wanted to go faster with less physical effort. Teenagers, Ian noted, were entranced with motor bikes because they cost much less than a car but gave many of the thrills of a car.

Checking with motor bike suppliers, Ian learned that he could easily become a dealer. As an experiment, Ian ordered two motor bikes. He was amazed with the results; he sold the two bikes from catalog descriptions before he received the bikes. Ian immediately ordered four more bikes and he sold these as fast as the first two.

Within a month Ian had a completely new group of customers—motor-bike enthusiasts. And, happily, not only was he selling motor bikes, he was also repairing and servicing them.

Ian's weekly income jumped from $1,500 to $2,000 within a few months. Had he stayed with only bicycles, Ian would be earning only about a quarter of that amount today.

You can enter new markets for your products or services in several ways:

* By selling similar or related items
* By expanding from specialized to general items
* By switching to unrelated products or services
* By selling to foreign markets

Pick the Best New Market for Your Business

Most home wealth builders find it a trifle easier to sell similar products or services, as Ian does, when entering new markets. If you switch from one type of product to another which is completely different you may run into problems. But if you carefully analyze the market and your ability to serve it, and find that you might make a success of it, then push ahead. You must have faith in yourself; if you lack faith and courage, don't try to enter new markets with your home products or services.

For a number of years I conducted seminars for top managers in a certain industry. After about five years it became a bit more difficult to find people to attend the seminars. Instead of making just one mailing to obtain 25 attendees, two mailings had to be made. Though the number of attendees didn't fall off, the handwriting was on the wall.

What to do? *Enter new markets.* But what markets? Looking over the seminar content, I quickly saw that, with only a slight change, the seminars could be made suitable for any industry. But to be sure there was a need for the seminars in the general market I made a test mailing to 100 firms.

The response was enormous. I quickly saw that there was enough of a demand to keep me busy seven days a week for the rest of my life. So I am now promoting my seminars throughout industry and have more customers than I can handle. But it took faith and courage to make the switch. Later in this chapter I will show you an easy and low-cost way to make meaningful and helpful surveys.

So have courage—enter new markets. By doing so you may convert your home business from a local neighborhood shop to a nationwide or worldwide organization. I've seen many home wealth builders do this within a year after they decided to enter a new market.

Two readers told me about their branching out to find new markets, saying, "In import-export I'm doing real fine. And as a Financial Broker I'm placing 85% of my loans." And "I have four people willing to invest in my real estate (rest homes for the elderly) at $50,000 per person. All this comes from your ideas on using OPM (Other People's Money) given in your Real Estate Kit. I'm also forming a mail order and export firm. Thanks."

From Farm Kitchen to Nationwide Market

An outstanding example of a home business that started small and grew large through expansion into new markets and new products is Pepperidge Farm Inc. This company bakes delicious bread, cookies, rolls, and similar products.

Maggie Rudkin, founder of the highly successful Pepperidge Farm bakery, started with a loaf of bread in her kitchen oven and built it into a $50-million-per-year business turning out some 70 million loaves of bread per year, besides cookies, rolls, etc. What's more, Maggie started her business the year she was 40, showing you that any age—young or old—is a good age to start your own home business.

Starting with little more than a cookbook (the *Boston Cookbook*), the memories of her Irish grandmother's cooking, and orders from her youngest son's doctor that he should be fed bread made of fresh stone-ground wheat, Maggie went to work. Adding a liberal pinch of her own baking knowledge, Maggie soon was turning out delicious bread. Her son's allergy, which led to her interest in home baking, seemed to disappear quickly. Soon the doctor who recommended that Maggie Rudkin prepare rich home-baked bread to relieve her son's asthma asked her to bake the same bread for some of his other patients.

Neighbors who tried Maggie's bread found it so good that she carried eight loaves to a local grocery store. The bread sold out quickly. With the demand for her bread increasing, Maggie decided she needed more room for baking than her home kitchen provided. So she moved her baking utensils into an abandoned stable on Pepperidge Farm. She also hired a neighbor, Mary Ference, to help her with the baking.

When she next expanded her sales outlets Maggie moved into the most competitive city in the world—New York. She personally sold her first loaf of bread in New York from a basket she carried it in. The buyer was the manager of a chain of specialty groceries. He ordered 24 loaves a day.

Maggie couldn't deliver these 24 loaves herself each day. So she asked her husband, Henry Rudkin, a partner in a Wall Street stock brokerage firm, to act as a delivery man. Every morning Mr. Rudkin carried the 24 loaves to the city on the 7:38 commuter train. At Grand Central Station Mr. Rudkin would meet a Red Cap who took the 24 loaves and delivered them to the grocer. Mr. Rudkin then took the subway to Wall Street.

This arrangement lasted only a few months before Maggie had to buy a truck to handle the expanding orders for her bread. She was delighted to see a steady flow of orders from Delaware, Florida, and nearby areas. Pepperidge Farm was steadily growing by expanding into new markets. In just one year, Maggie's home baking business grew from one loaf of bread to 4,000 loaves per day! Who says a home business isn't profitable?

At the time Maggie started her business (in the depression-ridden late thirties) most bread sold for 10¢ a loaf. Maggie's bread sold for 25¢ a loaf because it cost so much to make. Yet Maggie couldn't keep up with the demand—the more bread she baked the more people bought it.

From the stable, Maggie moved her baking plant to an abandoned service station. Soon she introduced some new products—melba toast and pound cake. A few years later, with her business still growing rapidly, Maggie had a modern bakery built to house the facilities for baking her many products. Later she also had similar modern bakeries in Pennsylvania and Illinois. Besides managing her highly successful baking business, Maggie authored *The Margaret Rudkin Pepperidge Farm Cookbook,* a popular best-selling cookbook.

Maggie's husband and two sons helped her in the business. When Mr. Rudkin met Wall Street friends and they asked him what sort of work he was doing he replied "I'm in dough!" He certainly was, thanks to Pepperidge Farms which started small and grew big by expanding into new markets and new products.

Set Up a Franchise System

Sometimes you can earn more money by expanding your business through a franchise system than you can by other means. Why? Because when you franchise your business ideas

* Other people pay you for your ideas
* Your costs are lower than for other methods
* Profits you earn are usually higher
* You need not spend money on machinery, land, etc.

Before you run out to franchise your home business, stop and ask yourself these questions.

Franchise Checklist

	Yes	No
1. Can other people run the same business I run?	....	....
2. Could other people earn a profit in my business?	....	....
3. Would my business succeed in other areas of the country?	....	....
4. Are highly specialized skills needed for this business?	....	....
5. Would I put a relative in this business?	....	....
6. Is the franchise investment needed less than $25,000?	...	....
7. Could franchises in other areas hurt my home business?	....	....
8. Is my business one which would interest other people?	....	....
9. Can my business be conveniently advertised?	....	....
10. Is there a chance for 20 or more franchises?	....	....

For an ideal franchise potential, your answers to questions 1, 2, 3, 5, 6, 8, 9, and 10 should be yes. The answers to questions 4 and 7 should be no.

If your answers differ slightly from these, don't be discouraged. Ask yourself: Would I invest in this franchise if these conditions existed? Try to remember how you felt when you started your own home business. If the answer to this question is yes, go ahead with your franchise plans.

There's Money in Franchises

Say you charge $5,000 for each franchise you allow to be set up. Your out-of-pocket costs might run $2,000 for each franchise. Since you'll probably run your franchise business out of your home, your fixed expenses (such as rent, light, heat, etc.) will not increase. Hence, your profit will be $5,000 — $2,000 = $3,000 per franchise.

If you can set up one franchise a month during the year you'll earn 12($3,000) = $36,000 per year from franchising alone. To this you should add the income from your other home business activities.

If you set up twenty or twenty-five franchises a year, as some home wealth builders do, your income would soon reach, or exceed, $100,000 per year in your own home business. Also, you might take a percentage of each franchisee's income. This is often done. It will increase your income enormously because you'll be earning money from the efforts of others with little additional investment of your time.

How to Do Low-Cost Research

You can research a new product or business by investing just a few dollars, if your product or service is the type that can be sold by mail order. Here are the ten steps to follow when you're doing low-cost research.

1. Decide which product or service you'll promote
2. Select a price for your product or service
3. Prepare a typewritten promotion letter. *Ask for a payment with the order*
4. Include an order coupon
5. Print, or reproduce 100 copies of your promotion letter
6. Choose 100 names to whom you'll send your promotion letter
7. Address the 100 envelopes for mailing
8. Mail your promotion letter
9. Keep accurate records of the orders and money you receive
10. Evaluate your results one month after you make your mailing

Let's look at this simple technique to see why, and how, it works.

First —you select a product or service to promote. Many people never even get this far. They dream about large incomes but never take steps to obtain it.

Second —you prepare a promotion letter which helps you understand your product or service better.

Third —you ask for money with the order. This may be a down payment or the full price of the product or service. *People who send you money through the mail for your product or service really want it.*

Fourth —you evaluate your results. Without a measurement of your efforts you have little to use as a basis for business decisions.

How to Project Research Results

Let's say you receive three orders on your mailing of 100 ads. This is a *return* of 3/100, or 3 per cent. If you mailed ten times as many ads, or 1,000, you could expect to receive ten times as many orders, or $10(3) = 30$. Knowing your costs, it's easy to figure if a 3 per cent return will make money for you. As a general rule, a 3 per cent return is considered to be excellent by experienced mail-order and direct-mail operators.

You'll have better results to project if you follow these hints in your direct-mail campaign:

(1) Use first-class mail for your test mailing
(2) Include an order coupon with the letter
(3) Provide a stamped addressed return envelope
(4) Use two-color printing for your letter
(5) Wait for one month after your mailing before projecting the results

A mailing of one hundred direct-mail ads will cost perhaps $500, tops. Yet the information you derive from the mailing can be worth thousands of dollars. Never scoff at the worth of low-cost research. It is another valuable way to pyramid your wealth by expanding your home business.

And if your research—no matter how little it costs—shows there is a market for your product or service, start promoting with more direct marketing. This is called "rolling out" by direct marketers. Why do we urge you to roll out your promotion? Because, at this writing, direct marketing consumer sales in the United States run at some $115 billion a year! More than half the people in the United States today (58% to be exact) buy direct—either through the mail or by phone. And almost all use their credit card to charge their purchases for payment at a later date. Use the *Mail Order Success Kit*, described at the back of this book, to get started in the booming direct marketing business. You can easily start in your own home.

12

How to Keep More

of Your

Business Profits

Reading this book could make you richer than you ever thought possible. If this happens, as I most certainly hope it does, you'll have another problem—high taxes. While we must all pay the taxes we owe, there is no need for us to overpay. For as the U.S. Supreme Court said in a famous decision (293 U.S. 465) "The legal right of a taxpayer to decrease the amount of what otherwise would be his taxes, or altogether avoid them, by means which the law permits cannot be doubted." Or: To *avoid* is legal, but to *evade* is illegal.

Know the Tax Laws

Some people boast about their lack of knowledge of the tax laws. This is the silliest approach a businessperson can take. To be successful in your own home business you need not be a tax expert. But you should know something about tax laws and rules. If you don't, how can you check the work of your tax accountant?

"He's the expert," you say. "Let him worry." He may worry, I say, but he won't worry as much about your money as you will! That's why I've always been careful to try to know almost as much about tax laws as accountants do. Then I can easily check their work. Just because a person is an accountant is no reason for him or her being right all the time. Yet I always use, and recommend that you use, a good tax accountant or lawyer.

Build a Tax Library

You'll pay the majority of your taxes to the U.S. Government. Fortunately for all home businessmen like ourselves, the Government has excellent tax publications which can be purchased at low cost. Two of these publications you should buy right now are:

Tax Guide for Small Business, IRS Publication No. 334

Your Federal Income Tax, IRS Publication No. 17

Order both of these from the U.S. Government Printing Office, Washington, D.C. 20402.

There is one other tax publication which I recommend you purchase as soon as your home business income reaches $5,000 per year. This publication is the *Federal Tax Course,* Prentice-Hall. Using this excellent publication, which is much more than a course, can save you many dollars in taxes. When your annual home business income reaches the four-figure level you need the extra information this excellent publication provides.

Keep Up with the Tax News

Regularly read the business section of a good newspaper. Watch for items on new tax developments. Clip these articles, mark the date on the article, and then file it in a folder marked *Income Taxes.* Follow this practice for a few years and you'll acquire a ready knowledge of tax laws and rules. While you will not know enough to be a tax lawyer or accountant, you'll be ready and able to carry on an intelligent discussion with them at any time. Also, you'll be able to make an intelligent review of any tax accountant's work on *your* tax returns.

Obtain copies of state and city tax rules from your local tax offices. Typical local taxes you may have to pay, depending on the size and location of your business, are:

> Personal income tax
> Business income tax
> Commerical rent tax
> Sales tax
> Business occupancy tax

In general, if you operate your business in your own home, you will have to pay taxes related to business rentals, but only on that part of your home used for business. But the rules differ from one city to another—so check yours. Many cities and states have no business rent taxes of any kind.

Where to Find Tax-Free Dollars

Study your local and state tax laws as carefully as the Federal laws. In the area of taxes there is no substitute for accurate, first-hand knowledge. One home wealth builder who runs a wine service estimates that he saves $1,000 per year by keeping up to date on taxes. Why does he save so much? Because his service includes: a wine school in which he teaches people all about wine; six books on wine, several of which this home wealth builder publishes himself; wine dinners at which he shows people how to serve wine properly. Few tax accountants are competent enough to unravel such a complicated setup so this home wealth builder is his own tax expert and shows a profit on it. As he remarked to me recently: "Always remember—a dollar saved in taxes is a tax-free dollar."

Seven Steps to Greater Home Income

Recognize, here and now, that we all must pay taxes. In fact, as I travel around the world and see how other people live, I often say to myself: "I'm delighted to be a citizen of the United States because I'm proud of the many good things our nation has done throughout the world. Since taxes are needed to support these good works, I'm glad to pay my taxes."

Once you recognize that you *will* pay higher taxes as more money rolls into your home business, you can get ready to take action. Some home wealth builders, feeling that their home is sacred, resent paying taxes on the income they earn in this revered place. This is an emotional approach to a business problem. It will only make you unhappy, bitter, and less successful.

Rid yourself of foolish, juvenile income-tax attitudes, if you have them. Replace them with the recognition of the tax burden we all face. Once you do this you'll be happier, freer, and—best of all— you'll earn more in your home business.

Now here are *your* seven steps to the largest income you've ever earned in your entire life:

1. Search for legitimate business deductions
2. Use depreciation wherever possible
3. Explore research and development costs
4. Make your hobby a profitable business
5. Take full advantage of home deductions
6. Don't overlook special expenses
7. Profit from capital gains

Use these seven lucrative steps and your chances for outstanding income will zoom. Every big-money home wealth builder I know is a tax expert in his or her own field. That's one of the reasons why so few home businesses fail, compared with other businesses. Thus, surveys show that only 15 to 20 out of 100 home businesses fail during their first six years of operation. Compare this with the Commerce Department figures showing that 74 per cent of all new businesses fail during their first six years!

Why do home businesses last so long? There are two main reasons. (1) The owners of home businesses exert better control over costs; (2) the overhead in home businesses is lower than in any other kind of business. Since we've discussed item (2) elsewhere in this book, we'll concentrate on cost control, item (1), as related to taxes in this chapter. You'll soon see how the seven magic steps listed above can put you in the $500,000-per-year income bracket in your own home business.

Search for Legitimate Business Deductions

There are hundreds and hundreds of legitimate business deductions to which you may be entitled as a home business fortune builder. But you cannot expect the government to point out all these deductions to you. Instead, you must seek out these deductions yourself. Why? Because you, and only you, know the kinds of expenses you are incurring in your business. As a general rule, if you incur an expense to produce a profit, you are entitled to deduct that expense from your gross income when preparing your tax return.

To find the deductions to which you may be entitled read *every* entry in the Business Deductions list contained in *Tax Guide for Small Business,* referred to earlier. Did I hear you groan "Read *every* entry?" If you did groan, or if you just thought of groaning, the answer is yes—*read every entry!* If you want to earn big money at home, you have to work for it.

Why? Because by reading *every* entry you will obtain a broad understanding of the deductions the law entitles you to take in your home business. The list will, I know, suggest deductions you may have overlooked. Also, the list will suggest deductions you can take in the future which will probably be approved by the Government. Knowing what deductions are legitimate can serve as a guide to your future spending plans. Why spend money for nondeductible items when, with a slight change, you can spend the same sum on deductible items?

I wish we had space in this book to reproduce the entire list of legitimate business deductions. But we don't. So turn today to this list and study every item in it. I assure you that you'll find it exciting, interesting, and profitable. Every moment you spend studying this list will put extra cash in your pocket. Not only that, you'll be improving your general knowledge of business, taxes, and deductions quickly and easily. So listen to an experienced home fortune builder and do as he says—you won't, I assure you, regret it.

Use Depreciation Wherever Possible

Some home wealth builders are afraid of the word depreciation. To them it looks like a big word which is puzzling because it is difficult to spell. Don't be one of these frightened wealth builders because you'll lose out—dollars will drain out of your business while you work and sleep. These dollars could be yours to do what you want with them—

Deposit in your bank
Reinvest in your business
Invest in stocks or bonds
Finance other businesses
Spend on yourself or family

Just what, then, is depreciation? Briefly, it is nothing more than recovery of the money you invest in profit-producing equipment— machines, buildings, autos, trucks, typewriters, computers, printers, software, cameras, office furniture, business books, etc. In general, you can depreciate, for tax purposes, any major equipment you buy to produce taxable income. Or you can deduct—with certain limits on the amount—the cost of major equipment in the year you buy it. Just be sure to check the latest tax laws on the amount of direct deduction you can take in a given year. Small items—pencils, paper, staples, pens, blotters, etc.—are generally not depreciated. Instead, you deduct their cost from the gross income you earn during the year you purchase them.

Using Depreciation in a Home Business

As an example of using depreciation, let's say you buy a word processor for your home business. You pay $2,000. This payment may be in cash or you may finance the word processor, paying about $66 per month for 36 months. Either way, however, your cost is $2,000. (Any interest you pay is deductible on another part of your tax return.)

Now all businesspeople, and the Government, recognize that as you use this word processor it will depreciate—that is, it will get older and perhaps less useful. Hence, you should be able to take some money from your income to cover the cost of buying a new word processor at a later date when the present one is no longer usable. The money you take from your gross business income is tax-free—you don't have to pay taxes on it. This means you can recover your investment at no cost to yourself, other than the effort you put into earning the money to pay for the depreciation of this word processor or any other productive business equipment.

How do you recover the $2,000 you invested in this word processor? You set aside a certain amount of money each year until you've accumulated enough to buy another $2,000 word processor. The Government, through the Internal Revenue service, sets allowable "lives" for various types of business equipment. Typical lives currently allowed for various popular types of business equipment are:

Allowable Lives for Business Equipment[*]

Equipment	Life, Years
Tractors (on-the-road types), horses	3
Office equipment—typewriters, computers, copiers, word processors	5
Vehicles—autos, trucks, trailers	5
Office furniture, fax machines, cellular phones, dishwashers, refrigerators	7
Ships, barges, certain agricultural equipment	10

[*]According to the Modified Accelerated Cost Recovery System (MACRS).
Consult a Certified Public Accountant for the latest rules and lives.

One Way to Figure Depreciation[**]

From this list we see that the allowable life of word processors is 5 years. On a straight-line depreciation basis you are allowed to deduct $2,000/5 years = $400 per year to repay your investment in this word processor. Thus, you'll have $400 per year of tax-free income to use as you wish. This may seem like a small sum but as your investment in business equipment grows, so does your total legitimate deduction for depreciation. Hence, a home wealth builder who runs a furniture refinishing business in his basement has enough equipment to justify an annual depreciation deduction of $2,500. If he's in the 28% tax bracket, this is the equivalent of an $8,929 tax-free income.

Explore Research and Development Costs

Let's say that you invest in art—paintings, sculpture, drawings, etc.—as the way to build your home fortune. You buy art at a low price and sell it at a higher price. A number of home wealth builders earn an excellent income—more than $100,000 per year—in this business. Many of these wealth builders are women who enjoy being around art. Men, of course, can be equally successful in art, if they are interested in it.

As a home wealth builder you are entitled to spend money for business purposes on:

Research on new products
Development of new products

[**] Since *Tax Code* allowances change fairly often, consult a Certified Public Accountant (CPA) for the exact guidelines to use.

> Market research
> Market development
> Product improvement
> Ways to increase sales income

These expenses, and many other related and similar expenses, are legitimate deductions on your tax return if (a) you're in business to show a profit, and (b) you spent the money for business purposes and not for personal items.

You are, however, allowed a choice in how you charge off your research and development (R & D) costs. You can (1) charge them off completely—that is deduct them from your gross income *before* computing your taxes, or (2) you can charge off R & D expenses over a five-year period. In effect, when you use method (2) you are depreciating your R & D costs. The IRS, happily, allows you, as a home wealth builder, the right to choose method (1) or (2). Thus, you can base your choice on what is best for your business and your profits. But once you choose method (2) you must stick with it until the particular expense concerned is written off.

Note, however, that you can use method (1) alone, method (2) alone, or a combination of both methods for different R & D expenses. The choice is yours. And, if you build your tax knowledge as we're recommending in this chapter, you can make an intelligent and profitable choice for *your* business.

If, as was mentioned earlier, your home business is the buying and selling of art objects, you can usually deduct as R & D expenses:

> Professional books on the art business
> Entertainment costs related to business data collection
> Market research costs
> Travel costs to research or develop products
> Equipment for business research

Many other R & D expenses, too numerous to mention here, are also deductible. To learn what you are entitled to deduct, refer to the tax publications listed earlier in this chapter. Again, you *must*, at *all* times, have the advice and guidance of a qualified CPA when making tax decisions and preparing tax returns.

While we've used the art business as our example in this chapter, any other business could have been cited. So no matter what business you run in your own home, or you're planning to run, the general guides on handling R & D costs given in this chapter can be used. Wise handling of R & D costs can put extra money into your pocket.

Make Your Hobby a Profitable Business

Some of the greatest talent available in the world today is expended on hobbies. Look around you now. You'll probably see many people who are only mediocre successes in business, yet who are outstanding in their hobbies. Why should this be? If a person can be a standout golfer, why can't he be a good manager on his job? After all, it isn't easy to be a great golfer. To be a competent manager, some people believe, is much easier than to be a skillful golfer.

Many studies show that a person is most competent in those areas of his life in which he has the greatest interest, or from which he obtains the most joy. Hence, you might conclude that the topnotch amateur golfer is probably more interested in his hobby than his job, if he is less successful on his job than he is on the golf course. Why then doesn't he stop working at a job on which he turns in a second-rate performance and concentrate on golf? He'd probably earn much more while getting a larger amount of fun and pleasure from life. This man doesn't switch occupations because he probably never stops to think about changing his career.

The same reasoning, of course, applies to women and their jobs and hobbies. Many women are more successful at turning their hobby into a home business because they spend more time analyzing their needs and wants in life.

Avoid Tax Problems

Just think—if you convert a hobby you love into a profitable business, you'll be able to enjoy your hobby while having legitimate business deductions for tax purposes. You must, however, be engaged in the activity to earn a taxable profit. You *cannot* deduct expenses you incur in your hobby solely for pleasure. So don't try to deduct hobby expenses until *after* you've converted your hobby to a business. To do this:

1. Select a suitable business name
2. Register your business name with local authorities
3. Establish an office in your home
4. Set up account and record books
5. Advertise your business
6. Make some sales and obtain income

Once you're earning some taxable income from what was formerly your hobby, you will, in general, be entitled to take business deductions for tax purposes. Thus, you'll be able to enjoy your hobby while earning an income from it. Remember this every day you work in your home wealth business because this is an important principle:

> There is no law against your enjoying your work. Converting your hobby to a profit-making business is a completely legal step and you are entitled to take legitimate business deductions on your tax return once you begin to earn a profit.

How to Stay Out of Trouble

The way home fortune builders run into trouble with tax authorities is by trying to take a tax deduction on a hobby that they have *not* converted into a profit-making business. Another way home fortune builders run into tax trouble is by deducting business expenses for a hobby after they've converted it into a business but *before* they've begun to earn a profit.

Many home wealth builders do, and are allowed to, make deductions for business expenses before their hobby-converted-to-a-business earns a profit. However, some of these home businesspeople had to have long "discussions" with the IRS to obtain the right to deduct legitimate expenses. Others had to go to court before they could obtain the desired authorization. Their court costs were, of course, deductible.

If you want to try to deduct business expenses before you earn a profit but after you convert your hobby to a business, go ahead and try. You are not breaking the law in taking the deduction, if you are truly trying to earn a profit. The worst that can happen to you is that the deduction may be disallowed. Then you'll have to pay the additional tax due, plus a certain percent interest on the tax due for the time involved since the tax was first due. The interest you pay is, however, a legitimate tax deduction, regardless of the decision on your business.

But I want you to have a happy, carefree time in your home business. So I recommend that you *not* take any business deductions until *after* you earn a profit. Then there is little chance that your deductions will be disallowed. Why ask for trouble, lost time, aggravation, and other difficulties? Show a profit and you will, in general, be in the clear.

Take Full Advantage of Home Deductions

As a home wealth builder you have a rich person's right to deduct business-related expenses you incur in your home. These deductions can put many extra dollars in your pocket. To overlook these deductions, to which you are legitimately entitled, is to pass by one of the choicest plums available to the home wealth builder. Since I want you to get as rich as possible, as quickly as possible, in your own home, I am calling these deductions to your attention again, even though we briefly discussed them earlier in this book.

Once again, go back to your copy of *Tax Guide for Small Business.* It lists a large number of home deductions to which you are entitled. Study the list of deductions carefully. No doubt you will find listed there many of the expenses you incur. If there are other business expenses you incur in your home which are not listed, add them to the list.

Search out every home deduction to which you are entitled because you do business at home. Don't overlook the obvious—light, heat, repairs, etc. You will have no trouble justifying these expenses if you keep accurate records of what you spend, and what part is chargeable to your home business activities.

Watch Your Entertainment Expenses

Where you may run into trouble with home expenses you want to take as tax deductions is in the area of entertainment. When you entertain you will probably spend money for

> Food
> Beverages
> Party favors
> Special decorations
> Other entertainment items

If you can prove that you entertain solely to increase the taxable income your business is earning, you are legally entitled to deduct a portion* of the costs you incur. But there is a difference—and some-

*Consult a CPA for the latest rules on entertainment deductions.

times a very large one—between being legally entitled to a tax deduction and being allowed to take this deduction. There is nothing dishonest about entertaining for business purposes. However, entertainment expenses are probably subject to more inspection, review, and disallowance than any other business expense reported on tax returns.

My personal choice has been to ignore my entertainment expenses when preparing my tax return. As a result, I've never had an entertainment expense disallowed because such an expense has to be listed before the tax examiner can disallow it. True, if I took an entertainment deduction I could save some money on taxes. But my view is that the time and effort I *might* have to spend justifying the expense would be worth much more than the tax saving. So I simply omit the expense and avoid the aggravation and time loss. You may wish to do the same. Or you may wish to take every home deduction to which you believe you are entitled. Fine; but have the records to justify your claims.

Don't Overlook Special Expenses

Every home business incurs special expenses of one kind or another. It's easy for you to overlook these expenses when you're preparing your tax return. Typical special or unusual expenses include:

> Losses from thefts
> Storm damages
> Returns and rejects
> Bad debts
> Insurance
> Losses from operating your business
> Condemnations
> Involuntary exchanges

All these, and other, unusual expenses are discussed in the *Tax Guide for Small Business*, which should be your bible of tax facts every day you are in a home business. To identify your special expenses, *keep accurate records*. You needn't invest in an expensive accounting book to keep your records. The Dome *Simplified Monthly Bookkeeping Record*, which sells for less than $25, is an excellent record book. It contains spaces for a variety of special expenses and is so arranged that you won't overlook them while preparing your tax return. You can buy the Dome record book in any large stationery store.

By taking your legitimate deductions for special expenses you reduce your tax bill. So be sure to

(1) Keep records
(2) Begin preparing your tax return early
(3) Include all special expenses in your return

Only if you follow this sensible and proven procedure can you derive the maximum advantage from the legal business deductions to which you are entitled.

Profit from Capital Gains

You are in a home business to earn a profit. And profit is not, as some people believe, a bad word. Profit is the force which builds great nations, important societies, and large companies. Without profit the largest countries and companies will soon fail. So aim, every day of your home business life, at earning the largest profit you can. One way to do this is by profiting from capital gains.

You have a capital gain whenever you sell something—usually property of some kind—which you do not hold for your main source of income. To explain this, let's say you design clothes at home as your main source of income. Let's say you are currently earning $500,000 per year designing clothes in your home.

As a hobby you collect coins. One day, while on an overseas business trip, you come across a valuable 1904 $20 gold coin. You buy it for $45 because you think you may be able to sell it at a profit. Back home you check the price of your gold coin and find that you can sell it for $445. Before selling, however, you check the tax laws in *Tax Guide for Small Business.* This excellent guide shows that if you hold your coin for one year before selling it, you'll have to pay taxes at only 28% of your profit from the sale.* This sounds good, but exactly how do you figure the one-year holding period?

---

* *Holding time and portion of profit taxed depend on the tax law in effect at the time of the sale. Consult a CPA for guidance.*

How to Figure Your Capital-Gain Time

Let's say you bought the coin on October fourth, getting a receipt for your purchase. To figure the one-year holding period, begin with the next day, October fifth. The first month of your holding period ends November fifth; the second December fifth, and so on. Thus, your one-year holding period will be up on October fifth. Were you to sell the coin on October fourth your profit would be considered ordinary income and would be taxed as such.

Let's say you sell your gold coin on October fifth for $495, the price having risen since you first received a quotation on it. Your profit on the sale, assuming you had no other expenses connected with the coin purchase is $495 − 45 = $450. You insert this amount in the Capital Gain section of your tax return.

Keep More of Your Earnings by Using Capital Gains

Using the advantages of the capital-gain tax rules allows you to keep much more of your earnings. When using the capital-gains rule remember that it does not apply to items you buy and sell as part of your regular business activities. Thus, as a home clothing designer you might buy, for future sale, clothing designs from other firms. The capital-gains rule would not apply to these sales because this is your regular business. Any profit from the sales would be classed as ordinary income.

Incidentally, you may think that home clothing design is an impossible way to get rich in your own home. One designer who started work in her living room with no investment other than for pencils and paper was soon grossing one million dollars per year. Today, a few years later, her various clothing interests gross more than $14-million per year. Yet she still designs in her living room— the only difference is that today her design table is much larger than when she first started.

Make Your Future More Profitable

We come now to a point where we can summarize much of what

we've discussed in earlier chapters. For many reasons I wish that you were sitting here talking with me. Then I could say to you many of the things I'd like to. Why? Because if you've read this far you *must* be interested in building wealth in your own home business. Since I'm so interested in seeing you become rich in as short a time as possible, I'm summarizing here the 11 major steps you can follow in building home wealth. These steps are:

1. **Know the joys of getting rich at home.** Picture for yourself the many advantages of working at home. Read Chapter 1 again; make its words part of the force that pushes you on to greater wealth, more success, and positive security in the warmth and privacy of your own home. Use your dreams of wealth as another positive force to generate the energy you need to work for your goal. Keep pictures of your ultimate goals—a new home, auto, ski lodge, etc.—in front of you while you work, and in your mind at all other times.

Motivate yourself—you are the most powerful being on earth, as far as self-motivation is concerned. When you motivate yourself you take *your* future into your own hands, where it should be, instead of in the hands of a mean and selfish boss. If you don't motivate yourself, I guarantee you that there will be few other people who'll volunteer to take on the task of motivating you. So take your future into your own hands—learn the joys of becoming rich at home and make them the potent force which rockets you to great wealth.

2. **Believe you can and you will.** You *can* earn big money in your own home business. I can show you thousands of people regularly earning enormous incomes at home. And these people are of all types—from the brilliant, young, intellectual housewife-mother making expensive costume jewelry in the living room of her lower east New York apartment to the aging farmer who makes and bottles apple cider in his basement. In between these extremes are thousands of other useful, productive occupations you can follow at home to earn a large income. Believe you can and you will.

Some of the most successful home fortune builders are people who were *forced* to believe they could earn money at home. These people, many of whom were injured in an accident of some kind, have to stay home because they can't move around enough to qualify for a regular job. So they seek, and find, a way to earn money at home. Without knowing it, they apply many of the principles outlined in this book. Soon they have a booming, lucrative business at home because they were forced to believe they might be able to earn money at home. Believe you can and you will!

Others forced to seek a home business today are some of the millions of people laid off from their professional or blue collar jobs. No matter what words were used when these people were cut from the payroll—downsizing, reduction in force (RIF), early retirement, etc.— the cold fact is that they're out of work. They don't have an income once their unemployment benefits stop. So they turn to a home business because sending out resumes by the hundreds begging for job interviews seldom produces the wanted position.

3. **Know your income needs.** You *can* start a successful home business with the vague feeling that you need, and want, more income. But you can earn more, faster, if you know your income needs and have a goal to aim at. A goal acts as an incentive, a guide, and a target for your efforts. Without a goal, your efforts are directed in a loose fashion, with many chances of error. With a goal you make fewer errors. Also, you reach your desired income level sooner.

Never overlook the importance of knowing your income needs. While I make no pretence of being a psychologist, I am firmly convinced that when you know your income needs, and put them in writing, your mind and body reach out to achieve your goal sooner, with less effort, and with fewer troubles. A written goal for a known income need is the spark many people need to urge them on to achieve more than they ever have before in their lives.

If you've had trouble making things work out in your life, perhaps you lack a written goal of your income needs. You have nothing to lose and everything to gain if you:

(a) Analyze your home income needs
(b) Write out your income needs clearly and accurately
(c) Make a firm resolve to achieve your needed income

Try this technique—it works for thousands of others and *will* work for you, too.

4. **Pick your wealth-building home business.** Some beginning home wealth builders fuss and fume for years while they kid themselves into thinking they are looking for a business that is "just right" for them. Let me tell you something I've learned—*it really makes very little difference which home wealth business you choose,* if you're:

(a) Sincerely interested in earning more money
(b) Determined to succeed
(c) Willing to work long hours
(d) Ready to take a business risk

Look at a successful home wealth builder and you'll see a person who could hit it big in any business—from acorns to zoology. So don't worry for years about the perfect home business—there's no such business. Every home business has problems, headaches, and drawbacks. But when the greenbacks start flooding into your home you can put up with a great deal of trouble and still be happy. As one brilliantly successful home wealth builder remarked to me recently: "Everywhere I turn in my house I see money. The sight of all that money is just delightful. I'd put up with anything to keep it flowing in!"

5. **Start your home business for maximum profits.** Don't go into any home business with the idea that you're going to lose money for the first year or so. Instead, start your home business with the aim of earning a profit from the first day you're working. Why wait for years to earn a profit when, with the right planning, you can start earning profits the first day?

One home wealth builder heard me say this and snapped his fingers with joy. "I've been waiting to move from my boat to an apartment to start a music school and a mail-order business selling musical instruments. Instead of waiting any longer, I'll start my music school on the boat."

To save on advertising costs, he hung a sign in the boat basin and told local people about the music lessons he planned to give. Within a week he had six students and was earning a profit without having invested a cent. The profits from his music school enabled this home wealth builder to finance his mail-order musical-instrument business. Thus, he started both businesses for maximum profits and he began earning profits from the first day. You can do the same—whether you live in a city apartment, on a farm, in a home of your own, a house trailer, a boat, or anywhere else.

6. **Earn enormous income from good products.** Some production lines seem to run forever—for example Hershey Bars, Corn Flakes, Ford, Chris-Craft, etc. Develop a product like any of these and you never need worry again. Your only problem will be what to do with all the money that's pouring into your home business.

Products *are* profitable, if you find or develop them wisely, and market them carefully. Chapter 7 gives you a number of valuable hints for earning big money from products at home. Put these hints to work today.

7. **Use mail order to build home riches.** Mail order, and direct

mail, are powerful tools for building wealth in many home businesses. Viewed as businesses in themselves, or as new ways to promote product sales, mail order and direct mail can build your home wealth quickly and efficiently. But both require careful work and realistic planning if you are to achieve the greatest success.

Read several good trade magazines and newspapers serving the field. One excellent source you should be sure to read is *DM News*. It contains much useful information for you and your business.

You should try to attend important meetings of the industry. You'll find such meetings listed in your trade magazines and newspapers. Also, consider joining one or more of the direct-marketing associations serving the field. You'll derive many benefits from attending meetings and belonging to key associations. Your knowledge will increase, along with your ability to earn a larger income in your home business.

8. Get rich fast in home services. You can run almost any type of service business in your own home. Some people combine two or more service businesses in their home. Thus, one man runs a school for French cooking and a fine French restaurant on the first two floors of his modernized brownstone house. He and his family live on the third floor.

The need for all kinds of services grows and grows. So if you open, or buy, the right kind of home service business you are almost certain to hit the big money. Just use the many general-business hints in this book and you'll soon be on your way to enormous wealth in your own home business.

9. Build your daily income to the maximum. Rid yourself of useless, profitless habits that cause you to lose money. Replace them with the strong drive of the successful home wealth builder. Resolve to make every day a high profit day—a day during which you will outdo all your previous records.

Look upon each new day as a golden chance for great wealth for yourself and your family. Plan, early in the day, how you'll earn the maximum income during *this* day. Then go out and make your plan work.

By using this plan you make each new day a glorious beginning, a chance to set new records. Thus, one day's work triggers the next day's income. You soon have a self-propelled, money-earning machine—your own home business. Before you realize what has happened you're earning $25,000 per year in your own home business. This soon jumps to $50,000, $75,000, $100,000 — then $500,000. Why? Because you're building your daily income to the maximum. This is one of the greatest secrets of getting rich at home. Remember that you learned it in this book.

10. Pyramid riches by expanding your business. To earn the biggest profit possible, you must expand your business as the demand for your products or services grows. Expansion is the life-giving vitamin which builds your income, helps the business hold your interest, and gives you a potential capital-gains situation should you decide to sell your business. Without expansion your business has nowhere to go but down. With expansion your business can increase at a fantastic rate.

Expand carefully. Try to avoid taking on larger fixed expenses— rent, heat, light, etc.—when you expand. If you must increase your expenses when expanding (and you usually can't avoid increasing them), try to raise your variable or out-of-pocket expenses. Why? Because these costs are recovered on every sale you make. Also, you don't incur a variable expense until after you decide to make a sale.

If, on the other hand, you raise your fixed expenses, you may get into trouble. How will you pay higher fixed costs if your sales fail to increase? Careless increases of fixed costs without the supporting sales may break you sooner than you think. So be careful when planning any expansion of your business.

11. Keep more of your business profits. "There's only one thing worse than having to pay an income tax—and that's not having to pay any income tax at all," is the excellent observation made by people who've known the misery of not being able to find work of any kind. But you can, and will, make big money in your own home business. Hence, careful tax planning is a must.

Use the many hints given in this chapter. They'll pay off for you over and over again. Then you won't have to remark, as so many poorly informed people have, that "the taxes will kill you."

You Can Make $500,000 per Year at Home

It is easier than you think to earn $500,000 per year in your own home business. And you can reach this income level sooner than you think. This book shows you the way. Read it at least twice before you begin your business. Mark key passages with a red pencil or yellow highlighter. Then take the recommended action.

You can't lose when you build a profitable home business because people will continue to come back, again and again, for your products or services. Try it and see.

And when you're trying your own home business, don't overlook real estate income. It offers you many tax advantages. You may even want to make one of the properties your home. Then you'll be living on your job! But even if you do not live in one of your properties you may tell me, as these readers did:

> Your zero cash real estate writeups always turned me on. So I started looking for buildings in my city. I found a 50-unit building for $5,000 down. Not having cash, I borrowed the $5,000, most of it from a credit union. I took over the building and today my income is $24,000 a year ($2,000 a month) after paying *all* expenses, including the mortgage. And I'll have the $5,000 repaid soon, too!

Get Expert Tax Advice When You Grow

As your business expands you'll need the advice of an expert accountant or tax lawyer. These professionals can be worth their weight in tax savings to you. So don't try to pinch pennies as you grow bigger in your home business. Consult, and use, tax experts.

If you don't know any accountants or attorneys, call the local chapter of an accounting or legal association and ask for the names of several tax specialists. Call on these experts and ask them about their services. Engage, on a trial basis, the expert who impresses you most. Keep careful track of his or her work—in general, the results will delight you because for every dollar you pay him or her, you'll probably save several more.

Also, and most importantly, your expert will come to your aid should you ever be called in for a tax audit. Knowing the tax laws as well as he or she does, your expert will be a welcome friend in your moments of stress. You won't feel lonesome and your facts will be presented clearly and concisely. Your chances of coming out ahead are better because your situation will be described with greater accuracy and force. So consider getting expert tax advice as soon as your home business starts growing.

You're Now Ready to Start, and Prosper In, Your Own Home Business

You now have what you need to start your own home business. And I'm sure you'll prosper in that business—if you use the ideas in this book. But to be sure you really *do* earn money in your own home business, I—Ty Hicks—make this offer to you:

1. I'll be glad to help you in every way I can, either on the telephone or by mail or fax, if you're a 2 year, or longer, subscriber to my newsletter, *International Wealth Success*, described at the back of this book. The reason I suggest you be a subscriber is because you'll get hundreds of profitable ideas every year from this monthly newsletter. And it will motivate you to do more for yourself and your business—making *you* more successful!

2. If you have a good idea for a profitable home business I'll even consider financing it myself, or helping you get the financing you need—if you're a subscriber, as described above. While these services are also available to non-subscribers, I must admit that subscribing *can* be very helpful in terms of ideas you get from the newsletter.

3. If you want to talk to me personally, I'm as close to you as your own phone. Just pick it up and dial my number. Don't expect me to accept collect calls. If you want free advice as a subscriber (see No. 1, above), the phone call is on you! I'll spend as much time as you need and will answer every business question you ask. Remember, also, to be the courteous and businesslike person who identifies himself or herself when first contacting someone for advice. I won't talk to you unless you tell me your name, address, telephone number, and why you're contacting me. Why? Because I can help *you* more when I have this information. You'd demand the same from me if I were to call you unannounced! So adopt businesslike manners—it will really pay off in higher profits in your own home business.

4. If you write me, please include your phone number. I'll call you with my answers to your questions. Why do I prefer to call? Because when I'm writing letters I'm *not* writing books. And my reading public seems to want more books. I can talk to you a lot faster than I can write you. So have a heart, good friend, and let me help you—my way!

5. Lastly, you *do* have a good friend in Ty Hicks. I *will* talk to you on the phone, no matter how much you might disbelieve what I say. Some people call and say "Oh, I just wanted to see if what you say in your book is really true." Then they hang up, having wasted their time, my time, and the cost of the call. And I'm *not* a computer in Rocklin, CA, as some people believe! I have a wife, three kids, two cars, a beautiful home, and a great boat. So if you want a good friend who lives, breathes, and *will* help you, you have it in Ty Hicks!

13

Your Magic Checklist
to Home
Business Wealth

Checklists can be helpful to anyone seeking home wealth building ideas. That's why this checklist of more than 1,000 home businesses has been prepared especially for this book. If you use this checklist you may find, or have suggested to you by it, one or more businesses that will earn you $100,000 to $500,000 per year, or more, at home. So let's start right now to put this checklist to work.

How to Use This Checklist

Each entry in the home business checklist contains the name of at least one home business. Some entries—like *Rug cleaning, dyeing, shampooing* — actually list three businesses, i.e., Rug cleaning; Rug dyeing; Rug shampooing. Any of these businesses can be operated independently of the other, if you want to.

Method of Business Operation

You might also operate a business in one or more ways, as discussed earlier in this book. You might, for example, sell products directly to your customers from a store in your home. Or you might just service the products, or you might sell the products through mail order or by direct-mail promotion.

Since some businesses can be operated in more than one way, your checklist indicates this in a concise manner by the use of one or more letters. Thus, the three letters used in the Type of Operation column of the checklist have the following meanings:

P = product sale is a mode of operation
M = mail order or direct mail is a mode of operation
S = service is a mode of operation

Use of two or more letters—for instance, P, M, S as in *Binocular rental, repair, sales, service*—in your checklist indicates that the business could be operated as a product sales operation, a mail-order operation, a direct-mail operation, or a service operation, or all these ways. Thus, though only one business is listed in this main entry, you are actually given ideas for *three* businesses, if you regard mail order and direct mail as the same business. The second column of your checklist shows the type of home operation possible for each business listed.

Remember—this checklist is directed at home businesses. Hence, it has been specially prepared with the needs of the home business wealth builder in mind. So use the list to spark your mind with ideas for kinds of home businesses and ways in which they can be operated.

How Much Capital Do You Need?

Your checklist also shows the approximate amount of capital you'll need to start your own home business. The three letters—L, I, H—mean:

L = low, or $100–$500
I = intermediate, or $501–$5,000
H = high, or $5,001 and up

The capital needs listed are average values. You may find that local conditions in your area either reduce or increase the starting capital required. This can occur when averages are used. However, this book is distributed throughout the world and the checklist gives a good picture of the variations in local capital needs from one city to another. You can use the capital needs list with complete assurance of accuracy.

This capital needs list is, to the author's knowledge, the only such listing of home business money needs ever published. Use it as a guide and I guarantee that it will make you richer than you are today.

How Much Experience Do You Need?

You can open a frankfurter stand in your backyard and earn a good income from it with little previous experience. But if you plan to operate an air-taxi service, my advice to you is that you better have many years of experience before you put your first air taxi into service.

Your home business checklist shows you how much experience is generally needed to start and succeed in the businesses listed. While this list is accurate for every usual condition listed, there may be times when you hear of someone becoming a big success with less experience than indicated. Fine! In every home business there will be a few exceptions to one or more general rules.

The required experience is indicated in your checklist by three letters:

> N = none, or very little—less than 1 year
> m = a moderate amount—1 or 2 years
> W = wide, or several years

Use these general ranges as a guide when you are thinking of a new home business or planning to expand your present home business. Where N experience is indicated in the checklist, it is assumed that you will learn quickly once you start your home business. This often occurs in new businesses.

Now here's your complete checklist. Good luck in its use and in your search for home wealth!

Business Name	Possible Types of Operation	Capital Required	Experiences Required
Absentee home care	S	L	N
Abstracting written works	P,M,S	L	W
Academic costume manufacture, rental, sales, and repair	P,M,S	L	N
Accounting services	M,S	L	W
Acoustical consultant, product repair, sales	P,M,S	L	W
Acrobatic dancing lessons and performing	M,S	L	W
Acupuncture information, service	M,S	L	m-W
Adding machine rental, repair, sales, service	P,M,S	L	W
Addressing service	P,M,S	L	N
Adhesive (glue) sales and service	P,M,S	L	m
Adoption advice, service	P,M,S	L	m-W
Advertising agency, art, layout, checking, consultation	P,M,S	L	W
Aerial photography	P,M,S	I	W
Aerobics classes, instruction	P,M,S	L	N-m
Agricultural chemicals, sales and use	P,M,S	L	W
AIDS care	S	L	W
Air compressor rental, sales and service	P,M,S	H	W
Air conditioning rental, sales and service	P,M,S	H	W
Air pollution advice, services	P,M,S	L	m-W
Air travel ticket sales	P,M,S	L	W
Aircraft charter or parts sales and service	P,M,S	I	W
Airport transportation service	S	I	N
Album printing and sales	P,M,S	L	N
Altar linen manufacture and sales	P,M,S	L	N
Alterations to clothing	M,S	L	W
Aluminum awning, blind, screen, or siding sales or service	P,M,S	I	W
Ambulance service	S	H	N
Amusement device rental, sales or service	P,M,S	I	m
Anesthesia equipment rental, sales or service	P,M,S	H	W

Business Name	Possible Types of Operation	Capital Required	Experiences Required
Animal bedding, boarding, caskets, cemeteries	P,M,S	L-H	N-m
Animal food, hospital, rental, sales	P,M,S	L-H	N-m
Animated displays for advertising, shows, etc.	P,M,S	L	m
Anniversary card creation, sales	P,M	L	N
Announcement creation, printing, sales	P,M,S	L	m
Annual report preparation, printing, writing	P,M,S	L	m
Answer service for telephones	P,S	I	N
Antenna systems for radio, TV	P,M,S	L	W
Antique jewelry manufacture, sales	P,M,S	L	m
Antique repairing, restoring, sales	P,M,S	L	m
Apartment and house cleaning	S	L	N
Apartment renting or rental agency or finding service	P,M,S	L	m
Appliance refinishing, rental, repair, sales	P,M,S	I	m
Appraisal service for business, real estate, etc.	S	L	W
Apron manufacture, cleaning, sales	P,M,S	L-H	m
Aptitude tests	M,S	L	m
Aquarium sales, service, supplies	P,M,S	L-I	m
Arc welding equipment, sales, service	P,M,S	I	W
Archery equipment, range, sales, service	P,M,S	L-I	m
Architectural drawing, rendering, sketching	P,M,S	L	W
Architectural model construction	P,M,S	L	W
Art and craft sales, supplies	P,M,S	L	m
Art gallery, instruction, repairs, etc.	P,M,S	I	m
Art metalwork, needlework, restoring, etc.	P,M,S	I	m
Artificial limbs manufacture, sales, service	P,M,S	I	W
Artificial respiration equipment rental, sales, service	P,M,S	H	W

Business Name	Possible Types of Operation	Capital Required	Experiences Required
Ash and garbage removal	S	L	N
Athletic equipment, repairs, sales, service	P,M,S	L	m
Attic and basement cleaning, finishing, painting, repairs	P,M,S	L	m
Audio high-fidelity equipment sales, service	P,M,S	I	W
Audio-visual production, sales, rental	P,M,S	L	m
Autograph collection, evaluation, sales	P,M,S	L	m
Automobile appraisal, driving instruction, repair, sales, service, supplies, transportation	P,M,S	L-H	m-W
Awning manufacture, repair, sales, service	P,M,S	L	m
Baby carriages, cribs, foods, shoes, sitting	P,M,S	L	m
Back-number magazines	P,M,S	L	N
Badge manufacture, sales, service	P,M,S	L	m
Bag manufacture, sales, service	P,M,S	I	m
Bail bonds	S	H	W
Bait collection, sales	P,M,S	L	N
Baking sales, service	P,S	L	N
Ball bearing sales, service	P,M,S	L	m
Ballet dancing, instruction, supplies	P,M,S	L	m
Ballroom dancing, instruction, supplies	P,M,S	L	m
Bamboo and woven wood products manufacture, sales, service	P,M,S	L	m
Band equipment, instruction, instruments	P,M,S	L	W
Banquet catering	P,S	I	m
Bar rental, sales, service, supplies	P,M,S	I-H	m
Barber equipment, instruction, supplies	P,M,S	I	m
Barrel repair, rental, sales, service	P,M,S	I	N
Basement cleaning, excavating, finishing, waterproofing	P,M,S	L	N
Basket manufacture, sales, service	P,M,S	L	m

Business Name	Possible Types of Operation	Capital Required	Experiences Required
Bathroom remodeling, repairs, supplies	P,M,S	L	m
Baton twirling lessons	P,S	L	m
Battery equipment, sales, service	P,M,S	L-I	m
Bead assembly, sales, service	P,M,S	L	N
Beauty salon equipment, instruction, supplies, uniforms	P,M,S	L-I	m
Bed and bedroom equipment, renovating, rental, repair, supplies, wetting control	P,M,S	L	N
Bed and breakfast operation	S	I	N
Beefsteak parties	P,S	L	N
Beekeeping, sales, service	P,M,S	L	N
Beer equipment, sales, service	P,M,S	L-I	m
Bell manufacture, sales, service	P,M,S	L	m
Belt manufacture, sales, service	P,M,S	L-I	m
Bench manufacture, repair, sales, service	P,M,S	L	m
Beverage equipment, sales, service, supplies, vending	P,M,S	L-I	m
Bible sales	P,M	L	N
Bicycle rental, sales, service, supplies	P,M,S	L	N
Bill collection	S	L	m
Billiard equipment, sales, service	P,M,S	I	N
Binding of books, magazines	P,M,S	L	m
Binocular rental, repair, sales, service	P,M,S	L	N
Biological laboratory operation, supplies	P,M,S	I	W
Bird barriers, hospital, houses, supplies	P,M,S	L	N
Blackboard sales, service	P,S	L	N
Blacksmith	P,M,S	L	m
Blacktop installation, sales, service	P,M,S	I	m
Blanket repair, sales, service, supplies	P,M,S	L	N
Blueprinting sales, service	P,M,S	I	m
Boarding house	S	I	N
Boat covers, cushions, dockage, insurance, lettering, models, renting, repairs, storage, supplies, towing	P,M,S	L-I	m-W

Business Name	Possible Types of Operation	Capital Required	Experiences Required
Boating lessons	S	L-I	m-W
Bodywork for cars	P,S	L	m
Boiler cleaning, operation, repairs	P,S	L	m
Bonds for bail	S	L	N
Bookbinding	P,M,S	L	m
Book sales	P,M,S	L	N
Booking agent for entertainment	P,M,S	L	N
Bookkeeping service	M,S	L	m
Booths for exhibits — manufacture, sales, service	P,M,S	I	m
Boot sales, service	P,M,S	L	N
Bottle caps, sales, service	P,M,S	L	N
Boutique operation	P,M	L	N
Bowling apparel, accessories, instruction, refinishing, repairs	P,M,S	L-I	N-m
Box lunch preparation, sales	P,S	L	N
Box sales, service	P,M,S	L	N
Bread baking	P,S	L	N
Bric-a-Brac sales and service	P,M,S	L	N
Bridal consultant	S	L	N
Bridal service, supplies	P,M,S	L	N
Bridge instruction, parties, prizes, tables	P,M,S	L	N
Briefcase manufacture, sales, service	P,M,S	L	m
Broker for business, stocks, bonds	P,M,S	L	W
Buffing and polishing sales and service	P,M,S	L	N
Building cleaning and repair	P,S	L	m
Building inspection and appraisal	S	L	m
Building maintenance	P,S	L	m
Built-in furniture construction	P,S	L	m
Bulletin and directory board installation, sales, service	P,M,S	L	N
Burglar alarm system sales and service	P,M,S	L	m
Burial services (at sea, from air, etc.)	S	I	m-W
Bus charter and trip planning	M,S	L	N

Business Name	Possible Types of Operation	Capital Required	Experiences Required
Business chart preparation	P,S	L	m
Business consultant	M,S	L	m
Business gift sales and service	P,M,S	L	N
Business school operation	M,S	L	m
Button sales, service	P,M,S	L	N
Cabinet making for business and homes	P,M,S	L	m
Cab service	S	I	N
Cafeteria consultation, equipment sales, service	P,M,S	I	m
Cake baking, decoration, sales	P,M,S	L	N
Calculating machine instruction, sales, service	P,M,S	I	m
Camera repairing, sales, service	P,M,S	L	m
Camp information agency	M,S	L	N
Camp operation	M,S	L	N
Camping equipment rental, sales, service	P,M,S	L	N
Canary boarding, food, sales, service	P,M,S	L	N
Candy manufacture, sales, service	P,M,S	L	m
Canopy rental	S	I	N
Canvas products manufacture, sales, service	P,M,S	L	m
Cap and gown manufacture, rental, sales, service	P,M,S	I	N
Car driving instruction	S	L	W
Car leasing and renting	S	I	N
Car parking lot operation	S	I	N
Car repair and tuning	P,S	I	W
Car towing	S	I	m
Car upholstering	P,S	L	m
Car washing and polishing	P,S	L	N
Car wheel alignment	S	I	W
Carburetor sales, service, tune-up	P,M,S	I	W
Card table and chair rental, sales, service	P,M,S	L	N
Career guidance	S	L	m
Carpenter equipment sales, service	P,M,S	L	m

Business Name	Possible Types of Operation	Capital Required	Experiences Required
Carpet and rug cleaning, installation, sales, service	P,M,S	L-H	N-m
Cartoon preparation, sales	P,M,S	L	N
Cash register repair, sales, service	P,M,S	L	m
Cat boarding, breeding, hospital care, sales	P,S	L	m
Catalog preparation, sales, service	P,M,S	L	m
Catering service	S	I	N
Ceiling cleaning, painting, repairs	P,M,S	L	N
Cellar finishing, pumping, repairs	P,M,S	L	N
Cemetery decorations, equipment, supplies	P,M,S	L	N
Certificate design, embossing, printing	P,M,S	L	N
Cesspool building, cleaning, repairs	P,S	L	m
Chain saw rental, repair, sales, service	P,M,S	L	N
Chair building, rental, repair, sales	P,M,S	L-I	N
Chart sales for aeronautical, business, or marine use	P,M,S	L	N
Chauffeur service	S	L	m
Check cashing service	S	L	N
Cheese manufacture, sales	P,M,S	L	m
Chicken raising, sales	P,M,S	L	N
Child boarding, care, consultation, nursery	S	L	W
Children's clothing, toys	P,M,S	L	N
Chime and bell manufacture, sales, service	P,M,S	L	m
Chimney building, cleaning, repairs	P,M,S	L	m
Chinaware manufacture, sales, service	P,M,S	L	m
Chocolate sculpture, sales	P,M	L	m
Christmas decoration manufacture, sales, service	P,M,S	L	N
Church cleaning, maintenance, repair	S	L	N
Cider making, sales	P,M,S	L	m
Cigar and cigarette making, sales	P,M,S	L	m

Business Name	Possible Types of Operation	Capital Required	Experiences Required
Circular addressing, distribution, mailing	P,M,S	L	N
Circulating library operation	P,M,S	L	N
Civil service examination school	S	L	N
Claim adjuster, collector	S	L	m
Cleaning and dyeing of clothes, rugs	S	L	N
Clipping service for authors, business, churches, etc.	P,M,S	L	N
Clock repairs, sales, service	P,M,S	L	m
Closet construction, lining, supplies, design	P,M,S	L	N-m
Clothing consultant	P,M,S	L	m
Clothing manufacture, rental, sales, service, storage	P,M,S	L	m
Clown service for children's parties	S	L	m
Club operation	S	L	N
Clutch repair, sales, service	P,S	I	m
Coat and apron manufacture, rental, sales, service	P,M,S	L	N
Coffee break serving	P,S	I	N
Coffee roasting	P,S	I	m
Coin collection, sales	P,M,S	L	N
Cold storage of clothing	S	I	N
Collection of bills	S	L	N
Color analysis consultant	S	L	m
Color photo developing, printing	P,M,S	I	m
Commercial artist service	P,M,S	L	W
Compact disk sales, service	P,M,S	I	m-W
Compass adjustment, sales, service	P,M,S	L	W
Computer-aided design service	P,M,S	I	W
Computer consultation, debugging, programming	P,S	L	W
Computer games design, sales	P,M,S	L	m-W
Computing and calculating for architects, businessmen, engineers	S	L	W
Concert and theatre ticket sales	P,S	L	N
Concrete product manufacture, sales, service	P,M,S	L	m

Business Name	Possible Types of Operation	Capital Required	Experiences Required
Construction cost and time estimating service	S	L	W
Contest operation	S	L	m
Convalescent home operation	S	I-H	W
Convention services and conference planning	S	L	m
Cooking and cracker baking, sales, service	P,M,S	L	m
Copying service for business	P,M,S	I-H	m
Cosmetics manufacture, sales, service	P,M,S	L	m
Credit bureau operation	S	L	m
Crib rental, supplies	P,M,S	L	N
Cross (religious) manufacture, repair, sales, service	P,M,S	L	m
Curtain cleaning, installation, manufacture, sales, service	P,M,S	L	N
Cushion cleaning, manufacture, sales, service	P,M,S	L	N
Cutlery sales, sharpening	P,S	L	N
Dance-band instruction	S	L	W
Dancing instruction	S	L	m
Date arranging for singles	S	L	N
Day camp operation	S	L	m
Day care center operation	S	L	M
Debugging software	P,S	I	W
Decoration design, installation, repair, sales	P,M,S	L	m
Delivery service for business	S	L	N
Demonstration of merchandise, samples	S	L	N
Dental supply sales, service	P,M,S	L	m
Deodorizing service for business and homes	P,M,S	L	N
Design service for architects, business, engineers, homes, plants	P,M,S	L	W
Desk manufacture, sales, service	P,M,S	I	m
Desktop publishing	P,M,S	I	m
Detective force for business	S	L	m
Diamond appraisal, sales	P,M,S	I	W
Diaper service	S	I	N
Dictation and transcribing service	S	L	m
Diet control service	S	L	m

Business Name	Possible Types of Operation	Capital Required	Experiences Required
Diorama construction, instal-lation, repair	P,M,S	L	W
Direct-mail sale of products, services	P,M,S	L	N
Discotheque information, operation	M,S	I	m-W
Dish and chinaware rental, re-pair, sales	P,M,S	L	N
Dishwasher repair, sales, service	P,M,S	L	m
Disinfecting service for busi-ness, homes, ships	P,M,S	L	m
Display specialties construc-tion, sales, service	P,M,S	I	m
Dispossess service	S	L	m
Distribution service for busi-ness products, publications, samples	S	L	N
Diving (underwater) equip-ment, sales, service, supplies	P,M,S	I	W
Dog boarding, clipping, cloth-ing, food, hospital, rental, sales, training	P,M,S	I	m
Doll manufacture, repair, sales, service	P,M,S	L	N
Domestic help agency, service	S	L	N
Door products specialties	P,M,S	L	N
Dormer building, design, repair, sales	P,M,S	L	m
DOS® instruction	M,S	L	W
Drafting instruction, service	P,M,S	L	m
Drain pipe cleaning, repair, sales, service	P,S	L	N
Drapery cleaning, fireproofing, manufacture, sales	P,M,S	L	N
Dress design, manufacture, sales	P,M,S	L	N
Dressmaker training	S	L	W
Driftwood specialty item man-ufacture, sales	P,M,S	L	N
Driveway construction, design, repair, sales	P,M,S	L	m
Driving school for autos, boats, buses, trucks	S	L-I	W
Dry cleaning service	S	I	N
Dryer (clothes) repair, sales, service	P,M,S	L	m

Business Name	Possible Types of Operation	Capital Required	Experiences Required
Duck board, breeding, raising, sales, service	P,M,S	L	N
Dude ranch operation	S	I	N
Duplicating equipment sales, service, supplies	P,M,S	I	m
Earrings manufacture, sales	P,M,S	L	N-m
Earthenware manufacture, sales, service	P,M,S	L	N
Economics services — reports, research, surveys	P,S	L	m
Editing of manuscripts	S	L	m
Educational consultation, research, toys	P,M,S	L	m
Egg production, sales	P,S	L	N
Electric appliance rental, repair, sales, service	P,M,S	I	m
Electric design, installation, repair, services	P,S	L	m
Electric hair removal	M,S	L	W
Electric sewing machine rental, repair, sales, service	P,M,S	L	m
Electric tool rental, repair, sales, service	P,M,S	I	N
Electric train (hobby) rental, repair, sales, service	P,M,S	L	N
Electric typewriter rental, repair, sales, service	P,M,S	I	N
Electric welding service	S	I	m
E-mail sales, training, service	P,M,S	I	W
Embroidering of products	P,S	L	m
Employment advice	S	L	W
Employment agency operation	S	L	m
Enamel surface repairs, refinishing	S	L	m
Engine tune-up for cars, buses, boats, etc.	P,S	L	m
Engineering consultation, design	S	L	W
Engine rental, repair, sales, service	P,M,S	I	m
Engraving service for jewelry	P,S	L	m
Environmental advice, consulting	M,S	L	W
Estate appraisal, planning	S	L	W
Estimating service for architects, business, engineers	S	L	W

Business Name	Possible Types of Operation	Capital Required	Experiences Required
Etching framing, preparation, sales	P,M,S	L	m
Evening clothes manufacture, rental, sales	P,M,S	L-I	m
Executive search service	S	L	m
Exercise gym, lessons, machines	P,M,S	L	m
Export/import service	S	L	m
Express deliveries	S	L	N
Exterminating service for business, homes	P,S	L	N
Fabric dyeing, fireproofing, sales	P,M,S	L	N
Facial treatments	S	L	N
Factor for business	M,S	H	m
Factory cleaning, feeding, repair, maintenance	P,M,S	L	N
Factory location studies	S	L	m
Family counseling	S	L	W
Farm equipment, operation, sales, service	P,M,S	L	m
Fashion model agency	S	L	m
Favor products sales	P,M	L	N
FAX machine sales, service	P,M,S	L	W
Feed sales and service	P,S	L	N
Filling station operation	P,S	I	N
Film developing and printing	P,M,S	L	m
Financing consultation and service for business	S	H	W
Fire alarm system sales and service	P,M,S	I	m
Fire extinguisher sales and service	P,M,S	L	N
Fire investigation, loss adjustment	S	L	W
Fireplace and chimney cleaning, construction, repair	P,M,S	L	N
Fireworks manufacture, sales, service	P,S	L	W
Fish breeding, care, sales, service	P,M,S	L	m
Fishing bait, supplies, tackle	P,M,S	L	m
Fix-it store for business and home repairs	P,S	L	m

Business Name	Possible Types of Operation	Capital Required	Experiences Required
Flags, flagpole, and banner assembly, manufacture, sales, service	P,M,S	L	N
Flameproofing of fabrics, materials, trees, wood	S	L	m
Floodlight sales and service	P,M,S	L	N
Floor cleaning, covering, polishing, repairing	P,M,S	L	N
Florist sales and service	P,S	L	N
Flower bulbs, raising, sales, service	P,M,S	L	N
Foam rubber products manufacture, sales, service	P,M,S	L	N
Food locker rental	S	I-H	N
Food service for business, homes, pets	P,S	I	N
Foreign car rental, repair, sales, service	P,M,S	I	N
Foreign language translation service	S	L	N
Foundation building, repair, waterproofing	P,M,S	L	m
Fountain pen repairs, sales, service	P,M,S	L	N
Franchise rental, sales, service	P,M,S	L	N
Freezer rental, sales, service	P,M,S	I	N
Fruit basket preparation, sales	P,M,S	L	N
Fruit raising, sales	P,M,S	L	N
Fuel-oil burner repair, sales	P,M,S	L	m
Fund raising	S	L	m
Fur rental, repair, sales, service, storage	P,M,S	I	N
Furnace cleaning, repair, sales	P,M,S	L	N
Furnished room rental	S	I	N
Furniture manufacture, rental, sales, service	P,M,S	L	m
Game-room building, rental, repair, sales	P,M,S	L	N
Garage building, design, repair, sales, service	P,M,S	L	m
Garbage collection, disposal	S	L	N
Garden care, equipment, sales, supplies	P,M,S	L	N
Garment care, repair, storage	S	L	N
Gas station operation	P,S	I	N
Gasoline sales	P	I	N
Geese raising, sales	P,S	L	N

Business Name	Possible Types of Operation	Capital Required	Experiences Required
Gem engraving, repair, sales	P,M,S	I	m
Generator rental, repair, sales, service	P,M,S	I	m
Gift basket preparation, sales	P,M,S	L	N
Gift service for business, homes	P,M,S	L	N
Glass bending, blowing, repair, service	P,M,S	L	m
Glass, colored, making	P,M,S	L	N
Glass decoration manufacture, sales, service	P,M,S	L	m
Globe sales, service	P,M	L	N
Glove cleaning, making, repairs	P,M,S	L	N
Glue sales, service	P,M,S	L	N
Goldfish breeding, sales, service	P,M,S	L	N
Gold and precious metal sales	P,M	I	m
Golf instruction, supplies	P,M,S	L	m
Golf-range operation	S	I	N
Gown cleaning, manufacture, sales, service	P,M,S	L	N
Granite carving, cutting	P,M	L	m
Greenhouse rental, repair, sales, service	P,S	L-I	N
Greeting card design, manufacture, sales	P,M	L	N
Grinding of blades, tools	S	L	N
Grounds maintenance, planting, weeding	S	L	N
Guarding property, residences	S	L	N
Guest house operation	S	I	N
Guinea pig breeding, sales	P,S	L	N
Gun rental, repair, sales, service	P,M,S	L	N
Gutter (roof) installation, repair, service	P,S	L	N
Gymnasium equipment, operation, rental, sales	P,M,S	L	N
Gymnastics instruction	S	L	m
Hack operation, repair	S	L	N
Hair care, coloring, curling, cutting, dressing, drying	P,S	L	m
Hair removal, straightening, styling, tinting, treatment, waving	P,S	L	m

Business Name	Possible Types of Operation	Capital Required	Experiences Required
Hamburger stand franchising, operation	P,S	L	N
Hand-tool rental, repair, sales, service	P,M,S	L	N
Handbag manufacture, repair, sales, service	P,M,S	L	N
Handwriting analysis	S	L	m
Hardware supplies, sales, service	P,M,S	I	N
Harness (dog and horse) manufacture, sales	P,M,S	L	m
Harp instruction, rental, repair, sales, service	P,M,S	L	m
Hat cleaning, manufacture, sales	P,S	L	N
Hayride tours	S	L	N
Health food, gym, nursing home, resort	P,S	L-I	W
Health food manufacture, sales	P,M,S	L	m-W
Hearing aid rental, repair, sales, service	P,M,S	L	m
Hearse service	S	I	N
Heater rental, repair, sales, service	P,M,S	L	m
Hemstitching service	S	L	m
Hi-fi equipment rental, sales, service	P,M,S	L	N
Hobby supplies sales, service	P,M,S	L	N
Home cleaning service	S	L	N
Home maintenance, modernization, repair	S	L	N
Horn rental, repair, sales, service	P,M,S	L	N
Horse boarding, rental, riding instruction, training, transportation	P,M,S	L-I	m
Hosiery design, repair, sales	P,M,S	L	N
Hospital equipment and uniform sales, service	P,M,S	I	m
Hot-rod assembly, equipment, repair, sales, tune-up	P,M,S	I	m
Hot-tub manufacture, sales, service	P,M,S	I	m-W
Hotel equipment and uniform sales, service	P,M,S	I	m
Houseboat rental, sales	P,M,S	I	N
House cleaning service	S	L	N
House rental agency	S	L	N
House trailer rental, sales	P,S	L	N

Business Name	Possible Types of Operation	Capital Required	Experiences Required
Hunting equipment rental, repair, sales	P,M,S	L	N
Ice cream manufacture, sales	P,S	L	m
Ice cube vending machine operation	P,S	I	N
Ice skating instruction, rink operation, skate sales, sharpening	P,M,S	L-I	N
Ignition tune-up for autos	S	L	m
Illuminated-sign design, manufacture, sales, service	P,M,S	L-I	m
Import sales and service	P,M,S	L	N
Incinerator repair, sales	P,S	L	N
Income tax return preparation	S	L	m
Industrial catalog preparation, writing	P,M,S	L	m
Industrial clothing manufacture, repair, sales	P,M,S	L	N
Industrial consultation for business	S	L	W
Industrial design for business	S	L	W
Industrial feeding service	S	I	m
Industrial help-wanted agency	S	L	N
Industrial music playing systems	P,S	L	N
Industrial supplies rental, repair, sales, service	P,M,S	L	N
Industrial uniforms, wiping cloths, towels	P,M,S	L	N
Information service for business, homes, industry	S	L	m
Information superhighway sales, service	P,M,S	I	W
Insect extermination service	S	L	m
Instruction-book preparation, writing	P,S	L	m
Insurance sales, service	P,S	L	m
Interior decoration of business, homes	S	L	m
Interpreter of foreign languages	S	L	m
Introduction agency	S	L	N
Invalid care, equipment, home	P,S	L	m
Investigation service for business, individuals	S	L	m

Business Name	Possible Types of Operation	Capital Required	Experiences Required
Investment advisory agency, newsletter	S	L	W
Jade items — repair, sales, service	P,M,S	L	N
Janitorial agency for business, residential buildings	S	L	N
Jelly, jam, and condiments making, sales	P,M,S	L	N
Jewelry appraisal, making, repair, sales	P,M,S	L	m
Jiu-jitsu instruction, supplies	P,S	L	m
Job-finding agency, resumés	P,M,S	L	m
Jogging instructions, supplies	P,M,S	L	N-m
Jukebox rental, repair, sales, service	P,S	I	m
Junk collection, repair, sales	P,M,S	L	N
Karate gym, instruction, supplies	P,M,S	L	m
Kennel operation, rental, repair, sales, service	P,M,S	L	N
Key making, replacement, sales, service	P,M,S	L	m
Kindling wood collection, preparation, sales	P,S	L	N
Kitchen painting, remodeling, repair, spraying	P,S	L	N
Kitten boarding, raising, sales	P,S	L	N
Knitted-product instruction, manufacture, repair, sales, service	P,M,S	L	N
Laboratory equipment rental, repair, sales, service	P,M,S	L	m
Lace-product instruction, manufacture, repair, sales, service	P,M,S	L	m
Lacrosse instruction, supplies	P,M,S	L	m-W
Ladies-hat instruction (for making), manufacture, repair, sales	P,M,S	L	N
Laminating (plastic) equipment, repair, sales, service	P,M,S	I	N
Lamp and shade manufacture, repair, sales, service	P,M,S	L	N
Landscape gardening	S	L	m
Language interpretation, teaching, translation	S	L	m

Business Name	Possible Types of Operation	Capital Required	Experiences Required
Laptop computer sales, training, service	P,M,S	I	W
Laundry operation	S	L	N
Lawn cultivation, equipment, furniture, seeds	P,M,S	L	N
Leather-product instruction (for making), manufacture, sales, service	P,M,S	L	N
Lecture service for business, clubs, groups	S	L	m
Letter mailing, preparation, re-mailing, writing	P,M,S	L	m
Lettering for advertisements, drawings, signs	P,S	L	m
Library operation for business, homes	S	L	N
Life insurance sales, service	P,S	L	m
Limousine operation	S	I	m
Linen-products instruction, manufacture, rental, sales, service	P,M,S	L	m
Linoleum installation, repair, sales, service, waxing	P,M,S	L	N
Livestock feed manufacture, sales	P,S	L	N
Living room decoration, furniture, remodeling, repair	P,M,S	L	m
Loan agency for business, homes	S	I	m
Loan portfolio purchase, sales	P,M,S	I	W
Locksmith service	S	L	m
Logs for business and home fireplaces	P,S	L	N
Luggage manufacture, rental, repair, sales	P,M,S	L	N
Lumber sales, service	P,S	L	N
Machinery appraisal	S	L	m
Magazine binding	P,S	L	m
Magazine clipping agency	P,S	L	N
Magazine collection (of back-number), sales	P,S	L	N
Magic shows, supplies	P,S	L	N
Maid agency, uniforms	P,S	L	N
Mail addressing agency	S	L	N
Mail box center operation	S	I	m-W
Mail sorting agency	S	L	N
Mailing list compilation, sales, computerization	P,S	L	N

Business Name	Possible Types of Operation	Capital Required	Experiences Required
Make-up (facial) advice for women	S	L	N
Management advice and consultation for business	S	L	W
Mannequin rental, repair, sales, service	P,M,S	L	N
Mantleplace installation, rebuilding, repair, sales	P,M,S	L	N
Manufacturer's representative	P,M,S	L	m
Marble carving, repair, polishing	P,S	L	W
Marina operation, rental, repair, sales, service	P,M,S	L-I	m
Marine consultation, equipment, insurance, towing	P,M,S	L-I	m-W
Marriage broker	S	L	W
Mask (face) manufacture, repair, sales, service	P,M,S	L	N
Masonry work-cleaning, installation, repair, sales	P,M,S	L	N
Massage instruction	S	L	m
Maternity clothes design, manufacture, sales	P,M,S	L	N
Mathematical service for architects, business, engineers	S	L	W
Memory training lessons	S	L	m
Men's clothing design, manufacture, sales	P,M,S	L	m
Merger and acquisition (business) agency	S	L	W
Message and package delivery service	S	L	N
Microloan assistance, analysis	P,M,S	I	W
Microscope rental, repair, sales, service	P,M,S	L-I	m
Midget racing cars, parts, races, sales, service	P,M,S	L-I	m
Military equipment sales (new and used)	P,M,S	L-I	N
Milk sales, vending-machine operation	P,S	L	N
Mineral evaluation and identification	S	L	W
Miniature and par-3 golf course operation	S	L-I	N
Mirror repair, resilvering, sales, service	P,M,S	L	m

Business Name	Possible Types of Operation	Capital Required	Experiences Required
Mitten manufacture, repair, sales	P,M,S	L	N
Mobile home design, construction, repair, sales, service	P,M,S	L-H	m
Model and hobby center, equipment, instruction, supplies	P,M,S	L-I	N
Modem sales, training, service	P,M,S	I	W
Monogramming for clothes, luggage	P,M,S	I	m-W
Mortician	S	L	W
Mosaic design, preparation, sales	P,M,S	L	m
Mosquito control systems	P,S	L	N
Motel construction, design, operation, maintenance, repair, sales, service	P,M,S	L-H	N-m
Motivation investigation for business, institutions	M,S	L	m
Motor rental, repair, sales, service	P,M,S	L	m
Motor bike rental, repair, sales, service	P,M,S	L	N
Motor tune-up service	S	L	m
Moving advice, packing, transport	S	I	m-W
Music equipment rental, repair, sales, service	P,M,S	L	m
Musical instruction	S	L	m
Mutual fund sales	P,S	L	N
Nail care specialist	P,M,S	L	m
Nameplate manufacture, repair, sales	P,M,S	L	N
Napkin rental, repair, sales	P,S	L	N
Nautical chart, instrument, and supply sales	P,M,S	L	m
Necktie cleaning, manufacture, sales	P,M,S	L	m
Neon sign manufacture, rental, repair, sales	P,M,S	L	m
Networking instruction, meetings	P,M,S	L	m-W
Newspaper clipping, delivery, preservation	P,M,S	L	N

Business Name	Possible Types of Operation	Capital Required	Experiences Required
Notebook computer sales, training, service	P,M,S	I	W
Nursery and kindergarten operation	S	L	W
Nursing home operation	S	H	W
Nutrition advice, consultation, service	S	L	W
Nut sales to homes, restaurants	P,S	L	N
Obedience classes for dogs and other animals	S	L	m
Office decoration, design, remodeling, repair	P,S	L	m
Office cleaning service for business and professional suites	S	L	N
Office permanent and temporary help employment agency	S	L	N
Office record storage and shredding	S	L	N
Office rental agency	S	L	N
Office equipment and supply sales	P,M,S	L-I	N
Offset printing service	S	L-H	m
Oil burner rental, repair, sales, service	P,M,S	L	m
Oil delivery and storage	P,S	I	N
On-demand publishing sales, service	P,S	I	W
Online systems installation, instructions, repair	P,M,S	I	W
Orchestra instruction, leasing, training	P,S	L	m
Organ instruction, rental, repair, sales, service	P,M,S	I	m
Oriental products rental, repair, sales, service	P,M,S	L	N
Ornamental metal and wood products	P,M,S	L	m
Ostrich boarding, breeding, feathers, feed	P,M,S	L	N
Outboard motor rental, repair, sales, service	P,M,S	L	N
Overall rental, repair, sales	P,M,S	L	N
Package consultation, delivery, design, wrapping	P,M,S	L	N

Business Name	Possible Types of Operation	Capital Required	Experiences Required
Paint brushes, removers, supplies	P,M,S	L	N
Painting service for business, homes	S	L	m
Pamphlet production, writing	P,S	L	m
Paper (wall) hanging, repair, sales	P,M,S	L	m
Paper products — bags, cups, favors, hats, napkins, waste — sales	P,M,S	L	N
Parking (auto) lot operation	S	L	N
Party organization and operation for business, homes	S	L	N
Pastry making, sales	P,M,S	L	m
Patent application handling, consultation, defense, development	S	L	W
Pattern preparation for clothing	P,S	L	m
Pawnbroker service	S	L	m
Pearl collection, sales, stringing	P,S	L	m
Pen and pencil repair, sales	P,M,S	L	m
Pennant manufacture, sales, service	P,M,S	L	N
Pension and pensioned-persons consultant	S	L	W
Perfume collection, manufacture, sales, service	P,M,S	L	m
Personal assistance agency for business, homes	S	L	m
Personal communication system sales, service	P,M,S	I	W
Personnel advice, consultation, hiring, search	S	L	m
Pet boarding, breeding, feeding, hospitalization	P,M,S	L	m
Pet portrait photographer	P,M	L	m
Photography equipment rental, sales, service	P,M,S	L-I	m
Piano rental, repair, sales, service	P,M,S	L	m
Picture and painting framing, rental, repair, sales	P,M,S	L	m
Pie baking, sales	P,M,S	L	m
Plastic products manufacture, repair, sales	P,M,S	L-I	m

Business Name	Possible Types of Operation	Capital Required	Experiences Required
Plumbing service, supplies	P,M,S	L	m
Portable computer sales, training, service	P,M,S	I	W
Postage stamp collection, sales, appraisal	P,M,S	L	m-W
Poultry boarding, breeding, food, plucking, sales	P,M,S	L	m
Printing for business, homes, institutions	P,M,S	L-I	m
Private detective, process server	S	L	W
Public relations service for business, individuals	S	L	W
Publishing of books, magazines, newsletters	P,M,S	I	m
Pump rental, repair, sales, service	P,M,S	L	m
Purchasing agency for business, individuals	S	L	N
Quilt manufacture, sales	P,M,S	L	N
Rabbit boarding, breeding, food, sales	P,M,S	L	N
Racks for product display and sales in service stations, stores	P,S	L	N
Radio rental, repair, sales, service	P,M,S	L	W
Rag collection, sales	P,S	L	N
Real estate appraisal, sales	P,S	L	W
Record collection, rental, sales	P,M,S	L	N
Refrigeration equipment rental, repair, sales, service	P,M,S	M	m
Rental service — books, pictures, tools, etc.	S	L-I	m
Research agency for business, individuals	S	L	m
Riding (horseback) equipment, lessons, rental	P,M,S	L-I	m
Robot construction, supplies	P,M,S	L	m-W
Rock music sales, instruction, recording	P,M,S	L	N-m
Rug cleaning, dyeing, shampooing	S	L-I	N
Running instruction, supplier	P,M,S	L	m-W
Sailboat rental, repair, sales, training	P,M,S	L-I	m

Business Name	Possible Types of Operation	Capital Required	Experiences Required
Sales consultation, instruction, training for business, individuals	S	L	W
Sandwich delivery service to offices	S	L	N
Sauna supplies, operation	P,M,S	I	m-W
SBA loan analysis, assistance	P,M,S	L	W
Scalp care, products	P,M,S	L	m
School service — information, supplies, transportation	P,M,S	L	m
Scuba diving instruction, equipment rental, sales	P,M,S	L	m
Second-hand products collection, repair, sales	P,M,S	L	N
Secretarial agency for permanent and temporary help	S	L	m
Seed collection, sales	P,M,S	L	m
Sewing machine rental, repair, sales, service	P,M,S	L	m
Shade cleaning, manufacture, sales, service	P,M,S	L	N
Shirt cleaning, manufacture, sales	P,M,S	L	m
Shopping agency for business, homes, individuals	P,M,S	L	N
Sign manufacture, sales	P,M,S	L	N
Silver appraisal, collection, sales	P,M,S	L-I	m
Singing telegram service	S	L	N
Skin care instruction, supplies	P,M,S	L	m-W
Smoker's supplies — cigarettes, pipes, tobacco	P,M,S	L	N
Soccer instruction, supplies	P,M,S	L	m-W
Software development or service	P,M,S	I	W
Stop-smoking clinics, supplies	P,M,S	L	m-W
Stuttering correction	S	L	W
Sun-tanning salon	S	I	m-W
Surfing lessons, supplies	P,M,S	L	m-W
Swimming equipment, lessons, pool operation	P,M,S	L-I	W
Table (home and business) collection, manufacture, repair, sales, service	P,M,S	L	N
Tailor services for business, individuals	S	L	m

Business Name	Possible Types of Operation	Capital Required	Experiences Required
Tape recorder rental, repair, sales, service	P,M,S	L	m
Tapestry collection, manufacture, repair, sales, service	P,M,S	L	m
Tea room operation	S	L	N
Technical-manual production, writing	P,M,S	L	m
Telephone answering service	S	L-I	m
Telephone sales service	S	L	N
Television rental, repair, sales, service	P,M,S	L	m
Temporary employment agency	S	L	N
Tennis equipment, lessons, operation of courts	P,M,S	L	m
Terrace building, design, repair	S	L	m
Theatre and amusement ticket sales	P,M,S	L	N
Tool rental, repair, sales, service	P,M,S	L-I	m
Toupee and hair-goods manufacture, sales	P,M,S	L	W
Tour operator for travel	M,S	L	m
Towel service for business, industry	S	L	N
Towing service for autos	S	L-I	N
Toy rental, repair, sales, service	P,M,S	L	N
Trailer rental, repair, sales, service	P,M,S	L-I	N
Translation service	S	L	N
Travel consultant	S	L	N
Tree care, cultivation, sales	P,M,S	L	m
Tropical fish boarding, breeding, food, sales	P,M,S	L	N
Typing of documents, letters, manuscripts	S	L	N
Umbrella rental, repair, sales	P,S	L	N
Uniform rental, repair, sales	P,M,S	L	N
Unfinished furniture manufacture, sales	P,M,S	L	N
Upholstering service	S	L	N
Used equipment rental, repair, sales	P,M,S	L	N
Vacation counseling agency	S	L	N
Vacuum cleaner rental, repair, sales, service	P,M,S	L	N

Business Name	Possible Types of Operation	Capital Required	Experiences Required
Valence installation, sales	P,S	L	N
Valet agency	S	L	N
Vegetable cultivation, sales	P,S	L	N
Vending machine rental, repair, operation, sales	P,M,S	L-I	N
Venetian blind cleaning, repair, sales	P,M,S	L	N
Venture capital supply, instruction	P,M,S	L	W
Videocassette recorder rental, sales, repair	P,M,S	I	m-W
Videocassette rental, sales	P,M,S	I	N-m
Visual aid preparation, sales	P,M,S	L	N
Vitamin sales	P,M	L	m
Vocational advice, training	S	L	W
Voice mail sales, installation	P,S	I	W
Voice training	S	L	W
Wagon (toy) manufacture, sales, service	P,M,S	L	N
Wake-up service	S	L	N
Wall service — coverings, design, painting, washing	S	L	N
Washing machine rental, repair, sales, service	P,M,S	L	N
Waste collection and disposal	S	L	N
Watch rental, repair, sales	P,M,S	L	m
Water ski equipment, training	P,S	L	m
Wedding service — announcements, supplies, consultation	P,M,S	L	N-m
Weight control service	S	L	W
Weight-loss instruction, products	P,M,S	L	m-W
Wind surfing instruction, equipment rental, product sales	P,M,S	L	m
Window cleaning agency	S	L	m
Window display design, installation, sales	P,M,S	L	m
Windows® training, installation	P,M,S	I	W
Windsock manufacture, sales	P,M,S	L	N-m
Women's products sales and services	P,M,S	L	N
Wood finishing, working, preserving	S	L	N
Writing articles, books, manuals	P,S	L	m
Yacht rental, repair, sales	P,M,S	L	m

Bibliography

Profit-Building Tools from Tyler Hicks'
INTERNATIONAL WEALTH SUCCESS Library

AS THE PUBLISHER of the famous *INTERNATIONAL WEALTH SUCCESS* newsletter, Ty Hicks has put together a remarkable library of dynamic books, each geared to help the opportunity-seeking individual—the kind of person who is ready and eager to achieve the financial freedom that comes from being a SUCCESSFUL entrepreneur. Financial experts agree that only those who own their own businesses or invest their money wisely can truly control their future wealth. And yet, far too many who start a business or an investment program of their own do not have the kind of information that can make the difference between success and failure.

Here, then, is a list of publications hand-picked by Ty Hicks, written especially to give you, the enterprising wealth builder, the critical edge that belongs solely to those who have the *inside* track. So take advantage of this unique opportunity to order this confidential information. (These books are *not* available in bookstores.) Choose the publications that can help you the most and send the coupon page with your remittance. Your order will be processed as quickly as possible to expedite your success. (Please note: If, when placing an order, you prefer not to cut out the coupon, simply photocopy the order page and send in the duplicate.)

IWS-1   *BUSINESS CAPITAL SOURCES.* Lists more than 1,500 lenders of various types—banks, insurance companies, commercial finance firms, factors, leasing firms, overseas lenders, venture capital firms, mortgage companies, and others. $15. 150 pgs.

IWS-2   *SMALL BUSINESS INVESTMENT COMPANY DIRECTORY AND HANDBOOK.* Lists more than 400 small business investment companies that invest in small businesses to help them prosper. Also gives tips on financial management in businesses. $15. 135 pgs.

IWS-3   *WORLDWIDE RICHES OPPORTUNITIES*, Vol. 1. Lists more than 2,500 overseas firms seeking products to import. Gives name of product(s) sought, or service(s) sought, and other important data needed by exporters and importers. $25. 283 pgs.

IWS-4   *WORLDWIDE RICHES OPPORTUNITIES*, Vol. 2. Lists more than 2,500 overseas firms seeking products to import. (Does NOT duplicate Volume 1.) Lists loan sources for some exporters in England. $25. 223 pgs.

IWS-5   *HOW TO PREPARE AND PROCESS EXPORT-IMPORT DOCUMENTS.* Gives data and documents for exporters and importers, including licenses, declarations, free-trade zones abroad, bills of lading, custom duty rulings. $25. 170 pgs.

IWS-6   *SUPPLEMENT TO HOW TO BORROW YOUR WAY TO REAL ESTATE RICHES.* Using government sources compiled by Ty Hicks, lists numerous mortgage loans and guarantees, loan purposes, amounts, terms, financing charge, types of structures financed, loan-value ratio, special factors. $15. 87 pgs.

IWS-7   *THE RADICAL NEW ROAD TO WEALTH* by A. David Silver. Covers criteria for success, raising venture capital, steps in conceiving a new firm, the business plan, how much do you have to give up, economic justification. $15. 128 pgs.

IWS-8   *60-DAY FULLY FINANCED FORTUNE* is a short BUSINESS KIT covering what the business is, how it works, naming the business, interest amortization tables, state securities agencies, typical flyer used to advertise, typical applications. $29.50. 136 pgs.

IWS-9   *CREDITS AND COLLECTION BUSINESS KIT* is a 2-book kit covering fundamentals of credit, businesses using credits and collection methods, applications for credit, setting credit limit. Fair Credit Reporting Act, collection percentages, etc. Gives 10 small businesses in this field. $29.50. 147 pgs.

IWS-10   *MIDEAST AND NORTH AFRICAN BANKS AND FINANCIAL INSTITUTIONS.* Lists more than 350 such organizations. Gives name, address, telephone, and telex number for most. $15. 30 pgs.

IWS-11   *EXPORT MAIL-ORDER.* Covers deciding on products to export, finding suppliers, locating overseas firms seeking exports, form letters, listing of firms serving as export management companies, shipping orders, and more. $17.50. 50 pgs.

IWS-12 *PRODUCT EXPORT RICHES OPPORTUNITIES.* Lists over 1,500 firms offering products for export—includes agricultural, auto, aviation, electronic, computers, energy, food, health care, mining, printing, and robotics. $21.50. 219 pgs.

IWS-13 *DIRECTORY OF HIGH-DISCOUNT MERCHANDISE SOURCES.* Lists more than 1,000 sources of products with full name, address, and telephone number for items such as auto products, swings, stuffed toys, puzzles, oils and lubricants, CB radios, and belt buckles. $17.50. 97 pgs.

IWS-14 *HOW TO FINANCE REAL ESTATE INVESTMENTS* by Roger Johnson. Covers basics, the lending environment, value, maximum financing, rental unit groups, buying mobile home parks, and conversions. $21.50. 265 pgs.

IWS-15 *DIRECTORY OF FREIGHT FORWARDERS AND CUSTOM HOUSE BROKERS.* Lists hundreds of these firms throughout the United States which help in the import-export business. $17.50. 106 pgs.

IWS-16 *CAN YOU AFFORD NOT TO BE A MILLIONAIRE?* by Marc Schlecter. Covers international trade, base of operations, stationery, worksheet, starting an overseas company, metric measures, profit structure. $10. 202 pgs.

IWS-17 *HOW TO FIND HIDDEN WEALTH IN LOCAL REAL ESTATE* by R. H. Jorgensen. Covers financial tips, self-education, how to analyze property for renovation, the successful renovator is a "cheapskate," property management, and getting the rents paid. $17.50. 133 pgs.

IWS-18 *HOW TO CREATE YOUR OWN REAL-ESTATE FORTUNE* by Jens Nielsen. Covers investment opportunities in real estate, leveraging, depreciation, remodeling your deal, buy- and lease-back, understanding your financing. $17.50. 117 pgs.

IWS-19 *REAL-ESTATE SECOND MORTGAGES* by Ty Hicks. Covers second mortgages, how a second mortgage finder works, naming the business, registering the firm, running ads, expanding the business, and limited partnerships. $17.50. 100 pgs.

IWS-20   *GUIDE TO BUSINESS AND REAL ESTATE LOAN SOURCES.* Lists hundreds of business and real estate lenders, giving their lending data in very brief form. $25. 201 pgs.

IWS-21   *DIRECTORY OF 2,500 ACTIVE REAL-ESTATE LENDERS.* Lists 2,500 names and addresses of direct lenders or sources of information on possible lenders for real estate. $25. 197 pgs.

IWS-22   *IDEAS FOR FINDING BUSINESS AND REAL ESTATE CAPITAL TODAY.* Covers raising public money, real estate financing, borrowing methods, government loan sources, and venture money. $24.50. 62 pgs.

IWS-23   *HOW TO BECOME WEALTHY PUBLISHING A NEWSLETTER* by E. J. Mall. Covers who will want your newsletter, planning your newsletter, preparing the first issue, direct mail promotions, keeping the books, building your career. $17.50. 102 pgs.

IWS-24   *NATIONAL DIRECTORY OF MANUFACTURERS' REPRESENTATIVES.* Lists 5,000 mfrs.' reps. from all over the United States, both in alphabetical form and state by state; gives markets classifications by SIC. $28.80. 782 pgs., hardcover.

IWS-25   *BUSINESS PLAN KIT.* Shows how to prepare a business plan to raise money for any business. Gives several examples of successful business plans. $29.50. 150 pgs.

IWS-26   *MONEY RAISER'S DIRECTORY OF BANK CREDIT CARD PROGRAMS.* Shows the requirements of each bank listed for obtaining a credit card from the bank. Nearly 1,000 card programs at 500 of the largest U.S. banks are listed. Gives income requirements, job history, specifications, etc. $19.95. 150 pgs.

IWS-27   *GLOBAL COSIGNERS AND MONEY FINDERS ASSOCIATION.* Publicize your need for a cosigner to get a business or real estate loan. Your need is advertised widely under a Code Number so your identity is kept confidential. $50.

IWS-28   *WALL STREET SYNDICATORS.* Lists 250 active brokerage houses who might take your company public. Gives numerous examples of actual, recent, new stock offerings of start-up companies. $15. 36 pgs.

IWS-29 *COMPREHENSIVE LOAN SOURCES FOR BUSINESS AND REAL ESTATE LOANS.* Gives hundreds of lenders' names and addresses and lending guidelines for business and real estate loans of many different types. $25. 136 pgs., 8½ × 11 in.

IWS-30 *DIVERSIFIED LOAN SOURCES FOR BUSINESS AND REAL ESTATE LOANS.* Gives hundreds of lenders' names and addresses and lending guidelines for business and real estate loans of many different types. Does not duplicate IWS-29. $25. 136 pgs., 8½ × 11 in.

IWS-31 *CREDIT POWER REPORTS*—Five helpful reports to improve your credit rating and credit line. Report No. 1: *How to Get a Visa and/or Mastercard Credit Card.* $19.95. 192 pgs., 5 × 8 in. Report No. 2: *How to Increase Your Credit Limits, Plus Sophisticated Credit Power Strategies.* $19.95. 208 pgs., 5 × 8 in. Report No. 3: *How to Repair Your Credit.* $19.95. 256 pgs., 5 × 8 in. Report No. 4: *How to Reduce Your Monthly Payments.* $19.95. 192 pgs., 5 × 8 in. Report No. 5: *How to Wipe Out Your Debts Without Bankruptcy.* $19.95. 152 pgs. Each book is also available on a cassette tape which duplicates the entire content of the report. The tapes are priced at $19.95 each and run 60 minutes. Please specify which tape you want when ordering; the tape title duplicates the report title.

IWS-32 *GUARANTEED MONTHLY INCOME* gives you a way to earn money every month via mail order selling books and kits to people seeking a business of their own. With this plan the money comes to you and you keep a large share of it for yourself. $15. 36 pgs., 8½ × 11 in.

Newsletters

IWSN-1 *INTERNATIONAL WEALTH SUCCESS*, Ty Hicks' monthly newsletter published 12 times a year. This 16-page newsletter covers loan and grant sources, real estate opportunities, business opportunities, import-export, mail order, and a variety of other topics on making money in your own business. Every subscriber can run one free classified advertisement of 40 words, or less, each month, covering business or real estate needs or opportunities. The newsletter has a worldwide circulation, giving readers and advertisers very broad coverage. Started in January 1967, the newsletter has been published continuously since that date. $24.00 per year. 16 pgs. plus additional inserts, 8½ × 11 in., monthly.

IWSN-2 *MONEY WATCH BULLETIN,* a monthly coverage of 100 or more active lenders for real estate and business purposes. The newsletter gives the lender's name, address, telephone number, lending guidelines, loan ranges, and other helpful information. All lender names were obtained within the last week; the data is therefore right up to date. Lenders' names and addresses are also provided on self-stick labels on an occasional basis. Also covers venture capital and grants. $95.00. 20 pgs., 8½ × 11 in., monthly, 12 times per year.

Success Kits

K-1 *FINANCIAL BROKER/FINDER/BUSINESS BROKER/ CONSULTANT SUCCESS KIT* shows YOU how to start your PRIVATE business as a Financial Broker/Finder/ Business Broker/Consultant! As a Financial Broker YOU find money for firms seeking capital and YOU are paid a fee. As a Finder YOU are paid a fee for finding things (real estate, raw materials, money, etc.) for people and firms. As a Business Broker YOU help in the buying or selling of a business—again for a fee. See how to collect BIG fees. Kit includes typical agreement YOU can use, plus four colorful membership cards (each 8 × 10 in.). Only $99.50. 12 Speed-Read books, 485 pgs., 8½ × 11 in., 4 membership cards.

K-2 *STARTING MILLIONAIRE SUCCESS KIT* shows YOU how to get started in a number of businesses which might make YOU a millionaire sooner than YOU think! Businesses covered in this big kit include Mail Order, Real Estate, Export-Import, Limited Partnerships, etc. This big kit includes four colorful membership cards (each 8 × 10 in.). These are NOT the same ones as in the Financial Broker kit. So ORDER your STARTING MILLIONAIRE KIT now—only $99.50. 12 Speed-Read books, 361 pgs., 8½ × 11 in., 4 membership cards.

K-3   ***FRANCHISE RICHES SUCCESS KIT*** is the only one of its kind in the world (we believe). What this big kit does is show YOU how to collect BIG franchise fees for YOUR business ideas which can help others make money! So instead of paying to use ideas, people PAY YOU to use YOUR ideas! Franchising is one of the biggest businesses in the world today. Why don't YOU get in on the BILLIONS of dollars being grossed in this business today? Send $99.50 for your FRANCHISE KIT now. 7 Speed-Read books, 876 pgs., 6 × 9 & 8½ × 11 in. & 5 × 8 in.

K-4   ***MAIL ORDER RICHES SUCCESS KIT*** shows YOU how YOU can make a million in mail order/direct mail, using the known and proven methods of the experts. This is a kit which is different (we think) from any other—and BETTER than any other! It gives YOU the experience of known experts who've made millions in their own mail order businesses, or who've shown others how to do that. This big kit also includes the Ty Hicks' book *How I Grossed More Than One Million Dollars in Mail Order/Direct Mail Starting with NO CASH and Less Knowhow.* So send $99.50 TODAY for your MAIL ORDER SUCCESS KIT. 9 Speed-Read books, 927 pgs., 6 × 9 & 8½ × 11 in.

K-5   ***ZERO CASH SUCCESS TECHNIQUES KIT*** shows YOU how to get started in YOUR own going business or real estate venture with NO CASH! Sound impossible? It really IS possible—as thousands of folks have shown. This big kit, which includes a special book by Ty Hicks on *Zero Cash Takeovers of Business and Real Estate,* also includes a 58-minute cassette tape by Ty on "Small Business Financing." On this tape, Ty talks to YOU! See how YOU can get started in YOUR own business without cash and with few credit checks. To get your ZERO CASH SUCCESS KIT, send $99.50 NOW. 7 Speed-Read books, 876 pgs., 8½ × 11 in. for most, 58-minute cassette tape.

K-6   ***REAL ESTATE RICHES SUCCESS KIT*** shows YOU how to make BIG money in real estate as an income property owner, a mortgage broker, mortgage banker, real estate investment trust operator, mortgage money broker, raw land speculator, and industrial property owner. This is a general kit, covering all these aspects of real estate, plus many, many more. Includes many financing sources for YOUR real estate fortune. But this big kit also covers how to buy real estate for the lowest price (down payments of NO CASH can sometimes be set up), and how to run YOUR real estate for biggest profits. Send $99.50 NOW for your REAL ESTATE SUCCESS KIT. 6 Speed-Read books, 466 pgs., 8½ × 11 in.

K-7   *BUSINESS BORROWERS COMPLETE SUCCESS KIT* shows YOU how and where to BORROW money for any business which interests YOU. See how to borrow money like the professionals do! Get YOUR loans faster, easier because YOU know YOUR way around the loan world! This big kit includes many practice forms so YOU can become an expert in preparing acceptable loan applications. Also includes hundreds of loan sources YOU might wish to check for YOUR loans. Send $99.50 NOW for your BUSINESS BORROWERS KIT. 7 Speed-Read books, 596 pgs., 8½ × 11 in.

K-8   *RAISING MONEY FROM GRANTS AND OTHER SOURCES SUCCESS KIT* shows YOU how to GET MONEY THAT DOES NOT HAVE TO BE REPAID if YOU do the task for which the money was advanced. This big kit shows YOU how and where to raise money for a skill YOU have which can help others live a better life. And, as an added feature, this big kit shows YOU how to make a fortune as a Fund Raiser—that great business in which YOU get paid for collecting money for others or for yourself! This kit shows YOU how you can collect money to fund deals YOU set up. To get your GRANTS KIT, send $99.50 NOW. 7 Speed-Read books, 496 pgs., 8½ × 11 in. for most.

K-9   *FAST FINANCING OF YOUR REAL ESTATE FORTUNE SUCCESS KIT* shows YOU how to raise money for real estate deals. YOU can move ahead faster if YOU can finance your real estate quickly and easily. This is NOT the same kit as the R.E. RICHES KIT listed above. Instead, the FAST FINANCING KIT concentrates on GETTING THE MONEY YOU NEED for YOUR real estate deals. This big kit gives YOU more than 2,500 sources of real estate money all over the U.S. It also shows YOU how to find deals which return BIG income to YOU but are easier to finance than YOU might think! To get started in FAST

FINANCING, send $99.50 today. 7 Speed-Read books, 523 pgs., 8½ × 11 in. for most.

K-10   *LOANS BY PHONE KIT* shows YOU how and where to get business, real estate, and personal loans by telephone. With just 32 words and 15 seconds of time YOU can determine if a lender is interested in the loan you seek for yourself or for someone who is your client—if you're working as a loan broker or finder. This kit gives you hundreds of telephone lenders. About half have 800 phone numbers, meaning that your call is free of long-distance charges. Necessary agreement forms are also included. This blockbuster kit has more than 150 pgs. 8½ × 11 in. Send $100 *now* and get started in one hour.

K-11   *LOANS BY MAIL KIT* shows YOU how and where to get business, real estate, and personal loans for yourself and others by mail. Lists hundreds of lenders who loan by mail. No need to appear in person—just fill out the loan application and send it in by mail. Many of these lenders give unsecured signature loans to qualified applicants. Use this kit to get a loan by mail yourself. Or become a loan broker and use the kit to get started. Unsecured signature loans by mail can go as high as $50,000 and this kit lists such lenders. The kit has more than 150 pgs. 8½ × 11 in. Send $100 *now* to get started in just a few minutes.

K-12   *REAL-ESTATE LOAN GETTERS SERVICE KIT* shows the user how to get real estate loans for either a client or the user. Lists hundreds of active real estate lenders seeking first and junior mortgage loans for a variety of property types. Loan amounts range from a few thousand dollars to many millions, depending on the property, its location, and value. Presents typical application and agreement forms for use in securing real estate loans. *No* license is required to obtain such loans for oneself or others. Kit contains more than 150 pages., 8½ × 11 in. Send $100 *now* to get started.

K-13   *CASH CREDIT RICHES SYSTEM KIT* shows the user three ways to make money from credit cards: (1) as a merchant account, (2) helping others get credit cards of their choice and (3) getting loans through lines of credit offered credit card holders. Some people handling merchant account orders report an income as high as $10,000 a day. While this kit does not, and will not, guarantee such an income level, it *does* show the user how to get started making money from credit cards easily and quickly. The kit has more than 150 pgs., 8½ × 11 in. Send $100 *now* to get started soon.

K-14   *PROFESSIONAL PRACTICE BUILDERS KIT* shows YOU how to make up to $1,000 a week part time, over $5,000 a week full time, according to the author, Dr. Alan Weisman. What YOU do is show professionals—such as doctors, dentists, architects, accountants, lawyers—how to bring more clients into the office and thereby increase their income. Step-by-step procedure gets you started. Provides forms, sample letters, brochures, and flyers YOU can use to get an income flowing into your bank in less than one week. The kit has more than 150 pgs., 8½ × 11 in. Send $100 *now!* Start within just a few hours in your local area.

K-15   *VENTURE CAPITAL MILLIONS KITS.* Shows how to raise venture capital for yourself or for others. Gives steps for preparing an Executive Summary, business plan, etc. You can use the kit to earn large fees raising money for new or established firms. $100. 200 pgs.

K-16   *GUARANTEED LOAN MONEY.* Shows how to get loans of all types—unsecured signature, business, real estate, etc.—when your credit is not the strongest. Gives full directions on getting cosigners, comakers, and guarantors. $100. 250 pgs.

K-17   *IMPORT-EXPORT RICHES KIT* shows you how to get rich in import-export in today's product-hungry world. This big kit takes you from your first day in the business to great success. It gives you 5,000 products wanted by overseas firms, the name and address of each firm, procedures for preparing export-import documents, how to correspond in four different languages with complete sentences and letters, names and addresses of freight forwarders you can use, plus much more. Includes more than 6 books of over 1,000 pages of useful information. $99.50.

K-18   *PHONE-IN/MAIL-IN GRANTS KIT.* This concise kit shows the reader how to jump on the grants bandwagon and get small or large money grants quickly and easily. Gives typical grant proposals and shows how to write each so you win the grant you seek. Takes the reader by the hand and shows how to make telephone calls to grantors to find if they're interested in your grant request. You are given the actual words to use in your call and in your proposal. Also includes a list of foundations that might consider your grant application. $100. 200 pgs., 8½ × 11 in.

K-19   *MEGA MONEY METHODS* covers the raising of large amounts of money—multimillions and up—for business and real estate projects of all types. Shows how to prepare loan packages for very large loans, where to get financing for such loans, what fees to charge after the loan is obtained, plus much more. Using this kit, the BWB should be able to prepare effective loan requests for large amounts of money for suitable projects. The kit also gives the user a list of offshore lenders for big projects. $100. 200 pgs., 8½ × 11 in.

K-20   *FORECLOSURES AND OTHER DISTRESSED PROPERTY SALES* shows how, and where to make money from foreclosures, trustee sales, IRS sales, bankruptcies, and sheriff sales of real estate. The kit contains six cassette tapes plus a workbook containing many of the forms you need in foreclosure and trustee sales. Addresses of various agencies handling such sales are also given. $51.95. 80 pgs. and 6 cassette tapes, 8½ × 11 in.

K-21   *SMALL BUSINESS LOAN PROGRAM* is designed to obtain loans for small and minority-owned businesses doing work for government agencies, large corporations, hospitals, universities, and similar organizations. The small business loan program pays up to 80 percent on accounts receivable within 48 hours to manufacturers, distributors, janitorial services, building contractors, etc. Startups acceptable. You earn a good commission getting these loans funded, and receive an ongoing payment when the company places future accounts receivable with the lender. $100. 200 pgs., 8½ × 11 in.

K-22   *PHONE-IN MINI-LEASE PROGRAM* helps you earn commissions getting leases for a variety of business equipment—personal computers, copy machines, typewriters, laser printers, telephone systems, office furniture, satellite antennas, store fixtures, etc. You earn direct commissions of 3 percent to 10 percent of the cost of the equipment up to $10,000. You get immediate approval of the lease by phone and the lender finances the equipment for the company needing it. Your commission is paid by the lender directly to you. $100. 150 pgs., 8½ × 11 in.

K-23   *INTERNATIONAL FINANCIAL CONSULTANT KIT* shows how to make money as an international financial consultant working with large lenders who finance big projects. Gives the agreements and forms needed, fee schedule, lender who might work with you, sample ads, sample letters, plus much more. With this kit on hand, the beginner can start seeking large deals using overseas funding sources. The kit provides a variety of lenders for international deals in all parts of the world. $100. 200 pgs., 8½ × 11 in.

K-24   *PORTFOLIO NETWORK TRAINING LIBRARY KIT* shows you how to find collections of loans or receivables for real estate, retail and service businesses, automobile dealerships, and medical practices. You receive a handsome commission for referring the portfolio to investors. Two special bonus reports are included free when you purchase this kit. These bonus reports are "How to Purchase Real Estate from the Resolution Trust Corporation" and "How to Purchase Loan Portfolios from the Resolution Trust Corporation." You could make thousands of dollars just from these two reports alone. $295.00. 200 pgs., 8½ × 11 in.

ORDER FORM

Dear Ty,

Please rush me the following:

☐	IWS-1	*Business Capital Sources*	$15.00 ...... ―――――
☐	IWS-2	*Small Business Investment*	$15.00 ...... ―――――
☐	IWS-3	*World-wide Riches Vol. 1*	$25.00 ...... ―――――
☐	IWS-4	*World-wide Riches Vol. 2*	$25.00 ...... ―――――
☐	IWS-5	*How to Prepare Export-Import*	$25.00 ...... ―――――
☐	IWS-6	*Real Estate Riches Supplement*	$15.00 ...... ―――――
☐	IWS-7	*Radical New Road*	$15.00 ...... ―――――
☐	IWS-8	*60-Day Fully Financed*	$29.50 ...... ―――――
☐	IWS-9	*Credits and Collection*	$29.50 ...... ―――――
☐	IWS-10	*Mideast Banks*	$15.00 ...... ―――――
☐	IWS-11	*Export Mail-Order*	$17.50 ...... ―――――
☐	IWS-12	*Product Export Riches*	$21.50 ...... ―――――
☐	IWS-13	*Dir. of High-Discount*	$17.50 ...... ―――――
☐	IWS-14	*How to Finance Real Estate*	$21.50 ...... ―――――
☐	IWS-15	*Dir. of Freight Forwarders*	$17.50 ...... ―――――
☐	IWS-16	*Can You Afford Not to Be ... ?*	$10.00 ...... ―――――
☐	IWS-17	*How to Find Hidden Wealth*	$17.50 ...... ―――――
☐	IWS-18	*How to Create Real Estate Fortune*	$17.50 ...... ―――――
☐	IWS-19	*Real Estate Second Mortgages*	$17.50 ...... ―――――
☐	IWS-20	*Guide to Business and Real Estate*	$25.00 ...... ―――――
☐	IWS-21	*Dir. of 2,500 Active Real Estate Lenders*	$25.00 ...... ―――――
☐	IWS-22	*Ideas for Finding Capital*	$24.50 ...... ―――――
☐	IWS-23	*How to Become Wealthy Pub.*	$17.50 ...... ―――――
☐	IWS-24	*National Dir. Manufacturers' Reps*	$28.80 ...... ―――――
☐	IWS-25	*Business Plan Kit*	$29.50 ...... ―――――
☐	IWS-26	*Money Raiser's Dir. of Bank Credit Card Programs*	$19.95 ...... ―――――
☐	IWS-27	*Global Cosigners and Money Finders Assoc.*	$50.00 ...... ―――――
☐	IWS-28	*Wall Street Syndicators*	$15.00 ...... ―――――
☐	IWS-29	*Comprehensive Loan Sources for Business and Real Estate Loans*	$25.00 ...... ―――――
☐	IWS-30	*Diversified Loan Sources for Business and Real Estate Loans*	$25.00 ...... ―――――
☐	IWS-31	*Credit Power Reports*	
		Report No. 1	$19.95 ...... ―――――
		Report No. 2	$19.95 ...... ―――――
		Report No. 3	$19.95 ...... ―――――
		Report No. 4	$19.95 ...... ―――――
		Report No. 5	$19.95 ...... ―――――
☐	IWS-32	*Guaranteed Monthly Income*	$15.00 ...... ―――――
☐	IWSN-1	*International Wealth Success*	$24.00 ...... ―――――
☐	IWSN-2	*Money Watch Bulletin*	$95.00 ...... ―――――
☐	K-1	*Financial Broker*	$99.50 ...... ―――――
☐	K-2	*Starting Millionaire*	$99.50 ...... ―――――
☐	K-3	*Franchise Riches*	$99.50 ...... ―――――

☐	K-4	*Mail Order Riches*	$99.50	...... _____
☐	K-5	*Zero Cash Success*	$99.50	...... _____
☐	K-6	*Real Estate Riches*	$99.50	...... _____
☐	K-7	*Business Borrowers*	$99.50	...... _____
☐	K-8	*Raising Money from Grants*	$99.50	...... _____
☐	K-9	*Fast Financing of Real Estate*	$99.50	...... _____
☐	K-10	*Loans by Phone Kit*	$100.00	...... _____
☐	K-11	*Loans by Mail Kit*	$100.00	...... _____
☐	K-12	*Real Estate Loan Getters Service Kit*	$100.00	...... _____
☐	K-13	*Cash Credit Riches System Kit*	$100.00	...... _____
☐	K-14	*Professional Practice Builders Kit*	$100.00	...... _____
☐	K-15	*Venture Capital Millions Kit*	$100.00	...... _____
☐	K-16	*Guaranteed Loan Money*	$100.00	...... _____
☐	K-17	*Import-Export Riches Kit*	$99.50	...... _____
☐	K-18	*Phone-in/Mail-in Grants Kit*	$100.00	...... _____
☐	K-19	*Mega Money Methods*	$100.00	...... _____
☐	K-20	*Foreclosures and Other Distressed Property Sales*	$51.95	...... _____
☐	K-21	*Small Business Loan Program*	$100.00	...... _____
☐	K-22	*Phone-in Mini-Lease Program*	$100.00	...... _____
☐	K-23	*International Financial Consultant Kit*	$100.00	...... _____
☐	K-24	*Portfolio Network Training Library Kit*	$295.00	...... _____

TOTAL AMOUNT OF ORDER _____

Shipping:

Regular Mail:　　$2 first book; $1 each additional _____
　　　　　　　　$5 first kit; $4 each additional _____

Priority Mail:　　$4 first book; $2 each additional _____
　　　　　　　　$10 first kit; $6 each additional _____

I am paying by: ☐ Check ☐ MO/Cashier's Check ☐ Visa/MC

Name: _____

Address: _____

City: _____ State: _____ Zip: _____

Visa/MC #: _____ Exp: _____

Signature: _____

Send all orders to:
  Tyler Hicks, Prima Publishing
  P.O. Box 1260, Rocklin CA 95677
Or with Visa/MC, call orders at (916) 632-4400 Mon.–Fri. 9 AM–4 PM PST

Index